100 to 1
In the Stock Market

100 to 1
in the
Stock Market

---

by Thomas W. Phelps

*A distinguished security analyst
tells how to make more
of your investment opportunities*

ECHO POINT BOOKS & MEDIA, LLC

Published by Echo Point Books & Media
Brattleboro, Vermont
www.EchoPointBooks.com

ISBN: 978-1-62654-029-3

Cover design by Adrienne Núñez,
Echo Point Books & Media

Editorial and proofreading assistance by Christine Schultz,
Echo Point Books & Media

Printed and bound in the United States of America

Publisher's Note

As I write these words, *100 to 1 in the Stock Market* is out of print and the lowest priced new copy sells on Amazon.com for $683! Even a damaged, musty smelling copy without a cover sells for $73. Anyone who understands the 'wisdom' of markets recognizes that these high prices (accompanied by glowing reviews) suggest the great value within these pages. If you absorb and apply Thomas Phelps's guidance, even at $683, this book is a tremendous bargain for it has the potential to dramatically improve your long-term financial life. For those of us without extraordinary bankable talents, such as the ability to accurately throw or hit a 95-mile-per-hour fastball, there is no greater way to increase your wealth than to share in the equity and profits of a highly successful business.

What's so impressive about *100 to 1 in the Stock Market* is that its sound guidance has continued to hold up remarkably well for nearly half a century and counting. Of course, the stock prices and some of the famous companies referenced have changed since in the early 1970s, but the advice and wit within these pages continues to resonate. If anything, Phelps's advice is needed now more than ever. Overwhelmed by the onslaught of financial media and faster, more pervasive news cycles, investors now find it harder than ever to hold steady to an investing course, which is key to accrue large returns. To reap genuine riches, one must invest in long-term winners and hold on for compounded, tax-free growth. It is how investing standout Warren Buffet became one of the wealthiest humans on the planet.

There is one notable thing that is outdated about *100 to 1 in the Stock Market*: that is the dramatic shift in accessing investing information due to the Internet.

Modern readers can ignore any parts of the book that point you to acquiring annual reports or any other piece of paper. Company earnings, revenue results, and projections are easily found through search engines such as Yahoo Finance and Google, not to mention a plethora of smaller innovative websites. This is good news, as the Internet makes it much easier to apply the wisdom that Mr. Phelps has shared with us. The key is understanding what to do with the numbers, and that's where *100 to 1 in the Stock Market* is such a big help. Phelps's guidance is timeless.

As someone who has invested in the stock market for decades and managed millions of other's dollars, I only wish I had read *100 to 1 in the Stock Market* earlier in life. It takes a while to realize the value of planning and patience—of carefully and thoughtfully choosing what you invest in and then having the strength to stick with your insight as long as your most important metrics are being met. This clarity and discernment is important not just in the stock market, but in everything we do. It leads to greater rewards and less stress.

So may you enjoy the wit, wisdom, and profits offered in the pages that follow.

—Marshall Glickman

former stockbroker, author of *The Mindful Money Guide* (Ballantine Random House) and Publisher at Echo Point Books & Media, LLC

November 2014

Contents

TABLES

Preface

This is a story—fact, not fiction—of hundreds of opportunities to make a million dollars in the stock market by investing $10,000 in just one stock and holding on.

It was not necessary to pick the *one* right stock or tne *one* right time to invest. Starting with 1932 a different stock could have been bought in each of thirty-two different years, and every dollar invested would have grown to $100 or more by 1971.

The latest millionaire-maker security was available as recently as 1967 at 1 percent of its 1971 market value. The book lists more than 365 different securities valued in 1971 at more than 100 times the prices at which they could have been bought four to forty years ago. It tells how they looked before their big rise and suggests how the next potentially big winners may be recognized in advance.

100 to 1 in the Stock Market attempts to look to tomorrow and chart a course to help every investor, small or large, novice or professional, improve his score.

The author acknowledges with many thanks the help of the individuals cited in the book. He is particularly grateful to Scudder, Stevens and Clark for the charts reproduced herein and for access to the firm's vast research facilities, without which this book could not have been written.

To the author's wife, Christine Reed Phelps, this book is dedicated in recognition of her contribution of the title and her patience and inspiration while he did the research and hammered out the text.

–T. W. P.

100 to 1
In the Stock Market

CHAPTER I

Ask, and It Shall Be Given You

Five poor Arabs slept on the sand. A bright light woke them. Out of it came an angel.

"Each of you can have one wish," the angel said.

"Praise be to Allah," exulted the first Arab to catch his breath. "Give me a donkey."

Instantly a donkey stood at his side.

"Fool," thought the second Arab. "He should have asked for more."

"Give me ten donkeys," the second Arab begged.

No sooner said than done. He had ten donkeys.

The third Arab had heard and seen how the first two had fared.

"To Allah all things are possible," he said. "Give me a caravan with a hundred camels, a hundred donkeys, tents, rugs, food, wine, and servants."

They came so fast that the third Arab was ashamed to be seen in his rags before such an entourage. But his shame did not last long. Deftly his servants dressed him in robes befitting his new status.

The fourth Arab was more than ready when his turn came.

"Make me a king," he commanded.

So quickly did the crown appear on his head that he bruised his knuckles scratching where an instant before there had been nothing but an itch. The palace gardens stretched out before him almost as far as the eye could see, and the palace turrets reached so high their pennants were lost in the desert haze.

Having seen his companions in misery ask too little, the fifth Arab resolved to make no such mistake.

"Make me Allah!" he ordered.

In a flash he found himself naked on the sand, covered with leprous sores.

The moral, of course, is that those of us who ask little of life get little. Those who ask much get much. Those who ask too much get nothing.

But strange as it may seem, human greed being what it is, most of us make the mistake of asking for one donkey. Few ask too much.

Nowhere is this more true than in investing. Most try to make a few points quickly on their stock market speculations, or content themselves with 4 or 5 percent on their savings. Not one in a thousand seriously plans and acts as one must to make a fortune. Most do not believe they have a chance. When they see others do it, they salve their egos by crying "graft" or "inside information" or "born in the right bed" instead of trying to find out how it was done. Even when fate puts the prize in their hands, they throw it away, time after time. Some can't resist the urge to cash in their winnings, however small. Others sell a good stock to get into something that seems better, perhaps because it is moving. Theirs is the fate of the dog in Aesop's fable. You remember, the dog lost the piece of meat in his mouth by snapping at a seemingly larger piece reflected in the water.

Few businesses are more cursed by half-truths and specious maxims than Wall Street. But even there, where the competition in such matters is keenest, it would be hard to find a worse slogan than "You'll never go broke taking a profit."

Fortunes are made by buying right and holding on. Now that Wall Street is afflicted by having more business than it can handle, even brokers might preach this gospel with much benefit to their customers and no harm to their own long-range best interests. Few do.

Since 1932 more than 360 different securities have increased one hundredfold in market value in the United States—not to some interim price peak but to their value in 1971. Many have been much higher in prior years.

What nonsense it is to say that Opportunity knocks but once.

That beautiful lady has been banging incessantly on Everyman's door for more than a quarter century.

Starting with 1932 anyone could have made a million dollars on a $10,000 investment in a different stock in *each* of 32 different years, of which 1967 was the latest. To do it would have required neither the luck nor the skill to sell out at the right time. Every one of the more than 360 different stocks that could have been bought for $10,000 in 32 of the last 40 years was worth a million dollars or more in 1971. All that was required was to pick *one* of the hundreds of right ones and *hold on.*

Norris Darrell, senior partner in the great law firm of Sullivan & Cromwell, and president of the prestigious American Law Institute, told me this true story, changing only the name:

"An elderly client sought my advice on whether he should sell or give to his family a valuable piece of property. This involved estate planning, including calculations of alternative tax consequences. To do this properly I needed to know the old gentleman's net worth. When I asked him for this information, he insisted on giving me only an admittedly arbitrary figure to work with. This I used.

"Having been pleased with the help he received in the first matter, this same client later sought my help in planning his will and possible lifetime gifts to his children. I told him I would be glad to do this, but I emphasized the vital importance of my having accurate information as to his net worth. Still reluctant to disclose that information, he wanted time to think it over.

"A few weeks later, he came to my office with his middle-aged son. After the usual greetings, I waited to hear what the old gentleman's decision would be. There was a long pause. Then he turned to his son and said: 'Shall I do it?' 'Yes, father,' replied the son, 'I think you should.' Whereupon the old gentleman reached into his side pocket, pulled out a slip of paper, and handed it to me.

"I had suspected that the figure he had given me to work with in the earlier matter had been unduly low. But, when I saw the very large figure on the slip he gave me, representing primarily the value of his security portfolio, I whistléd and exclaimed: 'Mr. Blank, how did you do it?'

"To which he replied, 'I never sell anything.'"

Mr. Blank might have added that he had had the good judgment or good fortune not to buy what should have been sold.

Like Mr. Blank, Paul Garrett is a man who never wished for one donkey. Financial editor of the old *New York Evening Post,* he was wooed away by Alfred P. Sloan, Jr., to become a General Motors vice president in charge of public relations. Mr. Garrett was the first man to attain that title in large competitive industry. The story of his pioneering work there merits a book of its own, but here we are dealing with investing. In 1956, at the age of sixty-four, facing mandatory retirement at the end of the year, Mr. Garrett determined to make his last years his best years rather than sit out the rest of his life as so many pensioners do.

His first goal was to increase his capital in order to increase his power to help others. Having no children he was not heirselfish. He decided the way to increase his savings fast enough to count at his age was to invest in a fast-growing company. He began his search for one that met these four criteria:

1. It must be small. Sheer size militates against great growth.

2. It must be relatively unknown. Popular growth stocks may keep on growing but too often one has to pay for expected growth too many years in advance. Probably to meet this criterion the stock he wanted would be traded over-the-counter rather than on any stock exchange.

3. It must have a unique product that would do an essential job better, cheaper, and/or faster than before, or provide a new service with prospects of great and long-continued sales increases.

4. It must have a strong, progressive, research-minded management.

Put that way, the quest may sound easy. But even in that day there were more than fifty thousand stocks to choose from. The odds on finding a needle in a haystack would be about the same if one could hunt with a magnet.

Mr. Garrett had no magnet, but he did have friends in Wall

Street and in business. Some of them were advising or managing pension funds. Without seeking any confidential information Mr. Garrett asked for the names of any *smaller* than usual investments of institutional money. He was looking for stocks that professional buyers liked but were not sure of. Before he was through he had fifty stocks from which to choose. Since his goal was to make big money he did not make the common mistake of buying a little of each of the fifty. People who bet on all of the horses in a race always have a winner but never make any money.

Mr. Garrett winnowed out all but three by studying financial reports and analyses. Then he made what security analysts call field trips to those three, visiting with their chief executive officers. Finally he settled on one, Haloid, now Xerox, and invested $133,000 in its stock between 1955 and 1959. He has more than 63,000 shares which cost him $1 a share for stock which in 1971 sold above $125 a share.

Sounds easy, but Mr. Garrett first had to find the stock he wanted. Then he had to buy it in the face of recommendations against it by people who either knew nothing about it, or had pets they liked better, or believed in diversification no matter what. And finally, he had to hold on, and buy more, against repeated "sell" recommendations he began to receive even before the stock had doubled in price.

It would be misleading to other investors, though, and unfair to Mr. Garrett, if I left the impression that his fortune is all owed to a single lucky stock selection. He also owns 50,800 shares of Teleprompter at an average cost of 75¢ a share (it sold above $30 last year) and has a substantial block of McCulloch Oil stock. The real basis of his wealth is "buy right and hold on," a formula he has followed faithfully for many years. Does it work? Even after large institutional benefactions since 1969, his security holdings at the end of 1971 had a market value of more than $14,000,000. It is hard to argue with $14,000,000.

What does a man of eighty want with so much money? Doesn't he know he can't take it with him?

Mr. Garrett has an answer to those questions too. His wife died of cancer. One million dollars has gone into a cancer research fund with an unusual provision for the invasion of principal if in the opinion of the trustees a "breakthrough" seems near enough to warrant accelerating the program.

A second million dollars has gone to his alma mater, Whitman College, at Walla Walla, Washington, out of appreciation of the educational bargain he got there as a young man, and in the hope that he can give other men a better break.

A third million has been given to Columbia University's Graduate School of Business for a chair on "The Public Problems and Responsibilities of Business." Mr. Garrett's purpose and hope are to prepare business students to be corporate chief executives even though most of them never can be. The executive suite is not big enough. What matters is that those who *do* get there know the full dimensions of the job, and are qualified to handle it. Mr. Garrett is keenly aware that specialized training in finance, marketing, manufacturing, or even research, that most successful executives receive on their way to the top does not prepare them for the social and political challenges that confront the chief executive. As George V. Holton, retired chairman of what is now Mobil Oil Corporation, put it, "Unless a company operating in a foreign country is conducting itself so that the people of that country are better off net, after the company has realized its profit, than they would be if they nationalized the company and ran it themselves, that company is living on borrowed time." Mr. Holton added that such a company not only must operate to benefit the foreign country but must see to it that the people of that country know it is doing so. And even then, Mr. Holton concluded, a company operating abroad may find itself in hot water unless its representatives can win for themselves personally the respect and friendship of the nationals where they work.

Mr. Garrett goes even further. He thinks in our rapidly changing world Mr. Holton's words apply to domestic corporations as well.

When the chips are down, no man's title to any property—his home, his automobile, his stocks and bonds—is worth any more than the ability and willingness of his fellowmen to defend it. Mr. Garrett hopes that a higher proportion of the new breed of corporate executives may be educated to appreciate that *before* the chips are down.

Even at eighty Mr. Garrett is still looking for new financial worlds to conquer, not that he may die richer but that he may live more richly in terms of service to mankind. Withal he is a charmingly modest man. At our first meeting he admitted he had made $5,000,000. At our second conference he said $10,000,000 would be nearer the truth. Not until our third get-together did the $14,000,000 figure come out.

Few men have made their mark in more businesses than my longtime friend Karl Dravo Pettit. Industrialist, inventor, financier, and investment counselor, at eighty-two he still commutes daily to New York City from his Cherry Hill Farm estate near Princeton, New Jersey. He is not driven by necessity, nor has he ever been. Senior partner in Karl D. Pettit & Co., investment counselors, which he founded almost forty years ago, he is reputed to be the largest landowner in the Princeton area. He has sold some acreage for 100 times what it cost him. Yet probably no man in financial history has better reason to advise, "Buy right and hold on."

The story came out one day when we were lunching together. He paid me some undeserved compliment and I said, "Karl, you don't know how stupid I am. To get capital to go into the brokerage business in 1938 I sold, for $4,500, Dow-Jones stock now worth more than a million dollars."

"Except to learn from experience, one should never waste time looking back," Mr. Pettit replied. "In 1925 I personally owned 6,500 shares of Computing-Tabulating-Recording (now IBM). At that time there were only 120,000 shares outstanding. I sold mine for more than a million dollars—a lot of money in those days. Today they would be worth two billion dollars."

What did he learn from that experience? Two things:

1. Stay with your most successful stock investments as long as the companies are increasing their earnings.

2. Never forget that people whose self-interest is diametrically opposed to your own are trying to persuade you to act every day. *Who* is talking often means more than *what* is said. Try to identify people whose interests correspond with yours.

George Shea and I were news editors of The Wall Street

Journal in the mid-1930s. George has kept most of his Dow-Jones stock to this day. He now holds 9,520 shares worth more than 100 times his original investment of $4,200. That is after giving each of his two children 820 shares. He gets back in dividends *each year* more than twice his total cost.

Some of us are a little put off by such stories. It hurts our ego to see someone outdistancing us like that. Hence our resort to such ego balm as, "He had the inside track. He had the ten thousand dollars to get started. He had to pay no capital gains taxes. He had no family illnesses, no children to educate." Anything to make the point that those who did better than we had advantages denied to us. Besides, we tell ourselves, those success stories are ancient history. No one can do it now.

Unfortunately for our peace of mind, if we are hard up, not only does the record show constantly recurring opportunities in the past but strong indications that they are still popping up. Many stocks have grown in the last fifteen years at rates which if continued will produce one hundredfold appreciation in another fifteen or twenty years. If that seems too long to wait, remember the late George F. Baker's dictum: To make money in stocks you must have "the vision to see them, the courage to buy them and the patience to hold them." Patience is the rarest of the three.

Maybe you do not have ten thousand dollars. Many people don't. But one thousand dollars invested in any one of the more than 360 stocks that have gone up 100 for one since 1932 would be worth one hundred thousand dollars now.

You don't have even a thousand dollars? Sorry, there is no hope for you. I have it on the word of Andrew Carnegie.

"You want to know if you will be rich," he said. "The answer is, 'Can you save money?'"

CHAPTER II

Sinbad's Valley of Diamonds

Early in the summer of 1932 an oldtimer in Wall Street remarked to me, "Anyone who can put his hands on $10,000 to invest in the stock market at these prices is a rich man." At the time I likened his comment to the quip that if we had some ham we'd have some ham and eggs if we had some eggs. That was because I did not have $10,000 or anything like it. In fact the market was where it was because very few people did have $10,000 to invest.

Everyone knows now that the stock market in 1932 was literally studded with stocks in which an investment of $10,000 would be worth $1 million or more today. It was not even necessary to go outside the Dow-Jones Industrial Average to find them. Eastman Kodak was one. In July 1932, 144,000 shares changed hands at prices ranging from 35-1/4 to 45-5/8. Even at the month's high, $10,000 would have bought 219 shares of Eastman Kodak. Today the buyer of those 219 shares would have 14,191 shares without ever having invested another dollar or paid a penny of tax on his gain. Their 1971 value exceeded $1,400,000.

Most of the individuals who bought Eastman Kodak stock in July 1932 probably are dead by now but their heirs are alive, and so are most of the institutions which were in the market in 1932. I wonder if anyone, individual or institution, still has Eastman Kodak stock bought at 1 percent of its current market value. I doubt it, but would be glad to be proved wrong. And yet I know of no institution that has increased the value of its investment portfolio by anything like 100 times since 1932 without adding capital, and without paying any brokerage commissions or capital gains taxes.

It was not even necessary to buy Eastman Kodak in 1932 to make 100 for one on your money. Eastman Kodak stock could still have been bought on the New York Stock Exchange in 1933 at prices less than 1 percent of 1971 market values.

But this is hindsight. How did Eastman Kodak look in 1932 and 1933?

Per share earnings in 1932 were $2.52, down from $9.57 in 1929. But the price of the stock was 35-1/4 at the 1932 low, and 46 at the 1933 low, compared with its 1929 high of 264-3/4. Earnings were down 74 percent from their high, while the price was down 87 percent in 1932 and 83 percent in 1933 from the 1929 peak. The price-earnings ratio had dropped from about 28 times record high earnings to 14 times depression low earnings. (28 $\times$ $9.57 = $267. 14 $\times$ $2.52 = $35.)

Compared with the Dow-Jones Industrial Average, Eastman Kodak stock did very well in the 1929–32 bear market. As the relative price chart* shows, Eastman Kodak stock's price

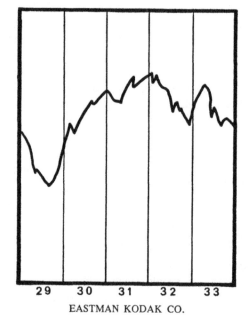

EASTMAN KODAK CO.

*For an explanation of relative price charts, see Chapter VII, *The Tree Does Not Grow to the Sky,* page 77.

improved sharply compared with the Dow-Jones average, from 1929 to 1932. The company had no near rival in the photographic business.

If for some reason one did not like Eastman Kodak in 1932, he could have bought the stock of the leading tire and rubber company—Goodyear. The stock sold at a low of 5-1/2 in May, a low of 6-1/8 in June, and a low of 6-1/4 in July 1932. Even at $9 a share, $10,000 would have bought 1,111 shares of Goodyear stock. Today the buyer of those 1,111 shares would have 32,441 shares, again without ever having put up another dollar. Those shares too were worth more than $1 million in 1971. Like Eastman Kodak, Goodyear was in the Dow-Jones Industrial Average. So was Sears, Roebuck. At its 1932 low, $10,000 would have bought 1,000 shares, now 24,000 shares. Their value in 1971 came close to $2,500,000.

Unlike Eastman Kodak, Goodyear reported a deficit of $850,000 for 1932. While Goodyear earned its fixed charges 1.06 times in that year, before minority interests, it failed by a wide margin to cover its first preferred stock dividends.

Again, unlike Eastman Kodak, Goodyear stock lost ground sharply compared with the Dow-Jones Industrial Average from 1929 to 1932, as the accompanying chart shows. Yet both Eastman Kodak and Goodyear have risen one hundredfold since 1932. Goodyear in fact sold in 1971 at more than 100 times its 1942 low.

Sears, Roebuck also reported a deficit for 1932, but its relative price went no lower than it had in 1930.

By hindsight, it was almost as easy to buy 100-to-one winners in 1933, before the bank holiday, as in 1932. Just to cite a few examples at random, $10,000 could have been invested in Melville Shoe, Newmont Mining, Philip Morris, or Pitney Bowes in 1933 to be worth more than $1 million in 1971. In the first three months of 1933, some 2,000 shares of Melville Shoe stock changed hands on the New York Stock Exchange at prices ranging from 8-3/4 to 10-7/8. At 9-7/8, approximately the average price, $10,000 would have bought 1,000 shares. Today, without ever having put up any more money, the buyer would have 18,800 shares valued in 1971 at more than $1 million.

The Newmont Mining story is much the same except that the

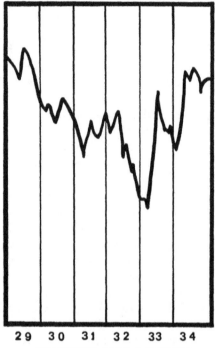

29 30 31 32 33 34

GOODYEAR TIRE & RUBBER

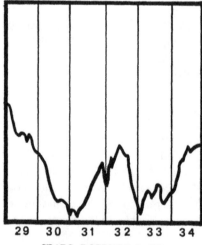

29 30 31 32 33 34

SEARS, ROEBUCK & CO.

buyer of the stock at the 1932 low would have had more than $3 million to show for this $10,000 investment while the buyer at the 1933 low would have had only $1,225,000. The 1933 low was 11-1/2. At that price $10,000 would have bought 868 shares. By 1971 the buyer of those 868 shares had 31,248 Newmont shares, without putting up another cent.

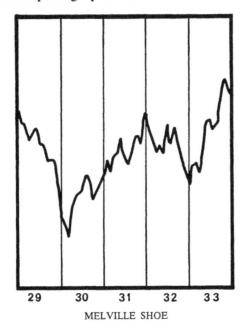

MELVILLE SHOE

How did Melville Shoe and Newmont Mining look in 1932 and 1933?

Melville Shoe earned $1.51 a common share in 1932. At its 1932 low of 7-7/8 the stock was selling 5.2 times its earnings for that year. Newmont Mining earned 22 cents a common share in 1932. At its 1932 low of 4-5/8 Newmont was selling 21 times its 1932 earnings.

Relative to the Dow-Jones Industrial Average, Melville Shoe's price by 1932 was about where it had been at the start of 1929. Newmont's relative price in 1932 was down precipitously from 1929.

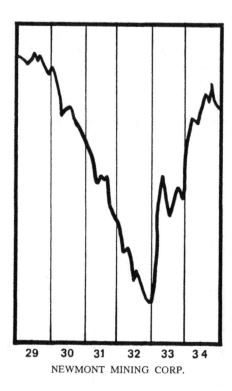

29   30   31   32   33   3 4
NEWMONT MINING CORP.

When you compare the five relative price charts as they looked in 1932 and 1933, bear in mind that, adjusting for stock dividends and stock splits, each of the five issues—Eastman Kodak, Goodyear Tire, Melville Shoe, Newmont Mining, and Sears, Roebuck—has risen to more than 100 times its 1932 and 1933 lows. Yet two of the five—Eastman Kodak and Melville Shoe—were in pronounced relative price uptrends by 1932. Two others—Goodyear and Newmont—could hardly have looked worse by mid-1932. Sears, Roebuck while down sharply from its 1929 high was finding support at its 1930 relative price low.

Their price-earnings ratios computed from their 1932 lows and their subsequently reported 1932 earnings were these:

Price-Earnings Ratio

Goodyear	Incalculable
Sears, Roebuck	Incalculable
Newmont	21 X
Eastman Kodak	14 X
Melville Shoe	5.2 X

If this disparity in relative price action and in price-earnings ratios suggests that there may be no surefire, simple rule of thumb by which a schoolboy can beat the market, the conclusion is yours. All I am trying to do is report fully and fairly. Millions of dollars worth of stocks change hands on the basis of such data, more often than not calculated from estimates of the murky future. Who am I to say there is no Santa Claus and bring Virginia and the ghost of the *New York Sun* down on my head?

Few people would have thought of Philip Morris in 1933 as a stock destined to multiply their investment by 100. Yet Philip Morris stock traded between a low of 8 and a high of 9 for the first three months of 1933. At the high of 9, $10,000 would have bought more than 1,100 shares. Without putting up any more capital, the buyer of those 1,100 shares would today have 20,790 shares. Their market value in 1971 was nearly $1.5 million. Even in 1934 Philip Morris still could have been bought for less than one percent of its 1971 value.

Philip Morris was much stronger than the Dow-Jones Industrial Average throughout the 1929–32 bear market.

At its 1932 low of $7 a share, Philip Morris stock was selling at less than six times earnings for that year.

Pitney Bowes is the last of the stocks I mentioned as having been available for purchase in 1933 at less than 1 percent of its 1971 market value. (As Table I—pages 54–75—shows, there were scores of others.) In the first three months of 1933, fully 8,500 shares of the stock changed hands at prices ranging from 2 to 3-3/8. At the low nearly 5,000 shares could have been bought for $10,000. Those 5,000 shares at this writing would be 32,000 shares. In 1971 they sold at more than 100 times their adjusted 1933 low.

Recitation of these big winners becomes tiresome not only because most of us failed to take advantage of them but also because this is all ancient history. What do we care if Peter Minuit bought Manhattan Island for $24 worth of trinkets? You and I must operate in today's real estate market.

Anticipating the first objection, I have shown in Table I that opportunities to invest $10,000 for one hundredfold appreciation have been present in 32 of the last 40 years—and as recently as 1967! The securities listed in Table II (see appendix) are the same as in Table I but they are listed alphabetically instead of being grouped by years of "purchase."

Many stocks other than those on my lists have risen more than 100 for one in price in the last forty years or less. To minimize hindsight I left out any that were not quoted in publications available to us all at the time the securities would have had to be bought to show one hundredfold appreciation by 1971. Every one I have listed was quoted in the *Wall Street Journal, Moody's* manuals, the *Commercial and Financial Chronicle,* or the *Bank and Quotation Record* when it was selling at one percent or less of its 1971 market value.

Because 1932 and 1933 were so long ago, with so little chance that we shall ever see their like again, it is profitless and possibly annoying to spend more time on what could have been done with $10,000 in those years. Suffice that the stocks I have mentioned are merely illustrations of the opportunities that abounded in those days. As you can see in Table I, there were many more. Remember, too, Table I is not all-inclusive even of issues that would meet my standards. I merely noted those that occurred to me. You may think of many that I have missed. But every one you add strengthens my basic thesis that the way to wealth is to buy right and hold on.

Opportunities to turn a $10,000 investment into a million dollars still were plentiful in 1934. Stocks which come to mind include Ex-Cell-O and Texas Pacific Coal & Oil.

Sometimes one can make a fortune in a liquidation. Texas Pacific Coal & Oil sold in large volume on the New York Stock Exchange in July 1934 at prices ranging from a low of 2-1/2 to a high of 4. As late as December 1934 it sold at a low of 2-7/8. In 1948 the stock paid a stock dividend of 100 percent, and in 1955 a second stock dividend of 100 percent. The result was that the buyer at 2-1/2 in 1934 found himself owning four times as many shares as he started with. At 2-1/2, $10,000 would have bought 4,000 shares. Multiplied by four those 4,000 shares became 16,000 shares. In 1953 and 1964 Texas Pacific Coal & Oil made liquidating distributions totaling $68.53 a share. Again the gain is more than 100 for one—without allowing for any return on the liquidating distributions since 1964. Adding interest at the rate of 5 percent compounded annually would raise the total return from $68.53 a share to $96.42, less taxes on the interest.

Please don't quibble about my failure to allow for brokerage charges on the purchase. The margin by which the stock's value exceeded $1 million in 1971 makes it unnecessary to split financial hairs over commissions.

Ex-Cell-O sold at a low of 3-3/4 on January 11, 1934, following a low of 1-1/4 on February 24, 1933. At the 1934 price $10,000 would have bought 2,660 shares. Today the buyer would have almost 16 times as many shares, or something over 42,300 shares. In 1971 their market value passed the million dollar mark. The profit opportunity in buying Ex-Cell-O in 1933 was three times as great, of course.

Turning to 1935, Skelly Oil could still have been bought on the New York Stock Exchange at less than 1 percent of its 1971 market value. The same opportunity, or even greater, had been provided by Skelly stock in 1934 and 1933. Its 1935 low was 6-1/2 in January. At that price $10,000 would have bought more than 1,530 shares. Today the buyer would have 22,400 shares valued in 1971 at more than $1 million.

What is now known as Sunbeam Corporation was called Chicago Flexible Shaft Company in 1935. The best market for the stock then was the Chicago Stock Exchange where it traded in January 1935, from a low of 13-1/2 to a high of 15. At 15, the month's high, $10,000 would have paid for 666 shares. Had the buyer held them until now, without ever paying a cent of capital gains taxes or making a dollar of additional investment, he would have 34,299 shares, again valued in 1971 at more than $1 million.

Except by hindsight these 100-to-1 opportunities in the stock market are hard to spot. It is even more difficult to spot them when they come via mergers. For example, another stock that could have been bought for $10,000 in 1935 to be worth $1 million in 1971 was Wilcox Oil Company. Wilcox Oil & Gas, as it was then called, sold at a low of $1 a share in March 1935. The high that month was $2. Subsequent stock dividends and a merger with Tennessee Gas Transmission Company (now Tenneco) in 1964 gave the buyer of one share of Wilcox in 1935 more than 3.8 shares of Tenneco in 1971. Their 1971 market value exceeded 100 times the 1935 purchase price. Those who bought Tennessee Gas Transmission Company likewise have made money but not nearly as much as the fortunate purchasers of Wilcox in 1935.

By 1936 the Dow-Jones Industrial Average had advanced to more than four times its 1932 low. Many of us felt that we had awakened too late to the opportunities to make a fortune in the stock market. But while we were bemoaning our inability or failure to buy more heavily in 1932, the year 1936 was presenting other stocks that would turn $10,000 into $1 million or more by 1971. One of them was Loft, now Pepsico. Loft sold on the New York Stock Exchange at a low of 2 on April 23, 1936, and ranged all year between that low and a high of 3-5/8. For $10,000 one could have bought 3,475 shares of Loft at 2-7/8, about midway between the year's high and low. Each of those shares would now be 6.06 shares of Pepsico. Thus the 1936 investor of $10,000 in Loft could have had 21,050 shares of Pepsico in 1971, worth nearly $1.5 million, without ever putting up another cent.

For the benefit of those of us who were asleep in 1935 and 1936, Loft sold in 1937 at a low of 1 and a high of 3-7/8. Then, almost as though the fates conspired to see that no one missed this opportunity, Loft sold in 1938 at a low of 75 cents a share. As a matter of fact, investors had to turn their backs on Loft each year for seven consecutive years from 1932 through 1938 to avoid the opportunity to turn $10,000 into more than $1 million. The stubbornness with which we mortals sometimes reject the blandishments of Dame Fortune has to be seen to be believed. Later on we shall examine more of these insistently persistent opportunity stocks.

The stock market broke sharply in the fall of 1937. At the time the decline was attributed to the Government's testing of its inflation brakes. Gold imports were sterilized, that is, prevented from increasing the money supply. The Federal Reserve raised reserve requirements of the member banks. And President Roosevelt "jaw-boned" against commodity price advances.

In the stock market there are often two explanations for a severe decline. The first one—that which I have just cited—is ostensible and satisfies the halfwise. The second one is the real reason which sadly seldom becomes apparent until too late to do most of us any good. In this case the real reason burst on the world with the beginning of the Second World War near the end of the summer of 1938.

The bear market of 1937 did not catch me by surprise. In a "Study in the Price Movement" published on the first page of the *Wall Street Journal* on September 8, 1937, I reported, "There seems no doubt that the major trend of the market is downward." The Dow-Jones Industrial Average closed the next day at 166. It was more than seven and a half years—May 1945—before the market sold that high again. Yet I would have been much better off if instead of correctly forecasting a bear market I had focused my attention throughout the decline on finding stocks that would turn $10,000 into a million dollars. Such opportunities were there in 1937, in 1938, in 1939, in 1940, in 1941, in 1942, in 1943, and in 1944, as Table I and Table II show with, to me, painful clarity.

There is another reason why professional investors, except those managing discretionary accounts, should de-emphasize market timing. That is because even if the market forecaster is right, he seldom can persuade others to act on his opinion. No one intends to buy stocks at the top of the market, or to sell them at the lows. On the contrary, bull market highs are made when the outlook for still higher prices is most broadly convincing. Conversely bear market lows are made when the likelihood of still lower prices seems overwhelming to the preponderance of reasonable, well-informed moneyed men. Since bull and bear markets are to a considerable extent manifestations of changes in mass psychology it is fatuous for anyone to believe that he can persuade a representative group of investors to sell stocks when that mass psychology is bullish, or to buy stocks when it is bearish. The wise professional, who understands this, concentrates on stock selection. Most investors are far less emotionally involved in deciding which stock to buy or sell than they are in deciding whether the market is going up or down. To clinch the argument, it is readily demonstrable that far more money can be made by good stock selection than by good stock market timing.

But let us return to the 100-to-one opportunities in 1937. Sharp & Dohme was actively traded on the New York Stock Exchange in that year. It sold at a low of 6-3/4 in September, 3-3/4 in October, 4-7/8 in November, and 4 in December. Thus it should have been easy to invest $10,000 in Sharp & Dohme at $6 a share. The buyer would have had 1,666 shares. In exchange for them he would have received in 1953 some 3,748 shares of Merck & Company. Those shares were split 3-for-1 in 1964, bringing the present total holdings to 11,245 Merck shares, valued at nearly $1.5 million in 1971. As late as 1943 Sharp & Dohme could still have been bought at less than 1 percent of the 1971 value of the Merck stock acquired in exchange. In fact we could have bought Sharp & Dohme in each of 12 consecutive years from 1932 through 1943 at less than 1 percent of its peak 1971 value. We could have bought it at the highs of six of those twelve years and still have had 100 for one on our investment. Score another knockout for Selection over Timing!

In 1938 I could have invested $10,000 in Beech Aircraft, or in Brunswick-Balke-Collender, or in Carnation, and had stock worth well above a million dollars in 1971. An investment of $10,000 in Loft at its 1938 low of 75 cents a share would have had a market value of more than $5.5 million last year.

In 1939 Columbia River Packers or Clark Equipment would have done the trick. In 1940 Merck itself would have given us 100 for one had we bought it and held it until now. (Actually at the 1971 high Merck was selling 164 times its 1940 low.) In 1941 (or 1943) one could have based his million-dollar fortune on a $10,000 investment in Gillette or Louisiana Land. In

1942, or as late as 1945, Plough (now Schering-Plough) would have done the job. In 1943 one might have chosen Maytag or Pfizer. In 1944 Black & Decker and Noxzema Chemical were available at prices less than 1 percent of 1971 market values. In 1945 Minnesota Mining and National Homes offered similar 100-to-one opportunities. And at the top of the market in 1946, and as late as 1948, Galvin (now Motorola) provided a vehicle for riding a small stake to a big fortune.

As you can see in Table I, pages 54–75, these were by no means the only 100-to-one stocks available in those years. They are merely illustrative of the goodies anyone could have had. All one had to do was recognize them, and stay with them.

CHAPTER III

Learning from Elephants

Like the builder who provides a landing on the stairs to avoid unduly fatiguing the climber, let us pause at this point to ask why, with so many 100-to-one opportunities around, even professional investors so seldom have increased their capital in these same periods by even 10 for one. The answer is to be found both in psychology and in statistics. Let us deal first with the psychological aspects of the problem, saving the statistical for another landing on the stairs.

Forty-six years ago, when I was paying my way through equatorial Africa by shooting elephants for ivory, I learned this simple principle: When looking for the biggest game, be not tempted to shoot at anything small. Elephants' ears are very keen. Never after firing a single shot at a guinea hen, a colobus monkey, or an antelope did I see an elephant that day.

In a way this lesson I learned in the Ituri forest is a variation of the story of the five poor Arabs. When I asked for one guinea hen, I got one guinea hen—no more.

Few investors, private or professional, seek the big game. They focus on chances to make five points here and ten points there. They rush to buy on information that the next quarter's earnings will show a good increase, or to sell because they hear that profit gains have slackened. Brokers used to fatten on this type of activity. Ultimately it became so great that scores of firms succumbed at a time when both the price and the demand for what they had for sale were the highest they had ever known. If it seems contradictory for brokers to fatten on transactions in stocks and then to succumb when they got more transactions than they could handle, you have noted one of the great paradoxes in the history of business. I can recall no other instance in industry or finance in which numerous firms choked to death on prosperity. The explanation was that they had overemphasized getting business (selling) and under-emphasized keeping track of it (bookkeeping). The in-and-out trading that first enriched and then impoverished so many brokers was all to the good for the tax collectors—federal, state, and in many cases city as well. What it meant for the investor is something else again.

For the individual or institution really out to make a fortune in the stock market it can be argued that every sale is a confession of error. I write this fully realizing that to err is human. I do not mean to criticize anyone for making a few errors of the kind I have been making for forty-five years. But a problem well-defined is half solved. Just as I garnered no ivory by counting guinea hens as elephants, so shall I gather no fortune in the stock market by counting lost opportunities as trading profits. The shorter the time a stock has been held before it is sold, the more palpable the error in buying it—go-go fund managers to the contrary notwithstanding.

Let this not be construed as advocating hanging on to everything willy-nilly. The only thing worse than making an investment mistake is refusing to admit it and correct it. Usually the faster an error is rectified the less it costs. But it is still an error, a lost opportunity, compared with buying right and holding on.

In a bull market correcting mistakes often means taking profits. But when we do so let us not kid ourselves we are making money. The truth is we are acknowledging missing vastly bigger opportunities, and incurring a capital gains tax liability to boot.

The big risk in correcting errors in the stock market is that stocks look best to so many of us when their prices are highest, and worst when their prices are lowest. Almost irresistibly we are tempted to shoot where the rabbit was, to do now what hindsight shows would have been the right thing to do yester-day, last year, or even five or ten years ago.

The ability to foresee the future is rare, the ability to rationalize the present all too common. Hence when a stock we bought after careful investigation declines in price we often find it less attractive than before.

That same housewife who buys three roasts of beef for her freezer because they are offered at a special low price will sell her Consolidated Doorknobs stock because it is trading at half what she paid for it.

Professional investors sometimes do the same thing. They reason, often correctly, that someone knows more than they do. Rather than wait for the "bad news" to become public, they sell, thus accelerating the decline in the price of the stock and possibly unnerving still other investors.

Let's face it. A great deal of investing is on a par with the instinct that makes a fish bite on an inedible spinner because it is moving.

The fish reasons: "The last thing I ate was moving. It was good. This thing is moving. It must be good."

The investor reasons: "The last stock I bought was rising. It was good. This stock is rising. It must be good."

Good stocks do rise, and rise, and rise. As we can see in Tables I and II, there are enough of them to keep alive the notion that any stock that rises must be good. Periodically, as in 1969–70, we rediscover that all is not gold that glitters.

More subtle fallacies likewise impede the investor's progress on the way to wealth. One is the notion that cash is safe while all investments are more or less risky. Yet in every successive 100-year period since 1820—that is, 1820 to 1920, 1821 to 1921, 1822 to 1922, 1870 to 1970—our dollar has lost something like 50 percent to 70 percent of its buying power. Over successive 100-year periods the rate of inflation has been relentlessly stable. I shall have more to say about that in the section on Inflation (page 151).

Another often unrecognized investment fallacy is that avoidance of risk is more important than seizure of opportunity. Consider first the arithmetic. If you had invested equal amounts of money in 100 stocks in any one of the years shown in Table I, and *if 99 of your 100 stocks had become worthless,* you still would have your original capital intact if you had bought just *one* of the 100-to-one stocks available in the year you chose. Admittedly picking a 100-to-one stock in advance is not easy. But it would also be difficult to pick 99 stocks in one year, *all* of which would become worthless. Anyone who could do that would be worth his weight in gold in Wall Street as a guide to profitable short selling.*

It follows from this second subtle fallacy that investors tend to overemphasize the risks of being in stocks, and underweigh the cost of not buying, or of selling too soon. One of Wall Street's most hackneyed references is to the beaming, bewhiskered, complacent old gentleman whose face is pictured over the words, "I sold too soon." I wonder how many millions of shares of unwarranted brokerage business that old codger has generated.

Selling too soon can be frightfully expensive. Some poor

STOCKS OFFSET DOLLAR'S FALL

*One who sells stock he does not own, in hope of buying it at a lower price later on, has engaged in short selling. He is "short" of the stock until he buys it. A short sale made in hope of profiting by a price decline comes close to being the opposite of a purchase made in hope of profiting by a price advance.

souls sold 700 shares of Computing-Tabulating-Recording stock in July of 1921 for $21,700. In 1971, now selling under the name IBM, those shares were worth more than $150 million.

To go from one to 100 in twenty-five years the price of a stock must increase at a compound annual rate of more than 20 percent, not including dividends. The seller of such a stock after twenty years gets less than 40 for one before taxes and brokerage commissions. The remaining 60 for one comes in the last five years if the rate of price increase is constant.

There is no reason, of course, to sell at any time just because one has a big profit, even a 100-to-one profit. In fact one of the basic rules of investing is:

Never if you can help it take an investment action for a non-investment reason.

What are some of the non-investment reasons for which tens of thousands of investors go wrong?

Let me cite just a few:

1. My stock is "too high."
2. I need the realized capital gain to offset realized capital losses for tax purposes.
3. My stock is not moving. Others are.
4. I cannot or will not put up more money to meet my margin call.
5. Taxes will be higher next year.
6. New management.
7. New competition.

The possibility that one or all of these reasons may warrant a sale or switch should be weighed carefully, of course. But the difference between a possibility and reality is roughly the difference between track-soup and moose steak. Track-soup is what hunters have for supper when they come home empty-handed.

Josh Billings once said of a man he admired with great restraint: "The trouble with him ain't that he is ignorant, but that he knows so much that ain't so."

Much has been said since 1932 about keeping investors fully informed. I sometimes wonder if we are not told more than is good for us. If each passenger on a 747 had a clear view of every instrument in front of the pilots, his worries would lag the corrective actions taken by the pilots. Such is the relationship between stockholders and a competent company management.

Investors should beware of confusing cynicism with sophistication. Sometimes what the salesman offers you in the stock market is as good or better than anything you could have found for yourself. Take the Schering Corporation stock offering of 1952, for example. Investors paid $30,800,000 for 1,760,000 Schering shares. If they still have it, their paper *profit* as of the 1971 high was more than $1,200,000,000. While Schering stock has not yet made its holders 100 for one, those who bought on the original offering less than twenty years ago already have seen their holdings increase to 41 times their purchase price. (Those who bought Plough, now part of Schering-Plough, at 13-1/4 in 1945 have gained one hundredfold. See Tables I and II.)

Schering was seized as enemy property at the outset of World War II. It was sold at competitive bidding in 1952 by the Attorney General of the United States. The winning bid, $29,131,960, was entered by a group composed of Merrill Lynch, Pierce, Fenner & Beane; Kidder Peabody & Company, and Drexel & Company. The second highest bid was $26,845,-544. The lowest bid was $14,080,000.

Do-it-yourself investors may be interested in the fact that the winning bid amounted to $66.20 a share for Schering stock which had a book value of $32.55 a share.

The winning bidders promptly split the stock 4-for-1, then sold the new shares at $17.50 a share. At that price their gross receipts were $30,800,000 compared with their purchase price of $29,131,960, a gain of $1,668,040. Their gross profit thus was about $1.40 on each $1,000 that the buyers of their Schering offering have made in the last nineteen years—assuming of course that the buyers have held on.

Some of them may have switched into "something better." I have often done that myself.

By the way, you did not need a friend in a brokerage house

to cut you in on this Schering "hot issue." The public offering at $17.50 was made on March 11, 1952. For the balance of the year the stock's price range was from a low of 13-1/4 to a high of 17-7/8. Had you been lucky enough to buy at the low, and patient enough to hold on until now, your stock at the 1971 high would have been worth more than 54 times what you paid for it.

You could even have waited a year and a half and bought the stock at $11 a share in September of 1953 and again in October of that year. From that figure your investment would have increased by 1971 to more than 65 times your cost.

This is not to recommend waiting for the bottom eighth.* If you really think a stock is attractive, buy it at the market. Then if it becomes available at a lower price buy more if you can. The difference between making 40 times your investment and 60 times your investment is not nearly as important as missing the opportunity altogether. There is much wisdom in the Wall Street saying, "There is room in the stock market for bulls and for bears, but not for hogs."

Other golden underwritings come to mind. On May 20, 1941, Goldman Sachs & Company and Lehman Brothers offered 202,372 shares of Merck & Company stock at $28.75 a share. The stock was split 2-for-1 in 1949, 3-for-1 in 1951, and 3-for-1 in 1964. Thus each share offered on May 20, 1941, is now 18 shares. Everyone who bought 100 shares of that Goldman Sachs–Lehman Brothers offering for $2,875 and held them until now has 1,800 shares with a peak 1971 market value of more than $236,000. At the current dividend rate of 55 cents quarterly, his entire original investment is being returned to him 1.37 times each year. Unfortunately those dividends are taxable. The gain is not.

The entire underwriting, by the way, which raised $5,818,000, had a peak market value last year of more than $478 million.

Almost as if the fates wanted to give everybody a second chance, the same underwriters came along with 30,000 addi-

---

*That is Wall Street jargon for the lowest price at which a stock sells in any period under discussion. Since price changes are expressed in eighths of a dollar, the bottom eighth must be the low.

tional shares of the same stock at $30 a share on December 17, 1941. No one likes to buy at $30 when he could have had it at $28.75 just seven months earlier, but each of those $30 shares had a peak market value in 1971 of 78 times their cost.

It is true that investors who waited for the Goldman Sachs and Lehman Brothers salesmen have not yet seen their Merck stock advance to 100 times what they paid for it. To achieve that happy result in 1971 investors must have bought Merck stock on their own in 1940.

Lest it be suspected that I used the Schering and Merck underwritings as examples because I had no better ones, let us turn to Pfizer. On June 23, 1942, a syndicate headed by F. Eberstadt & Co., New York, offered 240,000 shares at $24.75 a share. If you had been persuaded by the Eberstadt salesmen to buy 100 shares for $2,475, and if you had held them until now, you would be the owner of 8,100 shares. At their 1971 high their market value was $349,312, or 141 times your purchase price. Bear in mind you did not have to outwit anyone to buy that stock. The company wanted more money with which to operate. All you had to do to make your fortune in Pfizer was to accommodate the company and make a syndicate salesman happy.

I can and will cite other examples of fortune-making underwritings. The point is that it is not necessary to buy little-known stocks in the dark of the moon to get hold of a fortune-maker. Most of us have owned one or more of them at some time in our lives. Our failure has been to hold on.

Thinking too much about what the market is going to do can be expensive, even when one is right.

Just three weeks before the *Wall Street Journal* featured my 1937 bear market analysis under a two-column heading on the first page, Russell Maguire & Company, Inc., of New York, offered 83,333 shares of General American Oil Company of Texas at $6.50 a share. Suppose I had not been keen enough to see the 1937 bear market coming. Suppose, instead, like the hapless public, I had been persuaded to put my life's savings of $10,000 into General American Oil Company stock on the eve of a major bear market. What would have happened to me?

For $10,000 I would have bought 1,538 shares and had a few pennies left over. If I had put those shares away and forgotten them, 1 would now have 24,930 shares without ever having invested another cent in the company or paid out a thin dime in capital gains tax. In 1971 those 24,930 shares were valued on the New York Stock Exchange at more than $1,200,000. My cash dividends would have been just under $15,000 or at the annual rate of 150 percent on my original investment.

I doubt that anyone who bought any of those 83,333 shares of General American Oil Company of Texas on August 18, 1937, at $6.50 a share has held them until now. I likewise doubt whether anyone who did buy the stock in 1937 and subsequently sold it to invest in something better is as well off today as he would have been had he just sat tight for thirty-four years. If anyone does still hold General American Oil stock bought on that 1937 offering, he should be interviewed on TV.

Again many will say that this is all hindsight. But anyone who examines the list of more than 360 stocks that could have been bought in any one of thirty-two different years at prices 1 percent or less of their 1971 market values must concede that a great many people have had million-dollar fortunes in their grasp only to lose them by trying to be in something that was moving upward all the time.

GENERAL AMERICAN OIL OF TEXAS
MONTHLY PRICES RELATIVE TO THE DOW-JONES
INDUSTRIAL AVERAGE

To read this chart (and any other relative price chart) simply keep in mind that from any point forward in time, the Dow-Jones Industrial Average is a horizontal straight line. If the General American Oil relative price line falls below that horizontal straight line, the price of General American Oil stock has failed to keep up with the Dow from whatever starting point you have taken. Three illustrative dashed lines are shown on the chart. Each represents the Dow-Jones Industrial Average from the starting point shown. If you had bought General American Oil stock in June 1957 (Point No. 1 on the chart) your investment would have done poorly compared with the Dow-Jones Industrial Average. If you had bought General American Oil stock in May 1960 (Point No. 2) you would have made money much faster than the Dow. The same would have been true if you had bought in May 1965 (Point No. 3).

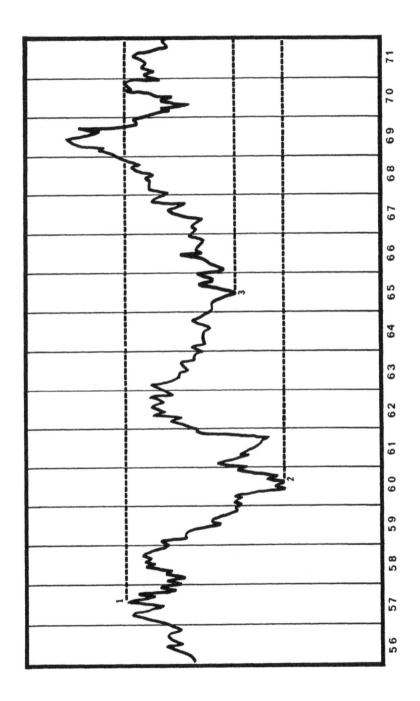

Bear in mind too that General American Oil Company of Texas stock is not a glamour issue. I have never seen it mentioned in the company of Polaroid, Syntex, and Xerox. But like the tortoise that won the race with the hare by keeping at it while the much faster hare explored the byways, the patient, stubborn and unflappable buyer of $10,000 worth of Russell Maguire's 1937 offering was a millionaire in 1971 if he never saved another dollar.

As is clearly shown by the accompanying chart* of the price of General American Oil relative to the Dow-Jones Industrial Average, no one demanding quarter by quarter, or even year by year, "performance" could have stayed with General American Oil until it made him a fortune. For sixteen years, from 1952 to 1968, the stock failed to keep up with the Dow-Jones Industrial Average. Few if any clients would have stayed with an investment advisor through such a period. Even fewer, I suspect, have done better with their investments since 1937 than the one hundredfold appreciation shown by General American Oil.

Someday "performance is the name of the game" will take its proper place in the history of the 1960s as an index of the speculative mania of that time. Investors have a right to expect results from professional counselors. But if the investors are wise they will encourage or at least permit their portfolio managers to seek results by way of increasing sales, earnings, and dividends regardless of market fluctuations, rather than by clever trading.

He who lives by the sword shall perish by the sword. When

---

*The chart shows the price of General American Oil stock month by month as a percent of the price of the Dow-Jones Industrial Average. For example, if General American Oil stock was selling at 40 and the Dow-Jones Industrial Average was at 800, the chart posting would be 40 divided by 800 = .05 or 5 percent. If the Dow-Jones Industrial Average advanced to 900 while General American Oil Stock sold at 81, the posting would be 81 divided by 900 = .09 or 9 percent. Between 1952 and 1960 the price of General American Oil stock failed to keep up with the price of the Dow-Jones Industrial Average so the relative price line declined as you can see. For that period the General American Oil stockholder would have been better off if he had owned the Dow-Jones Industrial Average instead. Since 1960 General American Oil stock again has outrun the Dow.

experienced investors frown on gambling with price fluctuations in the stock market it is not because they don't like money but because both experience and history have convinced them that enduring fortunes are not built that way.

Another fabulous underwriting was that of Air Products stock by Reynolds & Company of New York on May 6, 1946. The offering comprised: 100,000 Class A shares and 100,000 common shares in units of oné share each at $11 per unit; 150,000 common shares at $1 a share; 40,000 common shares aᴸ $1 a share for certain officers and employees.

Today each of those common shares is just over 2-1/2 shares valued at $144 at the 1971 high. If the officers and employees have held the stock they bought twenty-five years ago for $40,000, they now own 100,445 shares with a market value in 1971 of more than $5,800,000.

As for you and me, $10,000 would have bought us 10,000 shares. Today those 10,000 shares would be 25,111 shares valued in 1971 at $1,450,000.

I did not buy any. Four days after the Reynolds & Company offering, I wrote under date of May 10, 1946, a widely quoted market letter concluding, "Under the circumstances, retention of a fully invested position in common stocks would seem to be, like second marriage, 'a triumph of hope over experience.'"

I could hardly have been more right on the market. The Dow-Jones Industrial Average reached its 1946 high of 212.50 before the end of that month, and then declined 24 percent. Not for nearly four years did the Dow-Jones Industrial Average get back to the level against which I had warned. But by that time Air Products stock had trebled in price and another opportunity to make $100 on a $1 investment had escaped me.

The point I am trying to make, of course, is that even if one *knew* what the stock market was going to do, it could still be more profitable to forget it and concentrate on trying to find the right stock to buy.

Some will argue, as I have argued for many years, that good timing plus good selection is better than either alone. But bear market smoke gets into one's eyes and blinds him to buying opportunities if he is too intent on market timing. And the more successful one is at market timing, the greater the temptation to rely on it and thus miss the much greater opportunities in buying right and holding on.

Like an explorer going down an unmapped river in a dugout canoe, the investor must keep alert for the signs and sounds that warn of an undiscovered Niagara Falls. But in the last 100 years most investors have not encountered such all-engulfing liquidation more than once or twice in a business lifetime.

For the rest, if you are reasonably cool and skillful, history suggests you probably will do better to shoot the rapids in well-bought stocks than to portage around them in cash. But you must know yourself well enough to be sure you will not switch policies in mid-stream. Much profitless second-guessing, much shooting where the rabbit was, masquerades as adopting a new policy to meet changed conditions.

Most deception is bad but self-deception is worse because it is done to such a nice guy.

CHAPTER IV

Lemmings Follow the Crowd

To make the most money in the shortest possible time, you should buy a good stock when nobody likes it. The difficulty is that good stocks seldom are without friends.

What makes a stock good? When asked that question, most people think of earnings. They are right, to a point. But a stock also can be good because of assets even though those assets are earning nothing at the moment. Good assets are potential earning power. Since most people focus on earnings you can acquire assets at bargain prices once in a while because the companies owning them are operating at a loss and there is no sign of a change for the better.

Such was the situation in the coal industry in the 1930s. Oil was in abundant supply at what now seem incredibly low prices. Crude oil sold as low as 10 cents a barrel. Its many advantages over coal as a convenience fuel convinced many people that coal had no future whatsoever. From the point of view of the coal operators, the labor situation was bad, and with John L Lewis heading the United Mine Workers it promised to go from bad to worse.

As might have been expected, coal company securities were a dime a dozen. Old Ben Coal Corporation $1,000 1st Gold 6 percent bonds due 1944 could have been bought for $60 in 1932. Old Ben's Debenture Gold 7-1/2 percent bonds, due in 1934, sold as low as $30 for a $1,000 bond.

A capital readjustment plan in 1935 gave 14 shares of new common stock plus one $1,000 first income 6 percent bond of 1948 in exchange for each of the old 6 percent bonds. At the time, the new bonds were 17 bid and the new common was 5 cents bid.

Eleven years later the new bonds were retired at $1,010 each

35

Twelve years later the new stock was split 5-for-1 so that each of the old bondholders in addition to having already received $1,010 for his redeemed bond now had 70 shares of the new common stock. In 1968 that new stock was exchanged, share for share, for the common stock of the Standard Oil Company of Ohio. In 1971 those 70 shares sold as high as $6,440.

Had the holder of the Old Ben Coal bonds redeemed in 1946 reinvested the proceeds in Old Ben Coal Corporation common stock at the high of that year, he would have acquired 20-2/10 shares per bond. In 1947 those shares were split 5-for-1 giving him 101 shares, subsequently exchanged share for share foı Standard Oil of Ohio. Those shares sold in 1971 for $9,292.

Thus if a tax-exempt institution had invested $60 in one of the Old Ben Coal Corporation first 6 percent bonds in 1932, and had moved at every opportunity in the direction of the Old Ben Coal Corporation common stock, its holdings by last year would have reached a total value of $15,732, a figure 262 times the original investment. Even a private investor in the 50 percent income tax bracket in 1946 would have been able to get Standard Oil of Ohio stock worth 189 times what it cost him. The profit opportunity in the Old Ben Coal 7-1/2 percent Debentures of 1934, which could have been bought at $30 per $1,000 bond in 1932, was even larger. The points to remember for "next time" are these:

1. In 1932 the coal business was unpopular with investors.

2. Old Ben Coal Corporation owned 54,300 acres of coal lands of which 41,000 acres were unmined. It owned and operated ten mines with an annual capacity of 7 million tons of bituminous coal. Thousands of additional acres were held under lease. In other words the assets were there. The question was would they ever receive a higher market evaluation.

3. The American demand for energy was due to increase enormously.

There is a Wall Street saying that a situation is worth more tnan a statistic Certainly in this case the investor relying on growth trends, profit margins, rates of return on invested capital, and price-earnings ratios would have been left at the post. To buy Old Ben Coal in 1932 would have required extraordinary vision and great faith in America's future. Statistical analysis would have helped only to show how great were the speculative odds if that vision and faith proved correct.

Some of the great opportunities of the next ten, twenty, thirty, or forty years are bound to be realized only by investors with similar vision and faith.

There is small comfort to old-timers like myself in saying that no one had any money in 1932. The fact is that Old Ben Coal first 6 percent bonds could have been bought as low as $140 for a $1,000 bond in 1933, as low as $150 in 1934, and as low as $137.50 in 1935. For a tax-exempt fund the profit potential from the *highest* of those figures was more than 100 for one.

For out and out speculators the real killing could have been made by buying the new common stock of Old Ben Coal Corporation issued in the readjustment plan of 1935. As of September 19, 1935, that new common was quoted 5 cents bid. Assuming one could have invested $10,000 at *double* that price, he would have owned 100,000 of the new shares. They were split 5-for-1 in 1947 which would have brought his holdings to half a million shares. Those shares were exchanged share for share for Standard Oil of Ohio in 1968. Thus the man who gambled $10,000 on Old Ben Coal new common stock at twice the bid price of 1935 would have today half a million shares of Standard Oil of Ohio. They were valued in 1971 at $46 million. Our hypothetical speculator would have made that fortune without ever paying a cent of tax on his capital gain.

Actually it probably would have been impossible to make any such killing because there were only 194,037 shares of the new common stock of Old Ben Coal Corporation outstanding. But, for $5,000 a man in moderate circumstances might have bought 10,000 shares at 50 cents a share. In 1971 they would have been worth $4,600,000.

The point is that one need not have millions in order to make millions. As a matter of fact it is often easier to make a relatively small commitment of this sort than to invest a million dollars. The advantage the little man has over the big man in hunting elephants in Wall Street is that the little man's gun makes much less noise. Unfortunately if the little man's aim is good he soon loses that advantage by becoming a big man.

To make such a killing as I have recalled in Old Ben Coal

bonds or stock would have required the vision to see the opportunity, the courage and independence of mind to buy when almost no one favored doing so, and, most important of all, the patience to hold on through the bad business years of the late 30s, through World War II, and through all the slings and arrows of outrageous fortune since that time.

As the saying goes, "Patience is a virtue, have it if you can. Seldom found in women, never found in man."

Exceptions prove the rule. Paul Garrett is a notable current exception. But he is not alone.

When I was in the brokerage business in the 1940s the grapevine had it that Charles Stillman had taken a big position in Houston Oil for Time, Incorporated.

In taking that position in Houston Oil, Mr. Stillman avoided two of the most common investment errors. The first of those errors, which I have often made myself, is to devote a great deal of thought and study to arriving at an investment decision and then to act on that decision so cautiously that you won't be hurt if you are wrong. The converse, of course, is that it will not do you any significant good if you are right. When one owns more than 10 percent of a large company he can be hurt very badly if that company goes sour. But when the price of its stock advances more than 100 for one the rewards are significant even to an organization as big as Time, Incorporated.

As of February 1, 1955, Time, Incorporated owned 144,540 shares of Houston Oil stock, which was 10.73 percent of all the shares outstanding. At $166.50 a share, Time's holdings were worth more than $24 million in the final liquidation.

The second common investment error avoided by Mr. Stillman is to take small profits.

"Cut your profits and let your losses run," is one of the surest formulas for winning a place on the relief rolls.

Perhaps the greatest fortune-making opportunity of them all, gauged by return on investment, was afforded by the defaulted first gold 6s of 1946 of H. K. Porter Co. *Moody's 1933 Industrials* manual reports the 1932 price of the bonds at 5 bid. This meant $50 for each $1,000 bond. The bondholders' committee requested each depositing bondholder to pay $5 a thousand at the time of the deposit of his bonds, so anyone buying the bonds in 1932 may be assumed to have had a cost of at least $55 a bond. Moreover, since *Moody's* reports only a bid price, let us assume that to buy more than one or two bonds the buyer would have had to pay double the bid, making his total cost $105 per $1,000 bond deposited.

The face amount of the bonds outstanding was only $840,000. To have bought them all at $105 per $1,000 bond would have cost $88,200.

Under the plan of reorganization confirmed by the court in 1939, each $1,000 first gold 6 percent bond of 1946 received:

10 shares of 4 percent preferred convertible into 120 shares of common, and 5 shares of common, making a total of 125 common shares, assuming conversion of the preferred.

In 1945 the common was split 30-for-1, turning the 125 shares into 3,750 shares. In 1954 the common was split 4-for-1, turning the 3,750 shares into 15,000 shares. Three 2 percent stock dividends in 1958, 1959, and 1965 increased the common shares received in exchange for each of the defaulted 6 percent bonds of 1946 to 15,918 shares. In 1966 the common was split 6-for-5, raising the total number of shares received for each bond to 19,101.

At the 1971 high of 23-1/2 for H. K. Porter stock, the 19,101 shares had a market value of $448,873.

For anyone lucky enough to have bought the bonds at their 1932 bid price of $50, that meant $8,977 for each $1 invested.

For anyone who bought the bonds at double their 1932 bid price of $50 and paid the bondholders' committee $5 a bond besides, the 1971 market value was 4,274 times his total investment.

Moody's 1943 Industrials manual reported: "A substantial part of plant facilities has been converted to war materials." T. M. Evans was listed as president.

Moody's 1959 Industrials manual reported: "At Nov. 13, 1958, T. M. Evans owned of record and beneficially 815,436 shares (77 percent)." The list of officers showed Mr. Evans as chairman. His stock then had a market value of $42,402,000. If held until 1971 the 815,436 shares would have become 1,018,053 shares with a peak market value of $23,924,000, a decline that quickly showed signs of recovery.

CHAPTER V

Foresight vs. Tenacity

F ew stocks adorn a tale and point a moral better than Ogden Corp. Thirty years ago *Moody's 1941 Public Utilities* manual reported that as of the end of 1940 Atlas Corp. and its subsidiaries owned 2,584,160 Ogden Corp. shares, or 75.91 percent of the total. The stock's high that year was 3-1/2. Thirteen years later the same source reported that Allen & Company of New York owned approximately 80 percent of the outstanding Ogden Corp. shares. In the interim the market price of Ogden Corp. stock had declined to a low of 43-3/4 cents a share in 1950 and again in 1951. In 1950 a total of 97,900 Ogden Corp. shares changed hands on the American Stock Exchange at prices ranging from a high of $1.25 to a low of 43-3/4 cents. In 1951 there were 235,900 Ogden Corp. shares traded at prices ranging from a high of $1.75 to a low of 43-3/4 cents.

If you or I had bought all of the Ogden Corp. stock traded in 1950, and had paid the high of the year for every share, our total cost would have been $122,375. Had we paid the high of the year for all of the stock traded in 1951 our total cost would have been $412,825. We would have been the owners of 333,800 shares of Ogden Corp. In 1958 we would have received rights to buy 83,450 shares of Syntex at $2 a share. Had we exercised those rights our investment would have been increased by $166,900 to a grand total of $702,100. In 1971 our holding would have had a market value of more than $56 million. Had we bought midway between the low and the high prices of 1950 and 1951, instead of paying the year's high for every share, our total investment, including the cost of the Syntex rights, would

40

have been $506,634. The market value of our holdings in 1971 reached a figure 110 times that.

Had Allen & Company kept the Ogden Corp. shares *Moody's* said they owned seventeen years ago, and exercised all their rights to Syntex stock, their holdings last year would have been valued at more than $300 million. According to *Moody's 1959 Industrial* manual, however, by that time Allen & Co. no longer owned 80 percent of Ogden Corp., but only approximately 61 percent. Even with that sharply reduced holding, assuming exercise of all Syntex rights, the 1959 Allen & Co. holdings would have been worth more than $225 million in 1971.

What are the morals to be drawn from the Ogden Corp. story?

One is that no one can foresee for sure what the future holds. Atlas Corp. as owner of more than three-fourths of Ogden Corp. stock presumably was as fully informed about the company as anyone could be. But who could have foreseen in the 1940s that on December 29, 1953, Odgen Corp. would acquire a controlling interest in Teleregister Corp.? Who could have foreseen that in 1956 Ogden Corp. would acquire control of Syntex, S.A., Mexico City, pharmaceutical producer and distributor of steroids, and Caribbean Chemicals, S.A.? And even if one had foreseen those acquisitions, who could have foreseen the birth control pill and the market enthusiasm that greeted it?

Even in the bright light of hindsight it seems that the only way an investor could have made $100 for $1 in Ogden Corp. stock would have been to buy it in the belief that with Allen & Co. in the picture Ogden Corp. must have a bright future. Having done so the new Ogden stockholder would then have had to grit his teeth and hold on no matter what he heard or read for the next twenty years.

Maybe some brilliant traders have increased their capital one hundredfold in the last twenty years. Certainly none have done it for a publicly owned fund. But anyone who bought Ogden at the average prices of 1950 or 1951 could have accomplished the same thing by doing nothing except exercising his Syntex rights in 1958.

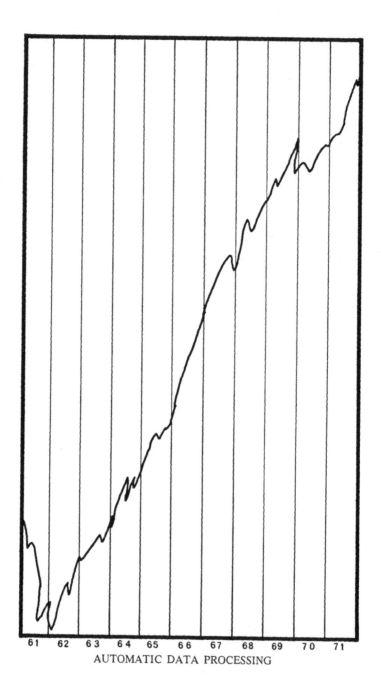

61   62   63   64   65   66   67   68   69   70   71

AUTOMATIC DATA PROCESSING

Again and again this survey of the big winners in the stock market emphasizes that it is more important to be right than to be quick. Take Automatic Data Processing for example. In less than seven years, since early 1965, the stock has advanced one hundredfold. Yet it was available for fifteen consecutive months—starting with April of 1961 and ending with June of 1962—at prices less than 1 percent of the market value reached in 1971.

Those who bought the stock in September of 1961 when it was first quoted in the *Bank and Quotation Record* at 4-1/8 bid, 4-1/2 offered, had their faith sorely tested when by the end of October 1962, the stock had declined to 7/8 bid, 1-3/8 offered. Yet even those who paid the asking price of 4-1/2 at the September 1961 high saw the market value of their investment 156 times their cost by 1971.

Here was a stock which declined 70 percent in market value in its first thirteen months of recorded trading, only to turn around and make $100 bills out of $1 investments between 1965 and 1971. It would be hard to find a better example of the hazards in relying on price movements alone as a guide to investment decision-making.

You may recall that patience was one of the three personality traits cited by the late George F. Baker as prerequisites to making a fortune in the stock market. Probably never has more patience been required by any stock than by Occidental Petroleum. Had anyone been able to invest $10,000 in Occidental Petroleum at its 1932 low of 25 cents a share, and held on, his Occidental Petroleum would have reached a market value of $3,367,000 last year. Meantime, however, he would have seen his $10,000 investment shrink in market value to a 1941 low of only $1,600. Even as late as January 3, 1956, after nearly a quarter century of waiting without dividends on his investment, his holdings had a market value of only $18,000, a gain of 80 percent. Meantime the Dow-Jones Industrial Average had risen to more than ten times its 1932 low.

In the period from 1932 through 1955, Occidental Petroleum stock could have been bought at the highest prices reached in twenty-two of those twenty-four years, and every share would have shown the buyer a profit of more than one hundredfold in 1971.

Beneath the surface something was stirring. More than 1,200,000 shares of Occidental Petroleum changed hands on the Los Angeles and San Francisco Stock Exchanges in the twelve years immediately preceding 1956 when the stock began its swift rise.

As is true of many of the other 100-to-one stocks, Occidental Petroleum showed that gain in 1971 even though at its high it was down nearly 60 percent from its record high reached in 1968.

In the stock market Fortune wears many disguises. Those disguises taken together with mankind's known inability to foresee the future clinch the case for buying right and holding on.

Dame Fortune never wore a more impenetrable disguise than that which kept so many investors from seeing the profit potential in Tampax.

As the list of 100-to-one stocks shows, Tampax could have been bought as late as 1949 for less than 1 percent of its 1971 value. But by 1949 the stock's low was $16.50 a share. Tampax stock could have been bought both in 1941 and 1940 at 1-7/8. At that price $10,000 could have made you and me the owners of 5,000 shares. Without our putting up another penny, those 5,000 shares would now be 45,000 shares, worth in 1971 well over $14 million.

For the benefit of those who scoff at "might have been" profits in buying stocks at the lows, because in real life no one can ever do that, let us note that the 1941 *high* for Tampax was $4 a share and the 1942 *high* $3.75 a share. If we had bought our stock at the *high* of those two years we would have acquired 2,500 shares. By now they would have increased to 22,500 shares with a market value in 1971 of more than $7,000,000. Bear in mind that this $10,000 investment would have grown to $7,000,000 had the original commitment been made at the *high* of two consecutive years. The conclusion seems inescapable that *what* one buys in the stock market is much more important than *when* he buys it. It would have been impossible for you or me to invest $10,000 in Tampax *anytime* from 1938 through 1948 without making more than 100-for-one on our investment by 1971, *if* we had just held on.

How did Tampax look to investors thirty years ago?

Moody's 1943 Industrials said: "Business: Manufactures and sells Tampax, a catamenial device used for feminine hygienic purposes."

The stilted reference to the Tampax product was symptomatic of the times. Hardheaded investors discounted the company's future because "they'll never be able to advertise it." Only the most imaginative and farsighted could have foreseen that by 1971 Tampax would be advertised on television.

One of the greatest speculative opportunities of all time was afforded by Tri-Continental warrants in 1941 and 1942. The warrants sold in December of 1941 and again in April of 1942 at 1/32 which is 3-1/8 cents each. Their 1971 high was $72.50. The increase in thirty years was not 100 times, nor even 1,000 times, but 2,320 times. In other words, for every dollar invested in Tri-Continental warrants at the 1941–1942 lows, the speculator who held on had $2,320 in market value thirty years later.

As with Tampax and Loft, it was not necessary to be alert to day-to-day market fluctuations to make a fortune in Tri-Continental warrants. While up from their lows, they could still have been bought in 1943 and in 1944 at less than 1 percent of their 1971 value. The 1944 low for Tri-Continental warrants was 68-3/4 cents. In 1971 they sold at 105 times that 1944 price.

Actually, for eight consecutive years, from 1937 through 1944, Tri-Continental warrants changed hands in large volume at prices less than 1 percent of their 1971 market value. Risking $10,000 on them in any of those years would have made you and me a million dollars. Timing did not matter except to gild the lily of opportunity. A million dollars was in store for the purchasers in any of those years. Perfect timing would merely have made the difference between making $1 million and making $23 million on a $10,000 investment.

Couldn't we have made just as much money without the speculative risk if we had bought Tri-Continental Corp. common stock?

Sadly, the answer is no. To have made $100 for $1 in Tri-Continental common we would have had to be inspired to buy it at its low of 62-1/2 cents a share, in 1941. Today we would have two shares for each one we bought in 1941, and those two shares last year sold as high as $64.50. The increase over the low is just 103 times.

Wall Street has its fads and fashions just as Paris does. A stock that is not in vogue may do a great job for its owners without attracting much speculative attention. One example is Square D. Certainly not unknown, Square D has received less market commentator attention than many glamour issues with inferior long-term records.

While Square D would have turned a $10,000 investment in 1935 into well over $4 million market value at the '1971 high, the real opportunity for a killing was in 1932 and 1933. In both years the stock's price range was from a low of 1/2 to a high of $2 a share. Volume of trading in the stock on the Detroit Stock Exchange totalled 3,529 shares in the two years. If you and I had bought every one of those shares at the *high* of those two years our total cost would have been $7,058. Without ever putting up another penny, our holdings today would be 375,450 shares valued at the 1971 high at well over $11 million—if we had just held on!

Probably everyone who has ever owned a share of stock knows about Xerox. As Mr. Garrett's experience demonstrates, it would be hard to find a better example of the value of buying right and holding on. But Mr. Garrett was a man of long experience in finance with many friends in high places. Not everyone could have found the Xerox opportunity the way he did.

But many people owned the stock before it became a market sensation. Are they all rich? Or did some of them take their profits when it moved up the first ten points? I know several who did. Do you know any? Most people do not like to think about it, so they make the same mistake again and again.

It was not even necessary to ferret out the Xerox opportunity. All anyone had to do was to say "yes" to a security salesman. Going way back to 1928, Steel & Stone Company, Inc., of Rochester, New York, offered 5,000 shares of Haloid (the old name for Xerox) 7 percent preferred stock and 5,000 shares of Haloid common in units of one share of preferred and one share of common at $110 a unit. All the preferred was redeemed at $105 eight years later. But each of those 1928 shares of Haloid common is now 540 shares of Xerox common with a market valuation in 1971 of more than $65,000. If anyone had been persuaded by the Steel & Stone securities salesmen to invest $10,000 in those units, he would have acquired 90-9/10 preferred shares and 90-9/10 common shares. When the preferred was retired in 1936 he would have gotten back all but $555 of his $10,000 investment. Had he continued to risk that remaining $555 in Haloid common stock, he would now own 49,086 Xerox shares whose 1971 market value topped $6 million.

Haloid, of course, did not have the fabulous Xerox copying machine in 1928. No one even imagined it. As late as 1933 *Moody's Industrials* said of Haloid: "Produces and markets photographic paper exclusively. Plant located in Rochester, New York, has the capacity for coating over ten miles long, 41 inches wide, of paper each day."

I know that more than half the people alive in the United States today were not even born by 1933 but they may be entertained by the thought of what grandfather could have done for the family by being nice to a security salesman in 1928.

Bear in mind, he could only have done it by holding on. Foresight could not have helped him. It was not until November 21, 1935, that Haloid acquired Rectigraph Company of Rochester, chief product of which was the Rectigraph photocopy machine.

Opportunity, like the postman, always rings twice, at least. Following a 3-for-1 split of Haloid stock in February 1936, Donoho, Moore & Company, of New York, and Mitchell, Herrick & Company of Cleveland offered 55,000 shares of the new stock at $20 a share. For $10,000 one could have bought 500 shares. Today those 500 shares would be 90,000 shares of Xerox with a market value in 1971 of more than $11 million. Somebody did buy those 55,000 shares. Only those who like Mr. Darrell's client "never sell anything" reaped the fantastic harvest fate put in their hands.

As late as July 1950, First Boston Corporation of New York

offered 10,911 shares of Haloid stock at $29.25 a share. For $10,000 one could have bought 341 shares. If he held them, he would now own 61,300 Xerox shares, valued in 1971 at more than $7,500,000.

You and I may not have been on the Xerox security sales-men's lists. Tough luck, not to be invited to that party. But we

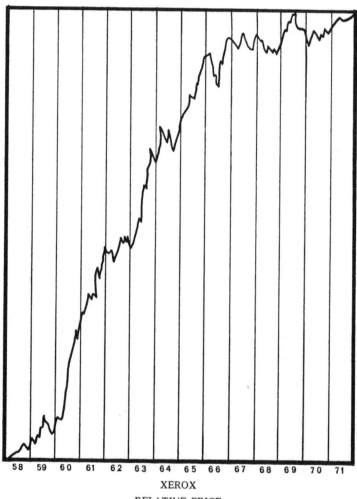

58   59   60   61   62   63   64   65   66   67   68   69   70   71

XEROX

RELATIVE PRICE

could have come uninvited as late as 1958, and still have made more than $100 for each $1 we invested in Xerox.

As the accompanying chart of the price of Xerox relative to the Dow-Jones Industrial Average clearly shows, by 1958 Xerox had begun one of the steepest price advances in stock market history. It was nine years before that advance relative to the Dow-Jones Industrial Average was interrupted for as long as twelve months. Bear in mind as you look at this relative price chart that the Dow-Jones Industrial Average was advancing at the same time. If Xerox had advanced as fast as the Dow but no faster this relative price line would have been norizontal and perfectly straight. Remember, please, these relative price charts show the price of the stock divided by the price of the Dow-Jones Industrial Average on the same day. If the stock sells at 90 and the Dow-Jones Industrial Average is at 900, the relative price is .10 or 10 percent. If the stock goes up to 150 while the Dow goes to 1,000, the relative price becomes .15 or 15 percent. Thus a rising relative price line shows that a stock has been advancing faster than the Dow, or declining more slowly than the Dow

Many will argue that no one could have foreseen the fabulous success of the machine which in a single decade made Xerox a synonym for copier just as Kodak has long been a synonym for camera. That may be true. The more nearly true it is, the stronger it makes the case for holding on. Fortunes made that way are what my old friend and colleague Dwight Rogers calls "triumphs of lethargy." In the same vein Decatur Higgins of Scudder, Stevens & Clark quotes a former associate as noting sadly, "I suffer from an absence of inertia."

CHAPTER VI

We'd Die for Dear Old Globe & Rutgers

In hundreds of different securities we have seen demonstrated the wisdom of buying right and holding on. The conclusion seems inescapable that if one can buy right, no amount of trading or switching thereafter is likely to produce results equal to what he can have by simply holding on. By doing so he avoids paper work, brokerage commissions, and capital gains taxes. He loses the fun of trading, of matching his hunches about what the market will do tomorrow against the hunches of everyone else who is trading, the self-satisfaction of making a fast buck out of thin air.

Not so obvious is the wisdom of holding on even when one has not been shrewd enough or lucky enough to buy quite right. A classic example of this is the market history of Globe & Rutgers Fire Insurance Company stock, now American International Group.

In the panicky market just after the bank holiday in 1933, Globe & Rutgers Fire Insurance Company common stock was quoted as low as 2-7/8 bid. Its high the year before, 1932, had been $257 a share. The *Bawl Street Journal,* Bond Club of New York parody of the *Wall Street Journal,* called attention to the price catastrophe in a page one advertisement at the top of column one. The ad read:

BANK AND INSURANCE STOCKS
We'd die for dear old Globe & Rutgers.
J. K. Rice, Jr. & Co.

Anyone who had been naive enough to buy Globe & Rutgers stock on reading that ad in 1933 would have paid something between $60.50 and $70.50 a share for it. Nine years later when Globe & Rutgers sold at a low of $5 a share the naive purchaser might have concluded that the *Bawl Street Journal* had indeed been joking. But the funny part of it is that anyone who bought the stock at say $65.50 on the strength of that *Bawl Street Journal* advertisement in 1933—and held on—would have had securities worth more than 48 times his purchase price by 1971. His 1933 $10,000 would have grown to $488,000, on a purchase that was atrociously timed.

Tri-Continental Corp. and its affiliate Selected Industries owned a total of 45,200 shares of Globe & Rutgers in 1943. At the high of that year the 45,200 shares had a market value of $723,200. If held until 1971 that block of stock would have amounted to 1,484,368 American International Group shares valued at more than $144 million. The latest Tri-Continental report shows just four names under "Finance and Insurance": American Re-Insurance, C.I.T. Financial, First National City, and Heller International. Their aggregate market value as of June 30, 1971, was $23,360,750, or 3.4 percent of the Tri-Continental portfolio of $679,553,693 investment assets.

As of the end of 1953, C. V. Starr & Co., Inc., held 151,584 Globe & Rutgers common shares, or 53.37 percent of the total. At that time the Starr block had a market value of $5,608,000. Eighteen years later that same block, increased by stock splits and stock dividends to 1,659,541 shares, had a market value of more than $160,000,000.

Another example of the value of hanging on through thick and thin is Kerlyn Oil Class A common, now Kerr-McGee.

In 1935 W. Earl Phinney & Co. of Chicago offered 118,898 Class A common shares at $5 a share. Each Class A common share was convertible share for share into Class B common. For $10,000 anyone could have become the owner of 2,000 shares.

Five years later their market value would have shrunk to $4,500. Many buyers of the 1935 offering doubtless sold out because their stock was not acting well though it did pay dividends at the rate of 35 cents a year. Others who failed to convert their Class A shares into Class B had them called in

1944 at $7 a share. They did not do badly. Anyone who bought $10,000 worth of Class A common on the 1935 offering and held on to the Class A stock not only received dividends at the rate of 7 percent annually but had a 40 percent capital gain by 1944—$14,000 for his $10,000 original investment.

But how about the person who bought 2,000 shares of Class A and converted them into Class B?

By the end of 1971, without ever putting up another cent or paying a dime of capital gains taxes, he was the owner of 35,180 shares of Kerr-McGee. Their market value had exceeded $1,700,000.

As in so many other cases, Opportunity knocked twice. In October 1936, Straus Securities Corp. of Chicago offered 125,000 Kerlyn Oil Class A shares at $6.50 a share. Any $10,000 investor in that offering who was tenacious enough to hang on through the 1940 decline to $2.25 a share, and courageous enough to convert his Class A shares into Class B, owned 27,053 shares of Kerr-McGee by the end of 1971 at a peak market value of more than $1,300,000.

I wonder if there is anyone alive who bought Kerlyn Oil shares on either offering and held on until now. I doubt it. Yet hundreds of people had fortunes in their grasp. All they had to do was hold on.

When I said Opportunity knocked twice, I did that good lady an injustice. She knocked three times. Five years after the 1935 and 1936 offerings of Kerlyn Oil stock anyone could have bought Kerlyn Oil Class A common shares in the Over-the-Counter market for half the first offering price. The gain on a $10,000 investment at either the 1940 or 1941 low, had the buyer elected to remain a shareholder until 1971, would have been more than $3,000,000.

In all the history of the stock market it would be hard to find a better example of the value of holding on through adversity than is provided by Richfield Oil's bonds.

In December 1925, Blair & Company, Inc., New York, offered $15 million of Pan American Petroleum Company of California 1st Convertible Gold 6s, due 1940, at $990 for each $1,000 bond. Pan American Petroleum was wholly owned by

Richfield Oil Company. In May 1929, $25 million of Richfield Oil's 1st Convertible Gold 6s, Series A, due 1944, were offered by Hemphill Noyes & Company, Hayden Stone & Company, Cassatt & Company, and Bank America-Blair Corp., all of New York, and Bond & Goodwin & Tucker, Inc. of San Francisco, and Hunter, Dulin & Company of Los Angeles. Those bonds likewise were offered at $990 for each $1,000 denomination.

By 1932 both Pan American Petroleum and Richfield Oil Company were in receivership. The Pan American 6s of 1940 sold on the New York Stock Exchange in 1932 at a low of $75 for each $1,000 bond while the Certificates of Deposit for the same bonds sold as low as $40. The Richfield Oil 6s of 1944 sold in 1932 as low as $57.50 per $1,000 bond while the Certificates of Deposit sold as low as $50 each. Thus the investors in the two bond issues had "lost" more than 90 percent of the value of their investment in three to seven years. Those who sold out in 1932 did indeed lose more than 90 percent of what they had paid for the bonds on the original offerings.

How about those who just gritted their teeth and held on?

In 1937 both Pan American Petroleum and Richfield Oil were reorganized. For each $1,000 Richfield Oil bond the holder received 48-1/2 shares of new Richfield Oil stock. Each Pan American Petroleum bond was exchanged for 43.45 shares of Richfield Oil stock. Today as a result of stock splits and the merger into Atlantic Refining, the Pan American Petroleum bondholder who held on has 147.7 shares of Atlantic-Richfield stock for each $990 invested in 1925. The Richfield Oil bondholder has 164.9 shares of Atlantic-Richfield stock for each $990 invested in 1929. At the 1971 high the investor who bought a Pan American Petroleum $1,000 bond and held on through its decline to $40 market value in 1932 owned stock valued at more than $11,500. Similarly, the buyer of a Richfield Oil $1,000 bond who held on in the face of a decline to $50 in 1932 owned stock valued last year at nearly $13,000. I doubt if Coney Island has a ride to equal that.

The two bonds are included in the list of securities that have risen more than one hundredfold in value because obviously anyone who had the money and the good luck to buy them in

1932 and has held on has made a good deal more than 100 for one on his investment. As an argument for buying right and holding on, however, it may be even more noteworthy that those who bought the bonds in 1925 and in 1929 when their timing could hardly have been worse—and did not let go— have likewise increased their capital by 11-1/2 to 13 times. Such a story may help you to understand how Mr. Darrell's client amassed wealth by never selling *anything*.

Before we leave this example, let me note that the 1932 prices were real. The bonds *could* have been *bought*. Between April 22 and June 10, 1932, no less than 60 of the Richfield Oil bonds changed hands on the New York Stock Exchange at an average price of less than $100 a bond.

Table I

365 MILLIONAIRE-MAKER STOCKS

When and Where You Could Have Bought Them,
Their Cost and Their 1971 Value

Here are the securities that would have (perhaps did) make you a millionaire if you invested ten thousand dollars in just one of them in the year indicated and held it until 1971.

Named in capital letters is the security that could have been bought in the year, on the market, and at the cost shown. If a name was changed subsequently, the 1971 name is shown underneath in brackets. Note that each 1971 value is at *least* 100 times the cost.

	Where Traded	Cost	1971 Value
1932			
AETNA CASUALTY & SURETY (Aetna Life & Casualty)	Hartford S.E.	$15.00	$ 1,998
AETNA LIFE (Aetna Life & Casualty)	O-T-C	8.25	934
AMERICAN BEET SUGAR (American Crystal Sugar)	NYSE	.25	80
AMERICAN CONSTITUTION FIRE INSURANCE (American International Group)	O-T-C	6.00	1,105
AMERICAN CYANAMID	Curb	1.63	303

	Where Traded	Cost	1971 Value
1932 (Continued)			
ARMOUR & CO. (ILLINOIS) CLASS A (Greyhound)	NYSE	.63	109
ARMOUR & CO. (ILLINOIS) PREFERRED (Greyhound)	NYSE	3.50	660
BLISS (E.W.) (Gulf & Western)	Curb	.63	80
BORG-WARNER	NYSE	3.38	387
BUTLER BROTHERS (McCrory Corp.)	Curb	.75	114
BYRON JACKSON (Borg-Warner)	San Fran. S.E.	.50	70
CARRIER CORP.	Curb	2.50	320
CELANESE CORP.	NYSE	1.25	223
CHICAGO RIVET & MACHINE	Curb	3.00	337
COPPER RANGE	Curb	1.13	139
CROWN CORK & SEAL	NYSE	7.88	935
CRUM & FORSTER INSURANCE SHARES (Crum & Forster)	O-T-C	3.00	428
CUTLER-HAMMER	NYSE	3.50	362
DOUGLAS AIRCRAFT (McDonnell Douglas)	NYSE	5.00	513
DOW CHEMICAL	Curb	21.13	2,854
DUNHILL INTERNATIONAL (Questor)	NYSE	.63	72
FANSTEEL	Curb	.25	67
HONOLULU OIL	San Fran. S.E.	4.75	663
INSPIRATION CONSOLIDATED COPPER	NYSE	.75	102
JOHNSON MOTOR (Outboard Marine)	Curb	.50	126
MAGMA COPPER (Newmont Mining)	NYSE	4.25	467
MARION STEAM SHOVEL 7% PFD. (Merritt-Chapman & Scott)	O-T-C	5.25	581
MENGEL (Marcor)	NYSE	1.00	155
MERRITT-CHAPMAN & SCOTT	Curb	.38	45
MIDLAND STEEL PRODUCTS (Midland-Ross)	NYSE	2.00	282

	Where Traded	Cost	1971 Value
1932 (Continued)			
MINNESOTA & ONTARIO PAPER 6s SERIES A 1931–45 (Boise Cascade)	O-T-C	40.00	5,501
NATIONAL AUTOMOTIVE FIBRES A (Chris-Craft Industries)	O-T-C	.50	55
NATIONAL BELLAS HESS CO., INC. 7% PFD. (National Bellas Hess, Inc. common)	NYSE	.13	28
NATIONAL CONTAINER $2 CONV. PFD. (Owens-Illinois-Glass)	Curb	8.13	841
NATIONAL STANDARD	Chicago S.E.	7.25	978
NATOMAS CO.	San Fran. S.E.	9.00	1,013
NORTH AMERICAN AVIATION (North American Rockwell, Sperry Rand)	NYSE	1.25	371
OLD BEN COAL 7.5% DEBS. 1934 (Standard Oil of Ohio)	O-T-C	30.00	10,994
PAN AMERICAN PETROLEUM (OF CAL.) CONVERTIBLE 6s 1940 (CERTIFICATES OF DEPOSIT) (Atlantic Richfield)	NYSE NYSE	40.00	11,557
PARKER PEN	Chicago S.E.	2.50	273
J. C. PENNEY CO.	NYSE	13.00	1,395
PHILLIPS PETROLEUM	NYSE	2.00	277
PORTER (H.K.) 1st 6s 1946	O-T-C	50.00	448,873
REPUBLIC GAS (Republic Natural Gas)	Curb	.13	26
RICHFIELD OIL OF CALIFORNIA 1st CONVERTIBLE 6s 1944 (CERTIFICATES OF DEPOSIT) (Atlantic Richfield)	NYSE	50.00	12,903
SCULLIN STEEL $3 PREFERENCE (Universal Marion)	Curb	1.00	124

	Where Traded	Cost	1971 Value
1932 (Continued)			
SHARP & DOHME $3.50 CONVERTIBLE PFD.A (Merck common)	NYSE	11.50	1,771
SHELL UNION OIL (Shell Oil)	NYSE	2.50	251
SLOSS-SHEFFIELD STEEL & IRON (A-T-O Inc.)	NYSE	3.75	411
STARRETT (L.S.)	NYSE	3.00	304
SULLIVAN MACHINERY (Joy Manufacturing)	Curb	3.25	329
SYMINGTON CLASS A (Dresser Industries)	NYSE	.50	52
THATCHER MANUFACTURING (Dart Industries)	NYSE	2.00	252
TRUAX TRAER COAL (Consolidation Coal)	NYSE	.25	61
TUBIZE CHATILLON (Celanese)	Curb	1.00	523
TUNG-SOL ELECTRIC (Studebaker-Worthington)	Curb	1.00	100
U.S. FREIGHT	NYSE	3.50	375
UNITED STATES RUBBER (Uniroyal)	NYSE	1.25	198
WAHL (Schick)	Chicago S.E.	.13	15
WESTERN AUTO SUPPLY CLASS A (Beneficial Corp.)	Curb	5.13	935
WESTVACO CHEMICAL (FMC)	NYSE	3.00	457
YELLOW TRUCK & COACH (General Motors)	NYSE	1.38	182
1933			
ALLEN INDUSTRIES (Dayco)	Cleveland S.E.	1.00	358
AMERADA CORP. (Amerada Hess)	NYSE	18.50	2,574
AMERICAN CHAIN & CABLE	NYSE	1.63	194

	Where Traded	Cost	1971 Value
1933 (Continued)			
AMERICAN INVESTMENT CO. OF ILLINOIS	St. Louis S.E.	3.00	347
AMERICAN MACHINE & METALS (Ametek, Inc.)	NYSE	.75	153
AMERICAN METAL CLIMAX	NYSE	3.13	315
AMERICAN METER (Singer)	Curb	5.00	573
AMERICAN SEATING	NYSE	.88	138
ARMSTRONG CORK	Curb	4.13	550
ART METAL WORKS (Ronson Corp.)	Curb	.63	149
ASSOCIATED TELEPHONE UTILITIES SERIES C 5.5% CONVERTIBLE BONDS (General Telephone)	Curb	50.00	5,087
BIRTMAN ELECTRIC (Whirlpool)	O-T-C	3.75	410
BRACH (E.J.) & SONS (American Home Products)	Chicago S.E.	3.75	789
BRIGGS & STRATTON	NYSE	7.25	888
BULOVA WATCH	NYSE	.88	271
BUTTE COPPER & ZINC (Jonathan Logan)	NYSE	.50	81
CATERPILLAR TRACTOR	NYSE	5.50	1,447
CELOTEX (Jim Walter)	NYSE	.50	97
CHICAGO PNEUMATIC TOOL	NYSE	2.13	343
CLIFFS CORP. (Cleveland Cliffs)	Cleveland S.E.	3.50	357
COLLINS & AIKMAN	NYSE	3.00	372
CONSOLIDATED AIRCRAFT (General Dynamics)	Curb	1.00	107
CONTINENTAL CASUALTY (CNA Financial)	O-T-C	5.00	754
CROWN ZELLERBACH	NYSE	1.00	186

	Where Traded	Cost	1971 Value
1933 (Continued)			
DAYTON RUBBER MANUFACTURING CLASS A (Dayco)	Chicago S.E.	1.00	119
DEERE & COMPANY	NYSE	5.75	668
S. R. DRESSER MFG. CLASS B (Dresser Industries)	NYSE	2.13	300
DUVAL TEXAS SULPHUR (Pennzoil United)	Curb	.50	300
EASTMAN KODAK	NYSE	46.00	6,480
EATON MANUFACTURING (Eaton Yale & Towne)	NYSE	3.13	358
ELECTRIC BOAT (General Dynamics)	NYSE	1.00	100
EVANS PRODUCTS	NYSE	.88	367
FEDERATED DEPARTMENT STORES	NYSE	7.50	1,027
GARDNER-DENVER	Chicago S.E.	7.50	1,012
GENERAL ALLIANCE (General Reinsurance)	O-T-C	5.00	656
GENERAL CABLE common	NYSE	1.25	131
GENERAL TIRE	Curb	23.00	3,209
GODCHAUX SUGARS (Gulf States Land & Industries)	Chicago S.E.	.25	62
GOODRICH (B.F.) COMPANY	NYSE	3.00	315
HANCOCK OIL (Signal Cos.)	Los Angeles S.E.	3.75	436
HOBART MFG.	Cincinnati S.E.	10.00	1,651
HOUDAILLE-HERSHEY CLASS B (Houdaille Industries)	NYSE	1.00	142
INDIAN REFINING (Texaco)	NYSE	1.13	178

	Where Traded	Cost	1971 Value
1933 (Continued)			
INTERNATIONAL COMBUSTION ENGINEERING CONVERTIBLE PREFERRED CERTIFICATES (Combustion Engineering Inc.)	NYSE	11.00	1,332
INTERNATIONAL PAPER & POWER CLASS A COMMON (International Paper)	NYSE	.50	170
INTERTYPE (Harris-Intertype)	NYSE	1.88	450
LERNER STORES	Curb	4.00	1,233
MARCHANT CALCULATING MACHINE (SCM)	San Fran. S.E.	.50	100
MASONITE	Curb	8.25	1,214
MC CRORY STORES (McCrory Corp.)	NYSE	.38	63
MC LELLAN STORES (McCrory Corp.)	NYSE	.25	37
MC LELLAN STORES PREF. (McCrory Corp. common)	NYSE	2.13	341
MELVILLE SHOE	NYSE	8.75	1,222
NATIONAL DEPARTMENT STORES 7% 1st PFD. (International Mining)	NYSE	1.25	268
NEWMONT MINING	Curb	11.50	1,413
NOBLITT-SPARKS INDUSTRIES (Arvin Industries)	Chicago S.E.	9.50	955
PACIFIC MILLS (Burlington Industries)	NYSE	6.00	721
PITNEY-BOWES	Curb	2.00	215
RELIABLE STORES	Curb	.88	123
REMINGTON-RAND (Sperry Rand)	NYSE	2.50	263
SAVAGE ARMS (Emhart)	NYSE	2.25	275

	Where Traded	Cost	1971 Value
1933 (Continued)			
SEARS, ROEBUCK & CO.	NYSE	12.50	2,499
SETON LEATHER			
(Seton Co.)	Curb	1.50	155
SMITH (HOWARD) PAPER MILLS			
(Domtar)	Canada	1.13	218
SNIDER PACKING FOODS			
(General Foods)	NYSE	.63	279
SPERRY			
(Sperry Rand)	NYSE	2.13	278
SPIEGEL, MAY, STERN			
(Beneficial Corp.)	NYSE	1.00	402
SUNRAY OIL			
(Sun Oil)	Curb	.25	52
SUNSTRAND MACHINE TOOL			
(Sunstrand Corp.)	O-T-C	1.50	233
UNION BAG & PAPER			
(Union Camp)	NYSE	5.50	1,005
UNITED-CARR FASTENER			
(TRW, Inc.)	NYSE	1.63	380
UNITED PAPERBOARD			
(United Board & Carton)	NYSE	.50	57
U.S. & FOREIGN SECURITIES			
(U.S. & International Securities)	Curb	.32	53
VAN RAALTE CO.			
(Cluett, Peabody & Co.)	NYSE	1.63	198
WALKER (HIRAM) GOODERHAM & WORTS	Curb	3.50	1,014
WESTON ELECTRICAL INSTRUMENT			
(Schlumberger)	NYSE	2.50	350
1934			
ABBOTT LABORATORIES	Chicago S.E.	40.00	4,302
ALOE (A.S.) CO.			
(Brunswick)	St. Louis S.E.	9.00	1,073

	Where Traded	Cost	1971 Value
1934 (Continued)			
AMERICAN HIDE & LEATHER 7% PREFERRED			
(Tandy common)	NYSE	17.75	1,912
BABCOCK & WILCOX	Curb	18.50	2,135
CONTAINER CORP.			
CLASS A (Marcor)	NYSE	6.13	777
EDISON BROS. STORES	Curb	8.00	1,199
EMPORIUM CAPWELL			
(Broadway-Hale Stores)	San Fran. S.E.	5.00	527
ENGINEERS PUBLIC SERVICE			
(Virginia Elec. & Power)			
(Gulf States Utilities)			
(El Paso Electric)	NYSE	3.15	387
EX-CELL-O	Curb	3.75	389
FEDERAL-MOGUL	Detroit S.E.	3.00	377
FOOD MACHINERY			
(FMC)	NYSE	10.50	1,226
GREYHOUND CORP.	Chicago S.E.	5.25	777
HOOVER BALL & BEARING	Detroit S.E.	1.13	237
HUSSMAN-LIGONIER			
(Pet Inc.)	O-T-C	1.00	177
LOCKHEED	Los Angeles S.E.	.90	102
MC GRAW ELECTRIC			
(McGraw-Edison)	Chicago S.E.	3.75	692
NATIONAL SHIRT SHOPS			
(McCrory Corp. common)	O-T-C	1.00	224
PHILIP MORRIS	NYSE	11.50	1,323
REECE BUTTON HOLE MACHINE			
(Reece Corp.)	Boston S.E.	10.00	1,140
TENNESSEE CORP.			
(Cities Service)	NYSE	3.13	372
TEXAS PACIFIC COAL & OIL	NYSE	2.50	385
UNION GAS OF CANADA	Canada	2.00	241
UNIVERSAL WINDING			
(Leesona)	O-T-C	11.00	1,275
WHITMAN & BARNES			
(TRW, Inc.)	Detroit S.E.	1.88	200

	Where Traded	Cost	1971 Value
1935			
AMERICAN MANUFACTURING	Curb	3.50	712
AMERICAN POWER & LIGHT $6 PFD.	NYSE	10.13	1,160
ANHEUSER-BUSCH	O-T-C	98.00	13,610
CHICAGO FLEXIBLE SHAFT (Sunbeam)	Chicago S.E.	13.50	1,622
CONTINENTAL BAKING (International Telephone)	NYSE	4.50	491
DR. PEPPER	St. Louis S.E.	16.00	1,938
ELECTRIC POWER & LIGHT $6 PFD. (Middle South Utilities) (Pennzoil)	NYSE	2.50	966
ELECTRIC POWER & LIGHT $7 PFD. (Middle South Utilities) (Pennzoil)	NYSE	3.00	1,062
GENERAL CABLE CLASS A (General Cable common)	NYSE	4.00	525
GIMBEL BROTHERS	NYSE	2.13	364
GRANITEVILLE MANUFACTURING (Graniteville)	O-T-C	34.00	6,170
LINE MATERIAL (McGraw-Edison)	O-T-C	3.63	536
LION OIL (Monsanto)	Curb	3.50	400
MIDDLE STATES PETROLEUM CLASS A (Tenneco)	Curb	.88	97
MINNEAPOLIS HONEYWELL (Honeywell)	NYSE	58.00	6,660
MOORE CORP. LTD.	Canada	17.00	1,842
OLD BEN COAL NEW COMMON (Standard Oil of Ohio)	O-T-C	.05	460
OLD BEN COAL FIRST GOLD 6s 1944* (Standard Oil of Ohio)	NYSE	137.50	15,732

*For tax-exempt fund, assuming reinvestment of 1946 bond redemption proceeds in Old Ben Coal common at 1946 high of 50. Individual paying 25 percent capital gains tax on bond profit would have only $13,754 in 1971.

	Where Traded	Cost	1971 Value
1935 (Continued)			
OUTBOARD MOTORS CLASS B			
(Outboard Marine)	Curb	.63	120
RUSTLESS IRON & STEEL			
(Armco Steel)	O-T-C	.75	111
SHAMROCK OIL & GAS			
(Diamond Shamrock)	Pittsburgh S.E.	.75	113
SIGNAL OIL & GAS CLASS A	Los Angeles		
(Signal Cos.)	S.E.	5.50	728
SKELLY OIL	NYSE	6.50	770
SQUARE D CLASS B— Common	Curb	17.00	3,361
STONE & WEBSTER			
(Stone & Webster)			
(Gulf States Utilities)			
(El Paso Electric)			
(Sierra Pacific Power)	NYSE	3.76	421
WILCOX (H.F.) OIL & GAS			
(Tenneco)	NYSE	1.00	112
1936			
HOLOPHANE			
(Johns-Manville)	Curb	6.50	752
LAWYERS TITLE INSURANCE			
(Richmond Corp.)	O-T-C	50.00	5,830
NEHI			
(Royal Crown Cola)	Curb	4.25	861
OUTBOARD MOTORS CLASS A			
(Outboard Marine)	Curb	11.00	1,269
1937			
BURLINGTON MILLS			
(Burlington Industries)	NYSE	5.75	656
COOPER INDUSTRIES	Curb	3.50	375
GENERAL AMERICAN OIL	Russell Maguire & Co. offering	6.50	825
PLACER DEVELOPMENT	Canada	2.00	231

	Where Traded	Cost	1971 Value
1938			
AMERICAN AIRLINES	Curb	8.00	877
AMERICAN HOME PRODUCTS	NYSE	30.75	3,384
BEECH AIRCRAFT	Curb	1.25	231
BRUNSWICK-BALKE-COLLENDER (Brunswick Corp.)	NYSE	5.50	751
CARNATION COMPANY	Curb	17.88	1,872
FAIRCHILD AVIATION (Fairchild Camera)	Curb	2.00	320
GENERAL AMERICA (Safeco)	O-T-C	46.00	4,686
LOFT INC. (Pepsico)	NYSE	.75	427
NESTLE-LE MUR	Curb	.25	29
THOMPSON PRODUCTS (TRW)	NYSE	8.13	1,003
1939			
BALDWIN (D.H.) CO.	Cincinnati S.E.	2.88	463
CLARK EQUIPMENT	NYSE	15.00	1,637
COLUMBIA RIVER PACKERS (Castle & Cooke)	San Fran. S.E.	4.00	429
HART SCHAFFNER & MARX	O-T-C	10.00	1,105
LINDSAY CHEMICAL (Kerr-McGee)	Chicago S.E.	1.88	285
LINEN SERVICE CORP. OF TEXAS (National Service Industries)	Company Offering	1.00	115
NEW YORK DOCK (Questor)	NYSE	1.75	220
UNITED CHEMICALS (FMC)	Curb	3.25	436
1940			
ABITIBI POWER & PAPER CO., LTD. 6% PFD. ($100 PAR) (Abitibi Paper common)	Canada	2.00	355*

*Assumes $100 cash received June 30, 1954, was reinvested in Abitibi common at high of ensuing week.

	Where Traded	Cost	1971 Value
1940 (Continued)			
CHICAGO, ROCK ISLAND & PACIFIC CONVERTIBLE 4⅛s, 1960 (Union Pacific)	NYSE	5.00	554
EDDY PAPER CORP. (Weyerhaeuser)	Chicago S.E.	11.50	1,245
FALCONBRIDGE NICKEL	Canada	1.43*	153*
INDIANA STEEL PRODUCTS (Electronic Memories & Magnetics)	Chicago S.E.	1.50	166
LEHIGH VALLEY COAL CORP. 6% $50 PAR CONVERTIBLE PFD. (Lehigh Valley Industries)	NYSE	2.00	205**
MERCK & CO.	O-T-C	43.00	7,087
MILLER WHOLESALE DRUG (American Home Products)	Cleveland S.E.	4.38	695
PANHANDLE PRODUCING & REFINING 8% PFD. (American Petrofina Class A)	O-T-C	13.00	1,598
PITTSBURGH RAILWAYS (CITIZENS TRACTION COMMON) (Pittway Corp.)	O-T-C	1.00	161
PYRENE MANUFACTURING (Baker Industries)	Curb	4.75	543
U.S. BOBBIN & SHUTTLE PREFERRED (Baker Industries)	O-T-C	20.00	2,073
VENTURES (Falconbridge Nickel)	Canada	1.57†	159†

*U.S. Funds
**Including $7.50 cash received in 1946 and compounded at 5 percent.
†U.S. Funds

	Where Traded	Cost	1971 Value
1941			
ALLEGHANY CORP. COMMON	NYSE	.13	18
APEX ELECTRICAL MFG. (White Consolidated Industries)	Curb	6.25	646
BROADWAY DEPARTMENT STORE (Broadway-Hale Stores)	Los Angeles S.E.	3.63	489
CESSNA AIRCRAFT	Curb	3.75	418
CHEMICAL RESEARCH (General Development)	Canada	.41	43
DOBECKMAN (Dow Chemical)	Curb	2.50	313
INTERNATIONAL VITAMIN (American Home Products)	Curb	3.13	423
SOSS MANUFACTURING (SOS Consolidated)	Curb	1.13	133
SOUTH COAST (Jim Walter)	Curb	1.00	124
TRI-CONTINENTAL COMMON	NYSE	.63	64
U.S. BOBBIN & SHUTTLE (Baker Industries)	O-T-C	1.00	128
U.S. STORES $7 FIRST PREFERRED (Thorofare Markets)	Curb	3.25	683
VENEZUELAN PETROLEUM (Atlantic Richfield)	Curb	.75	83
VENEZUELAN PETROLEUM (Sinclair Oil)	Curb	.75	90
WARNER BROS. PICTURES, INC. (Kinney National Service)	NYSE	2.75	278
WARREN BROTHERS (Ashland Oil & Refining)	NYSE	.38	39

	Where Traded	Cost	1971 Value
1942			
ABITIBI POWER & PAPER COMMON			
(Abitibi Paper Common)	Canada	.50	52
AIR INVESTORS			
(American Manufacturing)	Curb	.94	111
ASSOCIATED DRY GOODS	NYSE	4.25	535
AUSTIN, NICHOLS & CO.			
(Liggett & Myers)	NYSE	1.25	138
AYRSHIRE PATOKA COLLIERIES			
(American Metal Climax)	Curb	4.00	504
BURRY BISCUIT			
(Quaker Oats)	Curb	.25	50
CHICAGO & SOUTHERN AIR LINES			
(Delta Air Lines)	O-T-C	2.00	575
CITIES SERVICE	Curb	2.13	282
CLOROX	San Fran. S.E.	24.00	2,696
DELTA AIR LINES	O-T-C	8.00	1,443
DODGE MANUFACTURING			
(Reliance Electric)	Chicago S.E.	9.13	953
EASON OIL COMPANY	O-T-C	.38	100
ELECTRIC BOND & SHARE			
(Boise Cascade)	Curb	.88	115
ELECTRIC SHOVEL COAL PREFERRED			
(American Metal Climax)	O-T-C	6.00	1,012
EVERSHARP			
(Warner Lambert)	Chicago S.E.	2.25	262
GENERAL SHAREHOLDINGS			
(Tri-Continental)	Curb	.19	35
GOODYEAR TIRE & RUBBER	NYSE	10.25	1,029
GROCERY STORE PRODUCTS			
(Clorox)	Curb	.88	152
HOUSTON OIL	NYSE	2.25	340

	Where Traded	Cost	1971 Value
1942 (Continued)			
INDUSTRIAL ACCEPTANCE	Canada	5.90*	644*
INTERNATIONAL TEL & TEL	NYSE	1.50	282
INTERNATIONAL UTILITIES CLASS B	Curb	.04	5.38
JEANETTE GLASS	Curb	.82	97
KENDALL CO.	O-T-C	6.50	695
LANE BRYANT	NYSE	8.38	970
NINETEEN HUNDRED (Whirlpool)	Curb	5.00	799
NORTH AMERICAN CAR (Flying Tiger Line)	Chicago S.E.	3.88	409
PARMELEE TRANSPORTATION (Checker Motors)	NYSE	.32	81
PHILLIPS-JONES (Phillips-Van Heusen)	NYSE	6.13	690
ST. LAWRENCE CORP. (Domtar)	Curb	.75	85
SELECTED INDUSTRIES $1.50 CONVERTIBLE STOCK (Tri-Continental)	Curb	1.00	145
SIGNODE STEEL STRAPPING (Signode Corp.)	Chicago S.E.	9.75	995
SWEETS CO. OF AMERICA (Tootsie Roll Industries)	NYSE	3.13	444
TEXAS GULF PRODUCING	NYSE	2.00	239**
VIRGINIA CAROLINA CHEMICAL (Mobil Oil)	NYSE	1.00	144
VIRGINIA IRON, COAL & COKE 5% PFD. (Bates Manufacturing)	NYSE	14.00	2,007
WINN & LOVETT GROCERY (Winn-Dixie Stores Class B Conv.)	O-T-C	18.00	3,105

*U.S. Funds
**Liquidating payments 1964–67, not including any subsequent interest.

	Where Traded	Cost	1971 Value
1943			
ABITIBI POWER & PAPER CO., LTD. 7% PFD. ($100 PAR) (Abitibi Paper common)	Canada	12.50	1,606*
CONNECTICUT GENERAL LIFE INSURANCE (Connecticut General Insurance)	O-T-C	27.63	3,756
CONTINENTAL ASSURANCE (CNA Financial)	O-T-C	40.50	4,403
EASTERN GAS & FUEL 6% PFD.	Curb	19.75	2,322
ELECTRIC POWER & LIGHT COMMON (Middle South Utilities) (Pennzoil)	NYSE	1.25	151
ELECTRIC POWER & LIGHT $7 SECOND PFD. (Middle South Utilities) (Pennzoil)	Curb	7.00	1,034
EMPIRE TRUST CO. (Dome Petroleum, Ltd.)	O-T-C	43.50	4,681
GENERAL FIRE EXTINGUISHER (International Telephone & Telegraph)	O-T-C	10.63	1,096
GILLETTE	NYSE	4.75	610
INTERNATIONAL UTILITIES CLASS A (International Utilities Common)	Curb	3.75	753
KERLYN OIL CLASS A (Kerr-McGee)	O-T-C	3.13	861
KINNEY (G.R.) & CO. (Brown Shoe)	NYSE	1.88	256

*Assumes $187.50 cash received August 1, 1949, was reinvested in Abitibi common at $12.25 a share, high of week ended August 5, 1949.

	Where Traded	Cost	1971 Value
1943 (Continued)			
LINCOLN NATIONAL LIFE INSURANCE (Lincoln National Corp.)	O-T-C	28.50	3,630
LOUISIANA LAND	Curb	5.13	624
MAYTAG	NYSE	2.50	336
MC CORD RADIATOR & MANUFACTURING (McCord Corp.)	Curb	1.25	160
MC GRAW-HILL	NYSE	8.50	868
MERCANTILE STORES	Curb	21.00	2,702
MESABI IRON (Mesabi Trust)	Curb	1.00	121
MICHIGAN BUMPER (Gulf & Western)	Curb	.32	46
PACIFIC WESTERN OIL (Getty Oil)	NYSE	9.00	1,023
PFIZER (CHAS.) & CO. (Pfizer, Inc.)	O-T-C	29.00	3,493
PITTSTON CO.	NYSE	1 75	572
RAPID ELECTROTYPE (Rapid-American)	Cincinnati S.E.	2.38	413
RAYTHEON	Curb	2.75	420
SHARP & DOHME (Merck & Co.)	NYSE	8.63	885
STARRETT CORP. (Recrion)	Curb	.32	66
TRANE	Chicago S.E.	8.00	1,125
UNITED PIECE DYE WORKS COMMON	O-T-C	.10	51
UNITED PIECE DYE WORKS 6½% PFD. (United Piece Dye Works common)	O-T-C	1.88	724
U.S. FOIL B (Reynolds Metals)	Curb	2.63	342
VIRGINIA IRON, COAL & COKE (Bates Manufacturing)	O-T-C	1.00	143
WHITE SEWING MACHINE (White Consolidated Industries)	NYSE	2.63	287

	Where Traded	Cost	1971 Value
1944			
BLACK & DECKER	NYSE	16.50	1,835
EASTERN STATES CORP.			
(St. Regis Paper)	Curb	.63	67
HUNT BROS. PACKING	Los Angeles		
(Norton Simon)	S.E.	5.75	1,045
NATIONAL FIREPROOFING			
(Fuqua Industries)	Pittsburgh S.E.	.50	82
NOXZEMA CHEMICAL			
(Noxell)	O-T-C	4.50	501
PACIFIC PORTLAND CEMENT			
Ideal Basic Industries)	O-T-C	2.75	374
SELECTED INDUSTRIES			
(Tri-Continental common & warrants)	Curb	75	93
TRI-CONTINENTAL WARRANTS	Curb	.69	72
WEST VIRGINIA COAL & COKE			
(Eastern Gas & Fuel)	Curb	5.13	553
1945			
FEDDERS	Curb	9.50	1,000
MINNESOTA MINING & MANUFACTURING	Curb	60.00	6,480
NATIONAL HOMES	Kiser, Cohn & Shumaker, Inc. Indianapolis Offering	6.75	917
PHILADELPHIA LIFE INSURANCE	O-T-C	4.00	714
PLOUGH (Schering-Plough)	Curb	13.25	1,392
PRENTICE-HALL	Curb	51.00	5,452
1946			
AIR PRODUCTS & CHEMICALS	Reynolds & Co. Offering	1.00	144
JOHNSON & JOHNSON	NYSE	44.00	5,174

	Where Traded	Cost	1971 Value
1946 (Continued)			
KIRSCH COMPANY COMMON B			
(Kirsch Co. common)	O-T-C	5.00	671
KIRSCH CO. PREFERRED			
(Kirsch Co. common)	O-T-C	14.00	1,686
1948			
AMEREX HOLDING CORP.			
(American Express)	O-T-C	21.50	2,443
INTERNATIONAL BUSINESS MACHINES	NYSE	125.50	13,898
MOTOROLA	NYSE	11.25	1,184
NEW ENGLAND LIME			
(Pfizer Inc.)	O-T-C	4.50	582
ZENITH RADIO	NYSE	19.75	1,975
1949			
AMERICAN HOME FIRE ASSURANCE (American International Group)	O-T-C	7.00	1,043
EMERSON ELECTRIC	NYSE	8.50	912
FIDELITY UNION LIFE INSURANCE	O-T-C	42.00	4,425
FLYING TIGER LINE	O-T-C	1.00	123
GLOBE & RUTGERS FIRE INSURANCE (American International Group)	O-T-C	27.00	3,140
GOVERNMENT EMPLOYES LIFE INSURANCE	O-T-C	5.00	670
MAGNAVOX	NYSE	5.00	841
TAMPAX	O-T-C	16.50	2,961
1950			
DIEBOLD, INC.	O-T-C	11.63	1,594
MC DONNELL AIRCRAFT (McDonnell Douglas)	O-T-C	17.00	1,924

	Where Traded	Cost	1971 Value
1950 (Continued)			
VAN DORN IRON WORKS (Van Dorn Co.)	Midwest S.E.	6.25	714
1951			
GOVERNMENT EMPLOYES INSURANCE	O-T-C	38.00	3,938
OGDEN CORP. (Syntex) (Ogden Corp.) (Bunker Ramo)	Curb	.94	174
1952			
INTERCONTINENTAL RUBBER (Texas Instruments)	NYSE	3.00	322
1953			
GEORGIA-PACIFIC	NYSE	9.25	957
HENRY HOLT & CO. (Columbia Broadcasting System)	Amex	7.88	835
1954			
DISNEY (WALT) PRODUCTIONS INC.	O-T-C	3.63	1,630
SIMPLICITY PATTERN	Amex	4.88	772
1955			
AVON PRODUCTS	O-T-C	83.00	9,430
EMERY AIR FREIGHT	Amex	7.88	829
NEW PROCESS	Curb	58.00	7,380
POLAROID	O-T-C	42.88	5,622
1956			
BAXTER LABORATORIES	O-T-C	11.25	1,260
OCCIDENTAL PETROLEUM	San Francisco S.E.	.45	84
1958			
HALOID XEROX (Xerox)	O-T-C	47.50	7,605

	Where Traded	Cost	1971 Value
1959			
MONROE AUTO EQUIPMENT	O-T-C	10.50	1,346
1961			
MASCO SCREW PRODUCTS (Masco Corp.)	Detroit S.E.	6.25	729
1963			
SKYLINE HOMES (Skyline Corp.)	Amex	11.00	1,183
1964			
AMERICAN LABORATORIES (American Medical International)	O-T-C	.75	129
1965			
AUTOMATIC DATA PROCESSING	O-T-C	7.00	704
1966			
U.S. HOME & DEVELOPMENT	O-T-C	.63	78
1967			
DEVELOPMENT CORP. OF AMERICA	O-T-C	.38	74

It is painful for many of us to read such a record. Confronted with the star-studded backdrop of lost opportunities, we stand like Aristotle gloomily contemplating the Homeric bust of our vaulting financial ambitions. Some people doubtless will get mad at the writer. Kings in days of yore beheaded bearers of bad news. Their blue-blooded descendants—and some ordinary citizens too—vent their wrath on the inoffensive telephone receiver when they get a busy signal three times in a row.

But try to remember that denigrating or even exterminating the messenger will not alter or expunge the record. I have been a reporter for fifty years. Several times I have changed the name of my calling, and each time the price has gone up. But I am still a reporter and this is a report, not an opinion.

If you are not rich, and if you keep on thinking about investments as you have been thinking, this record could break your heart. But if this report should help you to look ahead instead of back, to think big instead of small, it could enable you to find the road to fortune. That road still lies open before us. I have never seen it closed.

Even if you are rich, a perusal of the record of the last forty years might help you better your investment score. Remember, please, a man does not have to be able to lay an egg to be qualified to tell a good one from a bad one.

Both rich and poor may be apprehensive lest they be led into an exercise in hindsight. Patrick Henry met that one head-on in a speech to the Virginia convention in St. John's Episcopal Church, Richmond, Virginia, on March 23, 1775: "I have but one lamp by which my feet are guided, and that is the lamp of experience. I know of no way of judging the future but by the past."

In subsequent chapters I shall try to point out what characteristics these 100-to-one securities have in common. I shall do this not only for the entire list of more than 360 but for those which have made 100-to-one fortunes since World War II. I shall try especially to show how these 100-to-one winners might have been detected in advance and to point out areas with similar promise today. The investor may ask a thousand questions, but "What shall I do now?" epitomizes them all.

Readers who want my answers without the reasons and the reasoning may jump now to Chapter XXVIII. Those who believe as I do that the reasons for any opinion are worth far more than the opinion itself will stay with me while we examine in more detail some of the fortune-making stocks of the last forty years.

CHAPTER VII

The Tree Does Not Grow to the Sky

Sometimes the argument as to whether one should buy growth stocks puzzles me. Money is made by buying anything that is going to be worth more in the future than one has to pay for it now. Since the past is visible to all, there is seldom much capital gain in buying stocks that continue to earn in the future what they have earned in the past. Everyone can see the past. Hence stocks that faithfully earn next year what they earned last year tend to be fully priced. That can also be true of stocks whose earnings continue to grow if the prospect of that continued growth is apparent to all. The only way to make more than the going rate of return on your capital is to buy values not apparent to most people at the time you buy.

Because every stock buyer wants to make money, it is almost a truism that nothing kills a money-making opportunity faster than its widespread popularity. This applies just as surely to growth stocks as it does to Florida real estate. What shall it profit a man to buy a stock whose earnings quadruple in the next ten years if he has to pay for four times the current earnings now?

It is true that time is on the side of the growth stock buyer *if* the growth and the expectation of growth continue. That is simple arithmetic. The price of a growth stock will increase year by year at whatever rate the earnings grow *if* the stock's price-earnings ratio remains constant. For example: Earnings this year $1. Price $25. Price-earnings ratio ($25 divided by $1) 25. If year-to-year earnings growth is 15 percent, earnings in the second year must be $1.15. If the price-earnings ratio

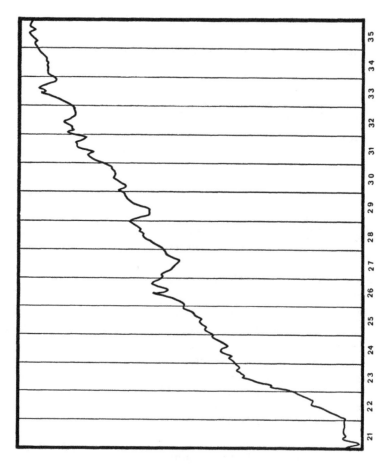

AMERICAN CAN
RELATIVE PRICE, 1921-1935

*Monthly postings on this chart show how American Can's price compared
with the price of the Dow-Jones Industrial Average. Each month the price of
American Can was divided by the corresponding price of the Dow-Jones Industrial Average. The resulting figures were posted on a scale that gives equal
percentage changes the same size. That is, an advance from 5 percent to 10
percent appears as large as an advance from 50 percent to 100 percent. American Can outran the Dow throughout 1921–35.*

stays at 25, the price must be 25 times $1.15 which equals $28.75. That, of course, is 15 percent over $25, the same percentage gain as shown by earnings.

Incontestably, growth stocks are highly attractive if they continue to grow as fast as or faster than they have been growing, and *if* buyers continue to expect them to continue to grow as fast or faster, and *if* the rate at which future earnings and dividends must be discounted does not increase materially. Those are three big "ifs," as we were sharply reminded in May 1970, when bond yields rose to historic highs while growth stock prices collapsed. No intelligent investment decision is possible without considering all three "ifs."

The mere fact that a stock has been a growth stock for ten or fifteen years is no warranty that it will continue to grow even one more year. Here is a relative price chart of a Big Board (listed on the New York Stock Exchange) blue chip (high quality, high-priced security) for fifteen years. People to whom I have shown the chart without identifying the company or the time period covered have usually exclaimed, "Yeah, that's Xerox."

What the chart shows is the market price of this stock divided by the Dow-Jones Industrial Average, month by month. If the stock had risen 20 percent when the Dow rose 20 percent, and fallen 25 percent when the Dow fell 25 percent, the relative price would be a horizontal straight line. For example: Stock price 10, Dow 100, stock price divided by Dow price *10 percent.* Stock price 12, Dow 120, stock price divided by Dow price *10 percent.* Stock price 9, Dow 90, stock price divided by Dow price *10 percent.* As you can see, for fifteen years, month in and month out, this stock went up more or declined less than the Dow, with the result that its relative price steadily rose.

The stock is American Can. The time is the fifteen years from the beginning of 1921 to the end of 1935.

Since 1935 American Can stock adjusted for all stock dividends and stock splits has fallen from more than 25 percent of the Dow to less than 4 percent. At the 1971 *high* the investor had stock worth about what he could have sold it for, forty-two years before. Meantime the Dow had increased about 2-1/2 times in price.

In 1936 American Can's price-earnings ratio was about 50 percent higher than the Dow's. That could only mean that investors were expecting American Can's earnings to increase relative to the Dow's. In 1936 American Can's earnings per share were more than 57 percent of the Dow's earnings. Five years later, in 1940, American Can's earnings were less than 37 percent of the Dow's. No wonder American Can's price declined relative to the Dow's. Computed on the same basis as in 1940, American Can's earnings had fallen to 27 percent of the Dow by 1970. So enduring was the halo American Can acquired back in the 1920s and early 30s, however, that the market did not stop putting a premium value on American Can's earnings until 1959. The halo was glorified hindsight.

From its 1903 low to its 1929 high American Can rose 369-fold.

From its 1911 low to its 1929 high the rise was 123 times.

From the end of 1920 to the 1929 high the rise was nearly 51 times.

From the 1929 high to the 1971 high the rise was zero.

Even for those who buy right, as Cinderella did, fine carriages turn to pumpkins if one stays too long.

Unlike dogs, not every stock has its day. In Wall Street a stock that does not have its day is called a dog.

Even when a stock does have its day, there is no assurance that the stock will be a leader forever.

How do I reconcile that statement with my advice to buy right and hold on? That's easy. As we have seen, hundreds of stocks have risen more than one hundredfold. A few have risen one hundredfold, and then have gone on to double or triple in price after that. But tomorrow is a new day for every company, every security. Eternal vigilance is the price not only of liberty but of solvency. My advice to buy right and hold on is intended to counter unproductive activity, not to recommend putting them away and forgetting them.

All anyone can buy in the stock market at any time is the unknown future. The past is not for sale. Someone already has had it. American Can's future was shaped by new competition, frozen foods, and plastic containers, none of which loomed large on the investment horizon in 1935. It would have been a mistake to buy American Can then even at a discount from the Dow. What made the buyers in 1935 doubled and vulnerable was that they paid for expected superior growth when they should have been anticipating a drastic decline in relative profitability.

In limiting myself as I have in this book to consideration of stocks that have appreciated one hundredfold, I do not want to give the impression that I am thinking small and ignoring opportunities to make a good deal more than 100 for one. Take Avon Products stock, for instance. You and I could have bought it in March 1955 for $83 a share. That was the offered price at the end of the month. Each of those shares, which have now become 84.2 shares, attained a market value of $9,430. Thus anyone who had invested $10,000 in Avon Products in the spring of 1955 had stock worth more than a million dollars in 1971.

To stop there would be to ignore the much bigger opportunity of buying Avon Products in 1948 or 1949. The 1948 low was 10-5/8, the 1949 low, 10-3/4. Anyone who invested $10,000 at that time got between 930 and 940 shares.

Without ever investing another penny, the buyer of those 940 shares would now have 88,172 shares of Avon Products stock. That stock reached a market value of more than $9,-875,000 in 1971.

The point I am trying to make is not how rich you and I could be if our foresight was as good as our hindsight. To think that way is an unpleasant as well as unprofitable way to spend time. No, the point is that someone did buy Avon Products at 10-5/8 in 1948, and someone did buy Avon Products at 10-3/4 in 1949. Someone also bought Avon Products in the spring of 1955 at $83 a share. Every one of those "someones" would be a millionaire or a multimillionaire today if, having made an initial investment of $10,000, he had just sat tight.

That in fact is the moral of this story of more than 360 stocks that in 1971 were worth more than 100 times what they could have been bought for in my active business lifetime. Someone did buy every one of those hundreds of stocks at less than 1 percent of what they were worth in 1971. The investment tragedy is that so few held them long enough to reap the reward already in their grasp.

In most cases only an unusually farsighted or stubborn investor could have stayed with his 100-to-one stock through the periods of adversity that have punctuated the histories of most of those issues. Avon Products was an exception. Anyone who had been watching its relative price for the last twenty years would have had little ground for uneasiness on that score. Compared with the Dow-Jones Industrial Average, Avon Products stock rose with extraordinary steadiness throughout the last two decades.

Does this mean that one should never sell anything? Mankind has made so many amusing and pathetic errors in underestimating the future of the human race that it is tempting to adopt the policy of Mr. Darrell's client who never sold anything. But let us fall back on the principle that when any rule or formula becomes a substitute for thought rather than an aid to thinking, it is dangerous and should be discarded. As we have seen, and shall see again and again, the tree does not grow to the sky.

To grow at the rate of 20 percent compounded annually for fifty years, a company must be 9,100 times as big at the end of the period as it was at the beginning. If you project that kind of growth for a company with $100 million of annual sales, you must expect those sales to reach $910 billion annually by the year 2021. If you start with a company whose sales already are a billion dollars a year, to count on 20 percent compounded annual growth for the next half century, you must foresee the sales of 9 trillion 100 billion dollars in the year 2021.

Ridiculous, you say. No practical man tries to look ahead that far. But 20 percent growth compounded annually will increase a company's size by more than six times in the next ten years. The significance of this, in a book advocating "buy right and hold on," is twofold:

1. In human relations, as in nature, there seems to be a law against limitless growth. Beyond a point, people simply won't

tolerate any more, whether the growth is in business, church, or state.

2. When you pay in advance for the earnings of a stock to triple or quadruple, as you do when you buy it at three or four times the price-earnings ratio of the Dow-Jones Industrial Average, you should foresee not only the growth you are paying for but further above average growth beyond that. This means that you must evaluate the competitive status of the company not as it is today but as it will be six to eight years from now, when it is three or four times bigger.

To win in the stock market, as in checkers, one must think at least one move further ahead than the other fellow.

I shall have more to say about this matter in the chapter entitled *Figuring the Odds*.

CHAPTER VIII

How to Argue and Win

You can win any argument if you are permitted to make the assumptions. Recognition of this simple fact is essential to an understanding of the stock market.

No one buys a stock to do someone else a favor. No one sells a stock to let someone else in on a good thing. Most trades are the result of head-on collisions between diametrically opposite opinions about the same security at the same instant in time. I refer of course to trades in stocks already on the market, not to new financing.

Often both the buyer and the seller are well informed. How can two well-informed people come to opposite conclusions about the same stock at the same price?

Usually it is because they have made different assumptions about its future. One may assume that its earnings will grow at the compounded annual rate of 15 percent for years to come. The other may apprehend a slowing down in the growth rate. Or one may be convinced that inflation in America is uncontrollable. The other may assume that while tne American people act slowly they act wisely and courageously when the peril becomes clear.

The point is that when you buy a stock all you are buying is the unknown future. The past, even the earnings reported this morning or the dividend declared one minute ago, is not for sale. The present owner already has had it. All he can sell you is whatever the future may hold for his stock. And neither he nor you can possibly know what that is.

Opinions carry little weight with the experienced investor. "Often in error, never in doubt" should be carved on the tombstone of many an investment advisor. But the reasons for an expert's opinion may be worth much more than their weight in gold. And when we say his reasons, we mean his assumptions and why he makes them.

I was disillusioned by experts as to the value of opinions per se. In the fall of 1929, when the Dow-Jones Industrial Average plunged from a high of 381 to a low of just under 200, the head of what was then the world's largest bank told us the stock market had undergone a healthy correction and the country was ready to move onward and upward to new heights of prosperity. The market rallied into the spring of 1930, then plunged to the depression low of 1932. It was seventeen years before the Dow-Jones Industrial Average got as high as 200 again.

In this same period we got the word from the floor of the New York Stock Exchange that a Morgan broker was bidding 190 for thousands of shares of U.S. Steel. U.S. Steel was a Morgan creation. No one knew more about it than the house at 23 Wall. But by 1932 the stock sold at a low of 21-1/4.

One day from 26 Broadway, the headquarters of Standard Oil, came the word that the founder, John D. Rockefeller, and his son, John D. Rockefeller, Jr., were meeting the press. "My son and I," the elder Rockefeller announced, "are bidding 50 for one million shares of Standard Oil of New Jersey." No one could be better informed about the oil business in general or Standard Oil of New Jersey in particular than its founder and principal shareholder. Yet after a brief rally Standard Oil of New Jersey stock sold down to 20.

The point is not that any of the men involved were willfully misleading the public. I believe they were all sincere. But those three experiences taught me this:

1. Never mind opinions. They are not worth a dime a dozen. Try to get the reasons for them, the assumptions underlying them.

2. No one knows or ever can know for sure what the future holds. If the Almighty had intended us to know that, He would have equipped us with another sense which none of us has. The Irishman highlighted the

matter when he said, "Sure and I wish I knew where I was going to die. I'd never go near the place." If we have no certainty as to when or where our own life will end, how can we presume to be sure of future developments with regard to matters not nearly so close to us?

Is this a counsel of despair? Not a bit of it. It is simply a recognition that in investing we deal always with probabilities and possibilities, never with certainties. It follows as night the day that in investing the odds are all important.

Hardwick Stires has been a partner in Scudder, Stevens & Clark, probably the world's oldest and largest investment counsel firm, for 40 years, the period covered by this book. For almost that many years he has been a member of the Business Council, one of the prime links between business and the Administration in Washington. His investment philosophy has been developed and tempered by two major depressions, the second World War and the still unresolved battle against inflation.

"Risk," he says, "is an essential element in the investment quest for capital gain. Don't be dismayed by a loss. Recognize it as one of the costs without which you could not have *net* gain."

At bridge I have been told that if I am not set occasionally I am underbidding—not risking enough to make the best possible score.

There is a legend that the founder of the Morris Plan banks once called a manager to account for having no losses.

"To make such a record," the founder said, "you must have been turning down good loans. Next year I want to see some losses—not too many, mind you, but enough to show that you have been risking something on your judgment."

This is not to say that the risk must always be commensurate with the profit. The art of speculation in one sense is the ability to recognize when a seeming risk is not a real risk or when a real risk is not nearly as great as the stock market anticipates. Even so an investor would have to be starry-eyed indeed to think that he could turn $10,000 into a million dollars without taking any chances of losing his money.

I know of no rule, system or philosophy that will keep an investor from making mistakes or hold him harmless when he is wrong. If we never risk our money, however, except when we are convinced the odds are heavily in our favor, our inescapable losses should look small beside our profits. But how can we figure the odds?

One of the most persistent illusions of the business of investing is that information is all you need to make money. Organizations that sell information foster that illusion. It is good for their business.

If one just stops to think about the two parties to every trade, the fallacy in this notion that information is tantamount to money-making investment decisions becomes painfully apparent. For every buyer there must be a seller. For every seller there must be a buyer. Sometimes an informed buyer has the good luck to meet an uninformed seller and vice versa. But it is a good guess that most of the time—practically all of the time where institutions are on both sides of the trade—both buyer and seller are informed. If information is everything, how can two informed professionals come to opposite conclusions about the same security at the same price at the same instant in time?

There are several answers. One is that the seller may think he has a better place to invest the proceeds, even though he likes the stock he is selling. I remember vividly back in 1949 when an enormously wealthy investor sold Socony Vacuum stock at what proved to be almost exactly the bottom of the market. Not until many months later did I hear that he had put the proceeds into Superior Oil which went up more than twice as fast.

A second reason why one informed investor may sell what another informed investor is buying is that no one can be informed about the future. Since all decisions as to the future *must* be based on assumptions, informed investors may make different assumptions and hence come to opposite conclusions about buying or selling a particular stock at a particular moment.

A third reason for differences of opinion among informed investors is that no one ever is or can be fully informed. The investor who is 98 percent informed may come to the opposite conclusion from that reached by one who is 99 percent informed.

The illusion that information is the be all and end all of the investment business logically leads to the imposition of penalties on those who seek to benefit from "sure thing" inside information. If you believe that information leads you in a straight line to correct investment decisions it follows that anyone who gets information ahead of you has an advantage which should not be allowed.

In 1961 when I was writing an article for the *Atlantic Monthly* entitled "The Hazards of the Stock Market" I asked Joseph P. Kennedy for an interview. I had first met him twenty-five years earlier when he was chairman of the Securities Exchange Commission and I was chief of the *Wall Street Journal's* Washington Bureau. Ours then was the first news gathering organization to assign a reporter full-time to the SEC.

Mr. Kennedy agreed to see me, but because his son was President of the United States the interview had to be off the record. Now that both father and son are gone, however, and ten years have elapsed since the interview I think I have historical license to report these two points:

1. When I asked Mr. Kennedy if he regarded inside information as a major problem or hazard for investors in the excited stock market of 1961 he burst out with this comment: "If I had all the money that has been lost on inside information I'd really be rich."

2. Regarding trading in securities, Mr. Kennedy volunteered the statement that he had not made a round turn in a single stock since he had become chairman of the SEC more than twenty-five years before. By that he meant that he had not even once sold a stock in hope of buying it back cheaper, and later bought it back.

At the time I was not perceptive enough to infer that Mr. Kennedy, like Mr. Garrett, bought right and held on.

Let no one distort my comments on information to allege that I belittle getting the facts. All I am trying to point out is that information at best is nothing but the raw material out of which some people will concoct good investment decisions and other people will make bad ones. From Clarence W. Barron, publisher of the *Wall Street Journal* when I went to work there in 1927, I learned, "The fact without the truth is false. Always connect."

Even if one's information is complete and accurate, it can still be misleading investmentwise if it is late. A lemon that has been flattened by a steam roller has more juice in it than a piece of information the stock market has already discounted. To use another analogy, the difference between fresh and stale information is like the difference between soda water that has just been uncapped and soda water that has been left standing open all night. Just as uncapped soda water soon loses its fizz, so uncorked news swiftly fades into history or oblivion.

How can one tell whether his information is fresh or stale? As is true of so many aspects of the investment business, there is no way to be sure. Even if 10,000 investors have heard the news ahead of you, it may still prove profitable to you if 10 million investors are going to hear it and act on it after you.

Perhaps the best justification for the use of charts as aids to investment decision-making is that in experienced hands charts of stock prices often suggest whether good news foreshadows an advance in the price or explains an advance that has already taken place. News is like gifts in the old adage, "Gifts in health are golden. Gifts in illness are silver. Gifts in death are lead."

Really fresh news—news to which the stock market has not reacted—can indeed be golden. News that comes as no surprise to substantial market interests may yet have enough kick in it to be silver to the remainder. News that has been fully discounted is lead and those who act on it are dead.

Since information never comes labeled grade A, grade B, or grade C, those who attempt to base investment decisions on it must devise means of their own to grade it. Charts and chartists are by no means infallible but they are a lot better than nothing when they show that bad news has been heavily discounted by a precipitous decline in price or that good news has been widely and even enthusiastically anticipated in the marketplace.

The market vibrates on Dow-Jones news all right, but not necessarily in step. When you read your morning newspaper never forget as you put the paper down that your homework has just begun. Herman Melville said it better when he wrote of "serenely concocting information into wisdom."

CHAPTER IX

Figuring the Odds

An erudite way of referring to the odds in stock investing is to talk about the opportunity-risk ratio. For example if you see a chance to make 100 points in a stock and a risk of losing 10 points, the opportunity-risk ratio is 10-to-1. Unfortunately figuring the odds is not that simple. Equally important is the *chance* of gain relative to the chance of loss. If there is one chance in ten that the stock will go up 100 points, and nine chances in 10 that it will go down 10 points, the so-called 10-to-1 opportunity-risk ratio ceases to be attractive. Meaningful opportunity-risk ratios relate the prospective gain and the probability of achieving it to the prospective loss and the risk that it will materialize.

Since we are dealing with the unknown future anyway, why bother to go through such exercises? Wouldn't we do just as well to blindfold ourselves, stick pins in the quotation page of the *Wall Street Journal,* and buy ourselves whatever stock we happened to hit?

The question reminds me of the story of the gambler who was arrested in a small town for violating an ordinance against games of chance. His defense was that poker was not a game of chance. To prove it he played all night with the prosecuting attorney, the judge, and a few of the town's leading citizens. In the morning, after he had given them back the clothing he had won from them, they dropped the charges and sped him on his way.

The point is that in the stock market as in poker the wise investor tries to make even money bets when the odds are heavily in his favor. How can this be done?

By seeing favorable probabilities that are greater than generally appreciated, or finding stocks priced at levels which discount rather fully the unfavorable probabilities apparent to all. In the first instance the buyer simply recognizes a value that others do not see. In the second case the buyer says in effect, "Since the price of this stock already is discounting the worst that can be seen for it, there is no downside risk. And since the soup is rarely eaten as hot as it is cooked, the buyer is likely to get more than he is paying for."

How can you measure what others are expecting? Who can read the minds of millions of investors, most of whom he has never even met?

Put that way the problem sounds insoluble. But there is a logical solution if we can agree on three simple premises. They are:

1. The value of any security is the discounted present worth of all future payments.
2   A dollar of income from one fully taxable source is worth as much as a dollar of income from any other fully taxable source.
3. Hence it follows that when investors pay more for a dollar of income from one source than they need to pay to get an equivalent dollar of income from another source they are expressing implicitly the opinion that the income stream from the first source will rise faster or dry up more slowly than the income stream from the second source. Otherwise what they do makes no sense.

Robert G. Wiese, scholarly Scudder, Stevens & Clark dean of investment research and partner in Boston, puts it more neatly: "Investors don't pay different prices for the same thing. When they seem to be doing so they are paying like prices for different anticipations."

Two commonly used gauges of differing anticipations are:
1. Relative yields on stocks and bonds.
2. Relative price-earnings ratios on stocks.

The principle of relative values is at least as old as the Bible. The man who buried the talents his master left with him preserved his capital but lost out in competition with others who had increased their capital.

All values are relative in all respects. In the country of the blind, the one-eyed man is king.

Bond values are relative to stock values, and vice versa. And stock values are relative to each other. A few years ago there were some stock men who paid no attention to bonds. Most of them are sadder and wiser now.

While nothing is sure in investing, perhaps tne least unsure of any of the assumptions we make is that highest grade bonds will pay their interest and principal when due. Provided such bonds are not callable for ten years or more, as is true of many of them, the buyer who invests his money to yield 8-1/2 percent is very likely to receive 8-1/2 percent through good times and bad until the bonds are redeemed or refunded.

The man who buys stocks yielding half tnat much must foresee a big increase in the dividends on his stocks or his action makes no sense at all. He may scoff at dividends because he is buying for capital gains but unless earnings and dividends rise, his capital gains will be as ephemeral as the oft-cited snowball in hell.

Late in 1961 when the stock market was exuberant I remarked to the first chairman of the SEC, Joseph P. Kennedy, "People don't care about dividends any more."

"Where are these people?" Mr. Kennedy challenged. "I never met one."

International Business Machines, the greatest growth stock of them all, sold twenty years ago to yield about 1-3/4 percent. Clearly, you might think, the people who bought it were not looking for dividends. But if they still hold the stock they bought at the 1951 high they are getting dividends, in cash, now at the rate of more than 70 percent on their 1951 cost. Without that increase in dividends, and in earnings out of which to pay them, the phenomenal rise in the price of IBM stock simply could not have taken place.

Wise investors do not buy a stock just because it is going up or is expected to go up. Wise investors buy because they foresee an increase in earnings and dividends that will make today's price look cheap in years to come. Even the wisest sometimes misjudge the future of earnings and dividends. Only fools—and perhaps some professional short-term traders—buy without giving that future a thought.

Over the years, comparing the yield on bonds with the yield on stocks has provided a remarkable gauge of investor optimism and pessimism, as the accompanying chart shows.

Between twenty-five and thirty years ago dividend yields on stocks were three times as great as interest yields on bonds. This made sense only if one assumed that dividends on stocks were highly undependable and very likely to decline over the years to come.

Actually, instead of declining, dividends rose steadily until about five years ago. At the same time the price per dollar of dividends rose relative to the price per dollar of bond interest. At the recent peak the investor could get almost twice as high a yield on the best corporate bonds as he could get on an average of fifty leading common stocks. In other words in a single generation the price of dividends rose from a third of the price of interest to almost twice the price of interest. It would be hard to imagine a more dramatic demonstration of the impact of a change from pessimism to optimism on security prices.

Just as it made no sense for dividend income to sell at a third the price of interest income unless one assumed a prolonged decline in dividends, so at the other extreme it made no sense for dividend income to sell at nearly twice the price of interest income unless one assumed a prolonged advance in dividends.

Over the last half century investors have tended to be optimistic about further increases in dividends when they should have been pessimistic. Likewise they have tended to be pessimistic about the future of dividends when in the bright light of hindsight we can see they should have been optimistic. They were, however, correctly optimistic about the future of dividends at the time the dollar was devalued in 1934, and again when dividends first sold at a premium over interest in 1958. Will their relative optimism today be justified? Only the

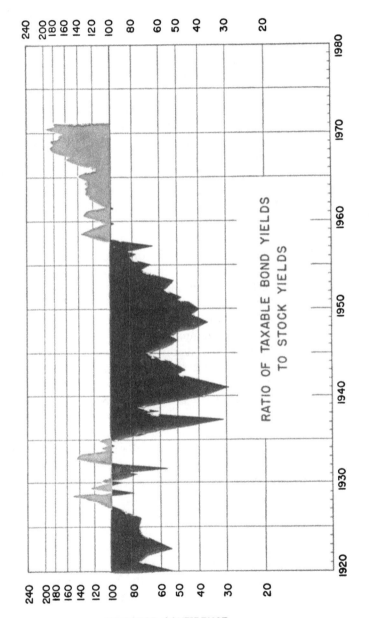

RATIO OF TAXABLE BOND YIELDS
TO STOCK YIELDS

INVESTOR CONFIDENCE

future can tell. What we do know is that dividends must increase just to give today's stock buyers what they already have paid for. From here the trend of the stock market will depend not on whether dividends increase—that is already in the price—but on whether the increase in dividends is *more* or *less* than is expected.

Just as the price of dividend income relative to the price of interest income reveals the stock market's expectations regarding the future trend of dividends, so do comparative prices of earnings of individual stocks reveal investors' expectations regarding their relative future trends.

In time most businesses develop their own jargon which is at best confusing and at worst incomprehensible to the uninitiated. Wall Street is no exception. Since the financial community talks of interest yields on bonds and dividend yields on stocks, it would be merely consistent to talk of earnings yields as well. But as though to avoid the imputation that consistency is a virtue of small minds, the financial community divides the dividend by the price to get the dividend yield, then turns around and divides the price by the earnings to get the price-earnings ratio. For example, if a stock pays $3.00 a year in dividends and sells at 100, its dividend yield is 3 percent. If the same stock earns $5.00 a share its price-earnings ratio is 20.

The meaning would be the same if Wall Street talked of a 5 percent earnings yield but that simply isn't the language used.

When one stock sells 10 times earnings while another sells 20 times earnings the inference is that the market (that is, the consensus of investor money) expects the earnings of the company selling at the higher price to increase much more rapidly (or decline much more slowly) than the earnings of the company selling at the lower price.

Using this method the investor still has to guess what the future holds, but he can be relatively precise in his calculations of what the stock market expects the future to hold.

Later on I shall point out some of the pitfalls in uncritical use of price-earnings ratios for comparative purposes. Like matches in the hands of a child, they can be deadly dangerous.

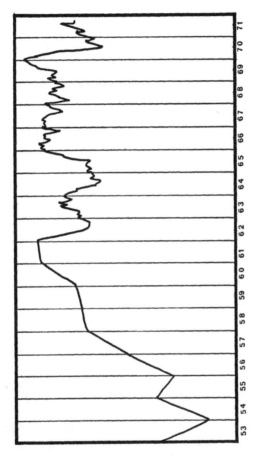

POLAROID HOPE CHART

Here, plotted monthly within each year shown, is the price-earnings ratio of Po-
laroid divided by the price-earnings ratio of the Dow-Jones. This is called
Polaroid's relative price-earnings ratio or relative multiplier. When this relative
price-earnings ratio is at the level of 1 on the scale on both sides of the chart,
the inference is that the stock market expects about the same rate of growth
in Polaroid's earnings as in the earnings of the Dow-Jones Industrial Average.
When this relative price-earnings ratio is at the level of 4 on the scale, the
stock market is paying four times as much for a dollar of Polaroid earnings as
for a dollar of earnings of the Dow. From that level Polaroid's earnings must
quadruple to give the buyer as much as he could have had by buying the Dow
instead.

To the expert they are an essential tool. Properly adjusted and related to a good general market gauge such as the Dow-Jones Industrial Average, they become Hope Thermometers.

No good doctor would prescribe for a patient on the basis of a thermometer reading alone. But I have seldom seen a doctor who did not take my temperature as part of his examination.

Good investment doctors use Hope Thermometers the same way. Because a picture is worth a thousand words, and can be read much more quickly, Scudder, Stevens & Clark keep Hope Thermometers on thousands of stocks. On page 97 is one on Polaroid for the last twenty years. It indicates that hopes for Polaroid's future earnings exactly equalled hopes for the thirty leading companies in the Dow-Jones Industrial Average.

Even at the 1970 low the market price of a dollar of Polaroid earnings was still more than twice the price of a dollar of earnings of the Dow-Jones Industrial Average. To warrant *that* relationship, Polaroid's earnings must more than double relative to the Dow-Jones Industrial Average earnings and do as well as the Dow thereafter. But there will be no sound basis for expecting Polaroid stock to outrun the Dow-Jones Industrial Average unless, after Polaroid's earnings more than double, the outlook is still more favorable for Polaroid than for the Dow. In effect, at the 1970 low, the Polaroid buyer was saying to the Polaroid seller: "I am so sure Polaroid's earnings will more than double relative to the Dow that I am willing to pay you now what Polaroid would be worth if they had already more than doubled. Why will I do that? Because I believe that after Polaroid's earnings have risen to the level I am now paying for, they will continue to rise faster than the Dow's."

All this shows a high degree of confidence in Polaroid's future, and great self-confidence in the buyer's ability to foresee Polaroid's future. Both may be justified. Time will tell. But as investors we play blind man's buff unless we thus define the implications of relative prices.

The careful observer will note that the price of Polaroid anticipated a record rise in its earnings relative to the average

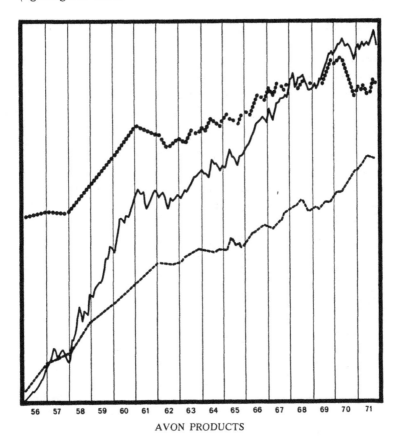

56   57   58   59   60   61   62   63   64   65   66   67   68   69   70   71

AVON PRODUCTS

of thirty leading stocks at the same time the price of leading stocks was anticipating a record rise in dividends—sort of a double whammy!

Because we have talked about relative prices, relative earnings, and relative price-earnings ratios or relative multipliers, it may be helpful to look at a chart which shows all three together. Here is one of Avon Products covering the 16-year period in which an initial $10,000 investment in the stock would have made us millionaires by 1971.

A stock's price may rise because its earnings rise, or because the price of each dollar of those earnings rises, or both. If a stock is earning $2 a share and selling at $20, the price of each dollar of those earnings is $10. If the stock earns $3 a share in the next year, and the price of each dollar of those earnings remains at $10, the stock's price will rise to $30. But if as often happens the price of each dollar of the stock's earnings rises too, say from $10 to $15, then the stock's price will rise to 15 times $3, or to $45 a share. Most great advances in the stock market result from some such combination of rising earnings *and* rising price-earnings ratios.

Likewise, the rise in the relative price of any stock must be derived from a rise in its relative earnings plus or minus any change in its relative multiplier or price-earnings ratio. That is simple arithmetic.

As the Avon Products chart shows, the great rise in the relative price of the stock was based on a steep and persistent advance in Avon Products' relative earnings. But without the accompanying advance in the relative price paid for each dollar of those earnings, the rise in Avon Products' relative price would not have been much more than half what it actually was.

This may seem to belabor the obvious, but many investors are so intent on earnings that they fail to appreciate the oft-times greater significance of changes in the market price of each dollar of those earnings. Price-earnings ratios and relative price-earnings ratios measure investor expectations. Ofttimes more than half of the rise in the price of stock is due to a change in investor psychology.

Paying attention to the psychological content of any stock price advance is important for two reasons:

1. What goes up on a rise in investor expectations can go down on a fall in those expectations. Both can occur without any change in reported earnings.

2. It is rare for seasoned stocks to have price-earnings ratios much over four times the Dow's. Hence when a stock sells at 60 times earnings while the Dow is selling at 15 times earnings, the prospective buyer is on notice (a) that his optimism about the stock's future is widely shared, and (b) that the chances of a further rise in the price of the stock due to a further rise in its relative price-earnings ratio are slim. What

this means is that the buyer must look to further increases in earnings to carry all of the burden of any further increase in the stock's price which heretofore has been lifted both by a rise in its relative earnings and by a rise in its relative price-earnings ratio.

A stock can rise one hundredfold if its earnings increase twenty-five fold while its price-earnings ratio increases fourfold. ($25 \times 4 = 100$). But if its price-earnings ratio remains unchanged, its earnings must increase one hundredfold to produce the same price advance. If, heaven forbid, its price-earnings ratio should be halved, its earnings must double just to keep its price unchanged.

It is no more unsound to buy a stock in anticipation of a rise in its relative price-earnings ratio than it is to buy a stock in anticipation of a rise in its relative earnings. Department store buyers would be stupid indeed if they paid no attention to fads and fashions. But it is unsound to buy any stock without knowing to what extent its price is based on its relative earnings and how much it is based on its relative price-earnings ratio.

There is no such thing as a "correct" price-earnings ratio. Nor is there a "correct" relative price-earnings ratio. All depends on what the unknown future brings forth. But one does not have to be a financial genius to realize that when he buys a stock at a very high relative price-earnings ratio he is paying someone hard cash now for what is hoped for in the rather distant future.

Turning again to the Avon Products chart, note that as late as 1957 Avon Products stock sold at a lower price-earnings ratio than the Dow-Jones Industrial Average. By the end of 1969 each dollar of Avon Products earnings was valued in the market at more than 4-1/2 times the price of each dollar of the Dow-Jones Industrial Average earnings.

If Avon Products price had advanced and declined proportionately to the Dow from 1955 to 1971 its relative price line would have been straight and horizontal. If Avon Products relative earnings had increased and decreased proportionately to the Dow's, Avon Products relative earnings line would have been straight and horizontal. Finally, if Avon Products price-earnings ratio had remained equal to the Dow's, that line too would have been straight and horizontal. Going forward in time from any point on any of the three lines, an advance above the horizontal or a decline below the horizontal shows that Avon Products' price, earnings, or multiplier has gained or lost compared with the Dow-Jones Industrial Average.

To me the picture suggests that:

1. Further rise in the price of Avon Products stock must depend largely on further gains in Avon Products earnings.

2. Investor confidence in those further gains in Avon Products earnings must stay high or go higher if the stock price-stimulus of rising earnings is not to be offset by a declining multiplier.

3. Avon Products' sales and earnings must grow to three or four times the greatest they ever have been just to support the 1971 price of Avon Products stock unless it is assumed that even after Avon Products has tripled or quadrupled in size its prospects for further growth still will be better than prospects for the Dow.

If these comments seem inconsistent with my theme of "buy right and hold on," I welcome the chance to make a point. Buying right will do you little good unless you hold on. But holding on will do you little good—and may do you great harm—unless you have bought right.

After a stock has risen to 50 times what you paid for it, you can be quite sure you have bought right. If it doubles once more, you have your 100 for one. You can afford to run some risks for a reward of that size.

The new buyer faces a different problem. He must ask and answer correctly the question: "What are my chances of making 100 for one from here?" As we saw in the case of American Can, history is no help. Only correct assumptions about the future are relevant. And unless those assumptions are materially better than the stock's price already is anticipating, there is still no profit in them.

Relative value analysis provides no final answers. It does help to define what is expected, and thus afford a benchmark against which the investor can gauge the profit potential in whatever assumptions he chooses to make.

In the bright light of hindsight it can often be seen that the stock market has gone to unjustified extremes. It is much safer for the investor to proceed on the basis that these unwarranted extremes result from the common human inability to foresee the future rather than from stupidity. As a matter of fact, in the stock market money tends to move from stupid to intelligent hands. The stupid round-lotter* becomes an odd-lotter.* The intelligent odd-lotter soon is trading in round lots. When one attempts to outguess the stock market he enters the lists against the distilled essence of the best financial brains of the world. It is a sobering thought. What should give the average man hope is the realization that the most expert, the most experienced are constantly retiring or dying, often being succeeded by inexperienced youngsters who insist on learning the hard way.

A further comforting thought is that since no one knows what the future holds, all of us are entitled to guess about it. We should not forget, though, that an informed guess has an edge over a wild one.

How can you calculate this hope element (relative price-earnings ratio) for yourself?

Every Monday, at the bottom of the first column on the next to the last page of the *Wall Street Journal,* is reported the price-earnings ratio for the Dow-Jones Industrial Average. Get the latest price for your stock from any newspaper. Divide that price by the per share earnings of the stock for the latest twelve months. If you are a stockholder you can get the earnings figure from the latest annual report. If you are only thinking of becoming a stockholder, you may find the latest twelve months' earnings a share reported in *Barron's Stock Market at a Glance.* If you have access to *Standard & Poor's* or *Moody's* manuals, you can find the earnings figures there. Your broker may be willing to look them up for you.

Let us suppose your stock is selling for $60 a share, and that its latest year's earnings are $2 a share. The price-earnings

---

* A round lotter is one who buys stocks 100 shares or more at a time. An odd lotter buys fewer than 100 shares, often just 10 shares. Since the odd lotter must pay slightly more per share than the round lotter, buyers who can afford to do so usually buy at least 100 shares at a time.

ratio then is 30 (60 divided by 2 = 30). Let us suppose that the latest price-earnings ratio reported for the Dow is 15. Divide 30, the price-earnings ratio for your stock, by 15, the price-earnings ratio for the Dow. The answer, of course, is 2. This means that the market is paying twice as much for each dollar of earnings of your stock as it is paying for each dollar of earnings of the thirty great companies in the Dow-Jones Industrial Average.

The inference is that the market (that is, the consensus of investor money) expects the earnings of your stock to increase much more rapidly (or decline much more slowly) than the earnings of the Dow-Jones Industrial Average. Using this method you still have to guess what the future holds for your stock, but you start from a factual base of what the market expects the future to hold for your stock relative to other stocks. If what you expect is better than what the market expects, you buy. If what you expect is less than what the market expects, you sell. But only if the difference between what you expect and what the market expects is great enough to give you a profit after allowing yourself a wide margin for error!

Having thus made a case for the use of price-earnings ratios, I shall now cite some of the hazards in doing so.

CHAPTER X

The Quality of Earnings Is Strained

Every age has its mass delusions. So, I suppose, does every race, nation, and occupation. While a delusion persists, it is lonesome, sometimes dangerous, and always unprofitable to say that the emperor has no clothes on. Nevertheless I shall put my head through the sheet and say that to my mind one of the worst delusions of the investment business is the uncritical use of price-earnings ratios, or more specifically the misuse of price-earnings ratios, to arrive at relative evaluations of various stocks and stock groups.

Basically the fallacy of using price-earnings ratios for comparative purposes is the implied assumption that the earnings are as comparable as the prices. We know that the prices are comparable, so long as the quotations are expressed in the same currencies. But the earnings of different companies vary so much in quality and hence in value that we might as well be comparing cows and horses on the basis of how fast they can run. When I see tabulations of stocks ranked according to the quotients of their prices divided by their latest year's reported earnings, I am reminded of the World War I veteran who lost his job and turned to begging under a placard reading:

> *Three years in the trenches.*
> *Two wounds.*
> *One wife.*
> *Four children.*
> *Seven months out of a job.*
> *Total seventeen.*
> *Please help.*

Let me make plain that I am not implying either originality or novelty for this idea that price-earnings ratios, like martinis, can be very deceptive. Nor do I mean to suggest that professional security analysts ignore the dangers in uncritical use of price-earnings ratios. Far from it. All I am questioning is whether as investors we try hard enough to allow for the differences in the quality of earnings. Do we perhaps sometimes pay lip service to these differences while using statistical procedures which ignore them? Does our pressing need to reach more investment decisions faster tempt us to gloss over differences in the quality of earnings because, after all, in this business one must be "practical"? Let's see.

There are two approaches to the problem. One might be called the accounting approach. The other is perhaps best described as conceptual.

The accounting approach is the better known but to my mind the conceptual approach is even more important. In saying that, I do not mean to belittle the significance of accounting variations and omissions. If the stock market clock ever strikes midnight again, as it did on September 3, 1929, Leonard Spacek, chairman of Arthur Andersen & Company, will be one whose C.P.A. coach should not turn into a pumpkin. No one has done more than he to deflate the "accepted practice" balloon which for so many years had lifted sharp practice to respectability.

I lack the accounting expertise to gild Mr. Spacek's lilies, but I do want to say an especially loud "Amen!" to his early criticism of corporate reporting of lease financing. If anything were needed to point up the gulf between the owners and the managers of some businesses, it could be supplied by the failure of some managers to tell the owners the amount and terms of lease financing in the same detail as they matter-of-factly disclose the amounts and terms of other long-term obligations.

The accounting profession weaseled out of this for decades by saying that it was not accepted accounting practice to show unaccrued rents as a liability. Accordingly when a corporation sold its headquarters building, or factory, or tanker, to an insurance company, then leased it back for a period of years at a rate sufficient to repay the entire purchase price plus interest, the transaction became off-balance sheet financing, the terms of which all too often were known only to the managers of the business.

These are material facts whose absence I am deploring. Take for example three companies with $100 million capital each. All wish to expand, because each is earning 20 percent before taxes on its invested capital. For this illustration let us assume that the effective tax rate is 50 percent.

The first of the three companies issues additional stock to increase its invested capital to $200 million. The second sells 8 percent long-term bonds to bring its invested capital to $200 million. In each case, whether we approve or not, we at least know what is going on. The first company, with all common stock capitalization, continues to earn 20 percent before taxes, 10 percent after taxes, on its invested capital and on its equity.

The second company continues to earn 20 percent on its invested capital, before taxes, but earns 16 percent on equity after taxes as a result of the capital leverage. That percentage is arrived at as follows: 20 percent of $200 million equals $40 million, less $8 million interest on $100 million of funded debt leaves $32 million less 50 percent corporate income tax leaves $16 million which is equal to 16 percent on $100 million equity.

The third company acquires $100 million of additional facilities by lease financing on terms which amount to 10 percent interest. Since neither the amount nor the terms of this lease financing are disclosed to the investing public, and since the lease obligations are not shown on the balance sheet, the investing public is encouraged to conclude that this third company now is earning 15 percent on invested capital and on equity. The 15 percent is calculated as follows: Earnings of 20 percent before undisclosed lease rentals and taxes on $200 million of assets amount to $40 million less $10 million of lease rentals leaves $30 million less 50 percent corporate income tax leaves $15 million which equals 15 percent on $100 million equity. Thus we have three companies each employing $200 million of assets, each earning 20 percent before taxes and undisclosed lease rentals on each dollar of assets employed in its business, but one apparently earning 10 percent after taxes on equity and on invested capital, another with disclosed leverage earning 16 percent on equity and 10 percent on invested capital, and the third with undisclosed leverage apparently earning 15 percent both on equity and on invested capital.

Suppose business turns bad, so bad that each of our three companies earns only 5 percent before taxes on each dollar of assets employed in its business. The first company with the all common stock capitalization earns 5 percent before taxes and 2-1/2 percent after taxes on both invested capital and on equity The second company with the $100 million of 8 percent bonds earns 5 percent before taxes on invested capital and 1 percent after taxes on equity. The figures are arrived at as follows: Pretax earnings of 5 percent on $200 million equal $10 million less $8 million bond interest leaves $2 million less 50 percent corporate income tax leaves $1 million which is 1 percent on $100 million equity. Security analysts could foresee the impact of the decline in business on the second company, of course, because they had the pertinent facts about the capital leverage. But how about the third company? Still assuming precisely the same conditions that we applied to the first and second companies, that is, a decline in pretax earnings on invested capital from 20 percent to 5 percent, the aftertax return on equity of the third company would plummet mysteriously from 15 percent to zero We arrive at that figure this way: Pretax earnings of 5 percent on $200 million of assets (before off-balance-sheet financing lease rentals) amount to $10 million. When we deduc $10 million of lease rentals from pretax earnings of $10 nillion, nothing is left.

If and when we manage to ferret out the details of lease financing, which is the villain in the cast, we discover that the return on the capital employed in the business is 5 percent but that the return on the equity has been wiped out by the necessity of paying 10 percent on the lease rentals.

Management, of course, is fully aware of all these lease financing details, but neither management, the company auditors, nor the S.E.C. thus far has seen fit to regard such vital statistics—vital to investors, I mean—as coming under the head of information which the owners of American business are entitled to have *in the same detail as debt.*

In times of long-continued prosperity, with prices, profits, and business volume all trending up, it seems old maidish to harp on such matters. Yet if we ignore these prior charges, we might as well ignore all others too, and henceforth consider only the equity. It is a pity for the business and financial community to leave undone those things which ought to be done. Sooner or later some reformer from outside grabs the ball and runs with it, upsetting the financial community's applecart as he goes. We can't block him because we know he's only doing what we should have done long ago. Many other examples could be cited, but they have all been in the news.

I said there are two approaches to this matter of the quality of earnings, one accounting, the other conceptual. Let's look at the conceptual:

Part of most companies' earnings is paid out in dividends. Those dividends are equal to each other, dollar for dollar. Your grocer never asks whether the money you pay him came from dividends or interest. He couldn't care less.

But how about the earnings not paid out in dividends? Suppose those retained earnings were stolen, what would they then be worth? More realistically, suppose they are invested in projects which do not pay off, with the result they add nothing to the company's earning power. What then is the proper price-earnings ratio at which such earnings should sell?

My feeling is that such plowed-back earnings are entitled to about the same multiplier as is given to the per share depreciation.

"That's nonsense," you may be thinking. "We don't apply any multiplier whatsoever to depreciation in figuring the value of a stock."

That is exactly the point I am trying to make. As investors, let us say we buy a company earning $1.00 per share, and paying us each year in dividends 50 cents a share. If at the end of five or ten years the company is still earning $1.00 a share and still paying us 50 cents a share in dividends, what has happened to the earnings retained each year? The answer may be that they have been required to maintain what we bought in the first place. But that comes close to being a definition of a charge for depreciation. Is it unrealistic therefore to disregard plowed-back earnings which fail to produce any improvement in the earning power of the business?

Let's not answer that question too hastily. Suppose we have two companies each earning $1.00 a share, each paying 50 cents a share in dividends, and each failing to show any growth in earnings as a result of the plowed-back profits. Before we conclude that one is as bad an investment as the other, let us note that the sales of the first company have been increasing at the rate of 10 percent compounded annually while the volume of business done by the second company has been declining 10 percent a year. Is it possible that the first company has been "buying" additional business out of its pretax earnings so effectively that if we capitalized the additional business fairly the adjusted earnings would have shown a nice increase? By the same token is it not possible that the second company has only managed to maintain its reported earnings at the starting level by in effect liquidating its business on the installment plan, thereby taking into the income account some money which in economic theory should have been return of capital?

Few would argue against the proposition that a dollar of earnings of the first company is worth more than a dollar of earnings of the second company. How much more is another question. The answer to that question depends primarily on how long one is prepared to assume the future will be like the past. The evidence is overwhelming that the future will be like the past for a little while. When the head of the Weather Bureau in New York City retired some years ago he was quoted as saying that a man could make a pretty good record as a weather forecaster by predicting that tomorrow's weather would be like today's. Since we tend to have periods of fair weather followed by rainy spells, weather forecasting based on nothing more than a look out of the office window would be right much more often than not.

Since for all men the visibility of the future is zero beyond this instant, assumptions as to how long observed trends will continue must be based on probabilities which in turn have been derived from the past and hence may not apply to the future. This is a long-winded way of saying that all estimates of the future are to some degree subjective.

The business of the stock market is to cash in on the future now. Accordingly it is really not as important, short term, to know what sales and earnings are going to be five and ten years hence as to know what other investors are going to think they will be. In general the longer a trend continues the more people can be found willing to risk their savings on the proposition that it will continue longer still. As a practical matter then we probably should assume that old trends will persist longer than new trends simply because, whether they do or not, more investors will be inclined to assume that they will.

Let us return for a moment to the two companies each earning $1.00 a share and each paying 50 cents a share in dividends, with no improvement in either over the last five years. Let us further assume that there has been no change in the relative sales of either company. Surely now we have the basis for a meaningful comparison of price-earnings ratios. If one of those two companies sells at ten times earnings while the other sells at twenty times earnings, our course is clear. Or is it?

Let us assume that one of the two companies has been spending $1.00 a share a year on basic research which thus far has been totally unproductive. The second company has been spending nothing on research. The first company's earnings obviously are worth more than the second company's earnings for two reasons:

1. The first company has a chance of striking it rich in research at any moment. The second company, doing no research, has no such chance.

2. The first company can discontinue the research program, in which case, other factors remaining equal, the money now being spent on research would be added to pretax earnings. The second company, doing no research, has no opportunity to cut expenses by eliminating its research program.

If instead of research you substitute prospecting for mineral deposits or wildcatting for oil, the comparisons between the two companies would be affected in much the same way.

Some readers may think I'm reciting things they have long known. Others may be feeling that the theoretical illustrations I have used are extreme and unrealistic.

"In practice," the latter may be saying to themselves, "such ariations do not amount to enough to alter my investment decisions."

I shall not argue against anyone who contends that *in most cases* such variations as I have cited would not alter an investment decision reached while ignoring such variations. Neither shall I argue that in most cases when you get into your automobile it does not matter whether you fasten your seat belt or not. But just as fastening your seat belt may at some time save your life, so scrupulous attention to the wide potential variations in the quality of earnings may someday save your fortune.

Let me cite two or three more ways in which $1 of reported earnings of one company may be found to be worth substantially more or less than $1 of reported earnings of another company in the same business at the same time:

1. Two companies each reporting the same earnings and paying the same dividends per share, each showing the same rate of sales growth, each spending the same amount on research or wildcatting, show sharply different trends in inventories and receivables. The first company has held its inventories and receivables in roughly the same relationship to its volume of business as in previous years. The second company has held down its unit cost of production by running its plants at a rate 10 percent higher than warranted by its sales with the result that its inventory has increased sharply. At the same time, as a sales gimmick, the second company has been selling its goods on extremely liberal credit terms with the result that its receivables have risen sharply in relation to the volume of business being done. Who would argue that the earnings of the second company are equivalent, dollar for dollar, to those of the first?

2. Two companies of equal size, with the same earnings and

dividends per share, each spending the same amount on research or wildcatting, each showing the same sales growth, each maintaining receivables and inventories at the same ratio to the volume of business being done, are surely near enough alike to make it meaningful to compare their price-earnings ratios.

But the first of the two companies has been a good citizen. Its waste water has been purified before being returned to the river on which its factory is situated. Obnoxious fumes have been removed from the gases billowing out of its chimneys. Soil turned over in its strip-mining operations has been landscaped and planted to trees and grass.

The second of these two companies has cut corners on all these matters. The day after the identical earnings reports are issued, the second company is hit by court orders requiring the remedying of the stream and air pollution. It is made defendant in damage suits brought by its irate neighbors in the name of ecology. Before the battle is over its earnings are half those of the first company, which took its ecological stitch in time.

3. Two companies report the same earnings. One does so after paying competitive wages and up-grading its key personnel. The other does so by squeezing its employees to the point where the best men leave and those who remain are ripe for a strike.

How can you as an individual investor adjust or correct reported earnings for such differences in quality? In reading annual reports you can look for such variables as I have just cited. It is no job for an amateur, though, particularly not after a big dinner. Close reading of the financial press will give you some professional help at low cost. Detailed criticisms of corporate accounting have been much in the news in recent years. *The New York Times* financial pages, *Barron's* and the *Wall Street Journal* all have carried such articles in the past year. Exposing accounting gimmickry has become an accepted part of the financial reporter's job. It is an important part of what a security analyst is paid for.

The best safeguard against sleight-of-hand bookkeeping is to have nothing to do with it, or with the men who practice it. See the chapter entitled *Profits in Ethics*.

CHAPTER XI

Manipulation Despite the SEC

Seventy years ago in a *Wall Street Journal* editorial Charles H. Dow wrote: "A method employed by some operators of large experience is that of responses. The theory involved is this: *The market is always under more or less manipulation. . . ."* William Peter Hamilton, who followed Dow as editor of the *Wall Street Journal,* while not denying the theory, declared: "Manipulation in the stock market is reported 20 times for once it occurs. It is the inefficient reporter's method of accounting for a stock market movement which he has not taken the trouble to understand."

For more than thirty-five years manipulation has been against the law. The Securities Exchange Commission both monitors the market and prosecutes manipulators. Is manipulation a thing of the past?

I cannot say, "Some of my best friends are manipulators." I do not know any. But nature abhors a vacuum. Where there are opportunities for profitable manipulation in a truly international market I assume there are manipulators, some of them beyond reach of our authorities and laws. My reasoning is the same as that which leads me to expect to find cockroaches in a dirty kitchen. What they feed on is there.

What are some of the more obvious opportunities for manipulation in the stock market?

S. A. Nelson's little book, *The ABC of Stock Speculation,* largely devoted to quoting Dow's editorials, cites the basic opportunity for manipulation in these words: "The great mistake made by the public is paying attention to prices instead of to values."

114

That is as true today as it was at the turn of the century, perhaps more true. The whole performance cult which dominated the stock market in the late 1960s was based on paying attention to prices rather than values.

But what do we mean by paying attention to prices rather than values? I quote *The ABC of Stock Speculation* again simply to emphasize that human nature is one of the few constants in an ever-changing world: "It is only fair to say that the public rarely sees value until it is most markedly demonstrated to them, and the demonstration comes generally at a pretty high price. It is easier for them, as experience shows, to believe a stock is cheap when it is relatively dear, than to believe it is cheap when it is more than cheap."

Shooting where the rabbit was, is one of the most common investment errors. I have said it before and shall say it again. Time after time, year after year, men who would think you were crazy if you fired your gun at the spot from which a rabbit jumped a moment before, buy stocks that have advanced and sell stocks that have declined. Even security analysts are not immune to this malady. Too many of them, possibly reflecting the attitudes of the investors they are supposed to guide, tend to like stocks better the higher they go, and to become increasingly disenchanted with them as their prices fall.

The stock market is almost unique in that the way to attract buyers is to mark up the price of the merchandise you want to sell. Conversely, if a large operator wanted to accumulate a position in a stock with great long-term potential the least effective thing he could do would be to bid up for it. On the contrary, if he could supply stock on each embryonic advance so that after a year or two speculators agreed that it was acting badly, they would sell him all they had at successively lower prices.

The money that has been lost by ill-advised sales of stocks in this great and growing country probably many times exceeds the money lost by unwise purchases. Yet the SEC so far as I know has never turned its beady eyes on a case of manipulation to drive or hold prices down, perhaps because it would be almost impossible to prove.

Dow wrote once that the elder Rothschilds are said to have acted on the principle that it was well to buy up property of known value when others wanted to sell, and to sell when others wanted to buy.

"There is a great deal of sound wisdom in this," Dow said. "The public, as a whole, buys at the wrong time and sells at the wrong time. The reason is that markets are made in part by manipulation and the public buys on manipulated advances and after they are well along. Hence it buys at the time when manipulators wish to sell and sells when manipulators wish to buy."

One area of possible manipulation and abuse of inside information to which so far as I know no official attention has been paid is via corporate acquisitions or mergers. Most managements scrupulously will avoid any personal investments in stocks of companies they might someday hope to acquire. But if all men were honest there would be less crowding in our jails.

The opportunity for the dishonest to play with marked cards in corporate acquisitions is great, as a perusal of Tables I and II will show. To cash in on such opportunities, top managers would not even have to buy up stocks in companies they planned to take over. They could make well-advised personal purchases of stocks their friends' companies were to acquire, and vice versa. Birds of a feather flock together.

Many people innocently assume that stock prices are manipulated simply by conspiracies to buy them so as to mark up their prices. Actually that probably never has been the prime tool of manipulators. It is much more effective to manipulate earnings.

In the bad old days of the 1920s, railroad reporters on the *Wall Street Journal* used to take it for granted that railroads would go through cycles of heavy maintenance expenditures and low earnings followed by light maintenance expenditures and high earnings. It was all done with a straight face. A new management would go over a railroad and "discover" that its roadbed was in poor condition. Years of expensive betterment would follow. Sometimes dividends had to be cut or omitted to pay for putting the track in good condition. Not surprisingly the price of the railroad's stock would decline.

Then would come a day when the property was in such good shape that maintenance expenditures could be reduced. Earnings rose, and with them the price of the stock. Investors who "understood" the program bought when earnings were depressed and sold when earnings were benefiting from subnormal maintenance ratios.

It is fair to say that some companies still manipulate their earnings, the SEC and the reformers in the accounting profession to the contrary notwithstanding.

Nothing is harder for security analysts to foresee than sharp changes in corporate earnings resulting from changes in the industry's pricing policies. Years of cutthroat competition suddenly give way to industrial statesmanship which could only have been foretold by mindreaders. The converse is often easier to anticipate because it follows overexpansion induced by a prolonged period of prosperity.

The moral of all this takes us back to Mr. Barron's, "The fact without the truth is false. Always connect." When you read a bearish story on a company whose stock has declined to a third of what it was two or three years ago, ask yourself not only whether the story rings true but also why it was published at this late date. It may be factual but still highly misleading to investors because of its timing. Good reporters know this and try to avoid being "used." Investors themselves must be the final judges.

But for the gullible there would be no manipulators. In Africa, where there are no antelope there are no lions.

CHAPTER XII

Keep Your Eyes Open on Those Random Walks

S tocks are bought and sold because *both* the buyer and the seller expect to benefit by their actions. Neither intends to do the other a favor. When a buyer and seller take the opposite action on the same stock at the same moment, as they must do to effect a trade, it's a good guess that they do not think alike. Without such differences of opinion the stock market as we know it could not be.

In a business thus based on a continuous flow of diametrically opposite opinions, it would not be surprising if there were differences of opinion about *how to decide* whether to buy or sell. There are. These differences of opinion about investment philosophies, methods, techniques, and procedures are many and varied. Among them I know of none more highly charged with emotion than the difference of opinion between the so-called fundamentalists and the so-called technicians.

I have been in both camps. My conclusion after forty-four years of observation and study is that technical work is not an alternative to fundamental security analysis. Rather it is a means of providing additional information of significant value in reaching profitable investment decisions.

It seems to me important for the professional investor to know at all times not only *what ought to be happening in the stock market,* as determined by fundamental security analysis, but also *what is happening in the stock market,* as determined by technical work. Good charts merely portray information any fully informed investor should have. Whether he gets this information in chart form or columns of figures is unimportant so long as he gets it. To me a picture is worth a thousand words. Hence charts save time.

There are two reasons why the fundamentalist security analyst needs technical assistance. The first reason is that no matter how good analysts are, there is always a chance that they do not know the whole story. When a stock persistently fails to act the way it should on the basis of the information I have, I conclude that I am missing something and redouble my efforts to find out what it is.

The other reason the fundamentalist security analyst needs technical assistance is to help him recognize when he is among the first to get the glad tidings, and when he is among the last. What difference does it make? Simply the difference between foretelling a price advance and explaining why one took place. The price-proof seesaw is always with us. The less the buyer has to go on, the airier the evidence, the lower the price. The more solid the proof, the higher the price.

Why do price movements sometimes reveal what investigation does not? Simply because no one except a manipulator lies to his broker. A man may mislead his competitors, hold out on his fellow directors, cheat his stockholders, and two-time his wife. But when he picks up the telephone and tells his broker to buy or sell he expresses the net of all he knows, hopes, and fears. Even manipulators know better than to try to make water run up hill. The composite of all this ultimate truthfulness tells a story that no businessman or investor can afford to ignore.

Neither can he afford to rely on market analysis alone. When the experienced hunter finds elephant footprints going up the side of a barn, he stops tracking and looks for a practical joker.

Getting the meaning out of almost infinitely varied price fluctuations is not easy. Sometimes I think it is as complex and difficult as any refining process I know of. Hundreds of individuals, scores of firms, have perfected methods of correlating market data which they regard as trade secrets. I shall not try even to suggest what they might be, though I suspect vast amounts of duplicate effort are involved.

For the individual investor it is enough to know two things:

1.   Most price charts fall into one of two classes,

       a. Actual prices, and

       b. Relative prices

2.   Even the most astute chart reader can only tell what the market seems about to do. Whether the market is right in what it does is another question.

Who cares whether the market is right in what it does, if only he knows it first?

My answer is that anyone trying to make $100 on an investment of $1 must care very much. Only by ignoring many unwarranted market movements can he achieve his goal, even if he has bought right.

In the bright light of hindsight, the general stock market decline from May 1946 to June 1949 was misguided, and could and should have been ignored by investors seeking to make their fortunes in the stock market.

A relative price is simply an absolute price expressed as a percent of another absolute price. I learned the logic of doing this from Francis I. du Pont, one of the three or four truly great men I have been privileged to work with.

"The trouble with economics and finance," Mr. du Pont said, "is that we are always working with dirty test tubes." Mr. du Pont knew something about test tubes because he founded the research department of E. I. duPont de Nemours.

The use of relative prices enables us to take some of the dirt out of our economic and financial test tubes. That is so because when we divide the price (or earnings) of an individual company's stock by the price (or earnings) of any good average of stocks, we take out of the record of that stock those ups and downs which are common to the whole economy. What we have left is peculiar to the subject under study.

Not only prices but earnings and multipliers or price-earnings ratios, when analyzed in this way, reveal much that is hidden when we examine only the actual figures.

As you might expect when one removes extraneous factors from the price history of a stock by dividing its price by the Dow-Jones Industrial Average, the relative price line thus

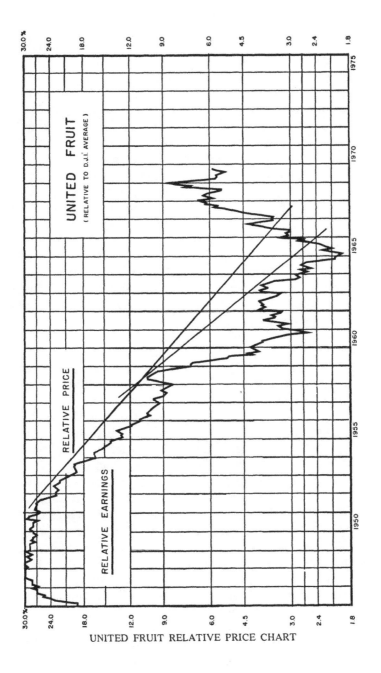

UNITED FRUIT RELATIVE PRICE CHART

obtained shows much more persistent trends than the absolu.e price line. This should surprise no one. Companies, like individuals, tend to run true to form. Here is a relative price chart of United Fruit. I chose a stock no longer traded because I wanted to provide an illustration without even an implied "tip."

This chart covers the period from the end of World War II to the end of 1968 when United Fruit was merged into AMK, now United Brands. The heavy black line is the price of United Fruit expressed as a percent of the price of the Dow-Jones Industrial Average at the end of each month. If the price of United Fruit had moved up and down proportionately to the changes in the Dow-Jones Industrial Average, the black line would be straight and horizontal.

Note the awesome persistency of the downtrend in United Fruit once it got under way in 1950. I wish I could say that I had consistently avoided the stock until it hit its relative price low fifteen years later. Unfortunately, at times I shared some of the hopes of the United Fruit management that this deteriorating situation could be turned around.

Note what happened once the relative price downtrend was broken. I have superimposed two straight lines (A and B) to emphasize how clear this downtrend was, and how unmistakable the change when the trend turned upward.

Relative price studies can be used not only to detect long-term trends but also as a gauge of what the stock market is expecting. To show what I mean let us go back in our memories to Monday, June 13, 1955. Union Carbide had just closed at 100, which is equal to 50 for the present stock which was split 2-for-1 in 1965. The Dow-Jones Industrial Average had closed at 440. Now let us suppose that our earnings forecasting was perfect. In other words let us assume that we *knew* that in 1966 Union Carbide's earnings would reach a record high 146 percent above what they were in 1954, and that we knew that earnings of the Dow-Jones Industrial Average would be up 102 percent. Or, putting it another way, suppose we knew in 1955 that Union Carbide's earnings would grow 7.8 percent compounded annually for the next twelve years.

Would you have bought Union Carbide?

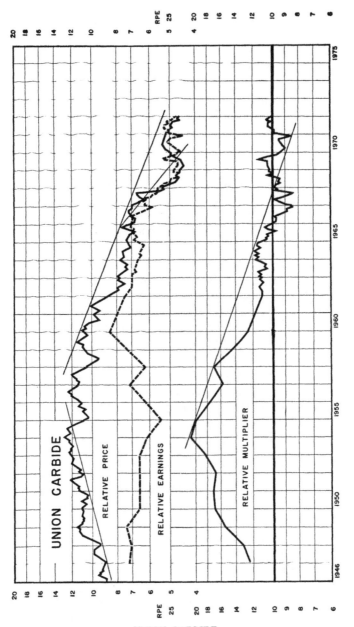

UNION CARBIDE

A great many people did. Yet by the end of 1966, despite an increase of 146 percent in its earnings, Union Carbide actually was selling 5-1/2 percent below the price at which it sold on that Monday the 13th of June, 1955. Meanwhile the Dow-Jones Industrial Average was up more than 78 percent.

How can such things be? On the face of it such market action would seem to be unfair to fundamental security analysts. There ought to be a law against such carryings-on in the stock market. But wait. When we look at the relative multiplier we see that the market in 1955 was paying nearly twice as much for each dollar of Union Carbide's earnings as for each dollar of Dow-Jones Industrial Average earnings.

On the basis of relative prices prevailing in mid-1955 the market was expecting Union Carbide's earnings to rise so much faster than the earnings of the Dow-Jones Industrial Average that the buyer of Union Carbide would be better off over the foreseeable future than the buyer of the Dow-Jones Industrial Average, even though the Union Carbide buyer was getting much less to start with. As you know now, Union Carbide's earnings did rise faster than the earnings of the Dow-Jones Industrial Average, but not enough faster.

The market reaction recalls the story of the happy boy and the sad boy at Christmas. Both received identical bicycles. One boy was happy because he had expected nothing but a candy cane. The other boy was in tears because he had thought he was going to get a Mustang. Relative multipliers measure expectations. What happens subsequently is bullish or bearish only if it is better or worse than what was expected.

What do I think of Union Carbide now? "Now" as I write and "now" as you read may be months or even years apart. Ask your current investment advisor. I can say, however, that the market is no longer expecting the stock's earnings to outgain the Dow's. Against that background of expectations, if Union Carbide's earnings should show relative improvement over the next ten years, the market's response could be quite favorable. A dozen years ago the market was expecting great things of Union Carbide and found merely good things to be bitterly disappointing. Now the market is expecting little from Union

Carbide. This means that good results could prove a delightful and even exhilarating surprise.

Just to emphasize again that relative multipliers are sometimes more important than any other investment consideration, here is a chart—What Makes Stocks Rise—of the relative prices of Standard & Poor's chemical average compared with Standard & Poor's electronics average, for the twelve years 1954 to 1966. You will note how profitable it would have been to switch from chemicals to electronics in 1954. How could we have known this at that time? A natural guess is that if we had known what the earnings would be we could have invested in the right group.

Actually earnings of the two groups started together and ended together. Most of the time the chemicals were doing better than the electronics.

Perhaps you are thinking that if we had been watching relative sales we might have gotten a clue as to what to do. Here again there was no material disparity.

What *did* make the difference? At the start of the period, the price-earnings ratio of the chemicals was twice that of the Dow, while the price-earnings ratio of the electronics was half that of the Dow. By the end of the twelve years, the price-earnings ratio of the chemicals was about the same as the Dow, while the price-earnings ratio of the electronics was twice that of the Dow.

Turning now to absolute price charts, they are studied for signs of accumulation or distribution, and for manifestations of the great law of action and reaction. To show you what I mean by trend, look at this fifty-year chart of the Dow-Jones Industrial Average. Note how the market advanced for a quarter of a century above the line drawn through the 1932 and 1942 lows. Since this is a chart drawn to a scale that gives equal amplitude to equal percentage price movements, the ability of the stock market to stay above this line means that for more than thirty-five years the price trend was upward at the compounded annual rate of nearly 9 percent a year. Thus a generation of men came to maturity and leadership in the financial community without ever experiencing any other trend but this.

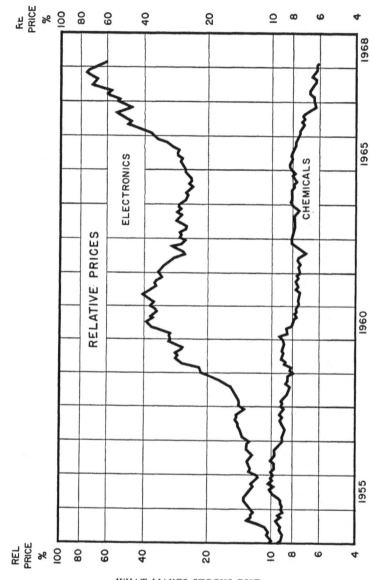

RELATIVE PRICES

ELECTRONICS

CHEMICALS

Rt PRICE %

REL PRICE %

WHAT MAKES STOCKS RISE

1968   1965   1960   1955

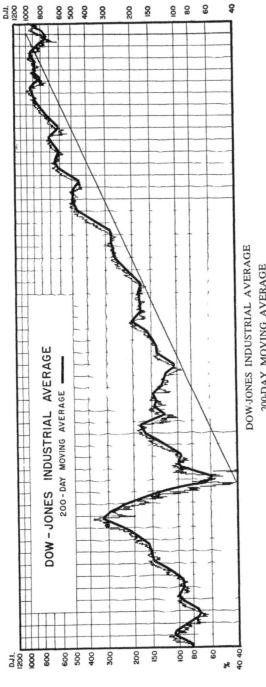

DOW-JONES INDUSTRIAL AVERAGE

200-DAY MOVING AVERAGE

3 - POINT REVERSAL

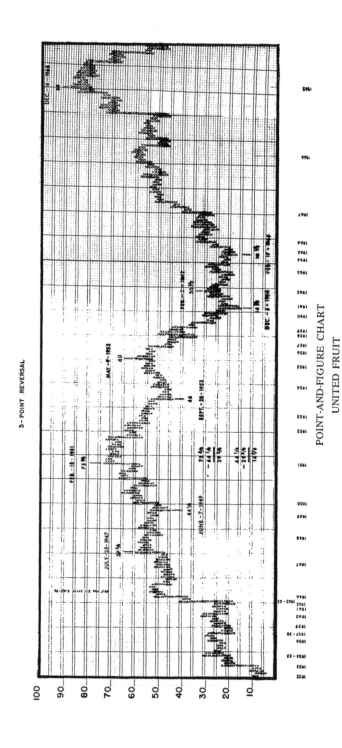

POINT-AND-FIGURE CHART
UNITED FRUIT

Some came to take it for granted, like summer and winter.

Probably the oldest and simplest form of keeping price records on the stock market is what is called the point-and-figure chart. This method records price fluctuations only, without any regard to the passage of time. If a stock should sell for the same price every day for a year no new mark would be made on its point-and-figure chart. When the market is active, as many marks may be made on a point-and-figure chart in a month as were made in five years back in the 1940s.

Traders find point-and-figure charts especially helpful for signs of accumulation or distribution, or for indications of action and reaction. Realizing that point-and-figure charts are probably the most controversial of the technical tools now in general use, and quite possibly the most abused, I am giving just one illustration. And to avoid the suspicion that I am trying to prove something rather than simply to be a good reporter, the example I have chosen is a point-and-figure chart on United Fruit—the same Boston-based company we have already seen in our relative price studies. It is now part of United Brands.

Point-and-figure buffs say that a classic sign of distribution in the stock market is what they call a head-and-shoulders top. This formation appears in the chart before you. Note the left shoulder at 59-3/4 on July 25, 1947, the left collar bone at 44-1/4 on June 7, 1949, then the head at 73-5/8 on February 21, 1951. You will note that the right shoulder at 60 on May 9, 1955, is exactly 25 cents higher than the left shoulder, while the right collar bone is precisely 25 cents lower than the left collar bone.

Head and shoulder tops are not always as symmetrical as that but such a nice balance between the left and the right is by no means unprecedented. Fundamental analysts "know" this is just coincidence. But when chartists see such a top, how much of a decline does it indicate to them? They take the distance from the left collar bone to the head and subtract it from the figure at the left collar bone. In this instance the stock advanced 29-3/8 points from the left collar bone at 44-1/4 to the head at 73-5/8. Subtracting 29-3/8 from 44-1/4 they got 14-7/8. That happened to be the precise low reached by the stock in December 1960, almost ten years later. At that time it was hard to find anyone to say a good word for the issue. Yet anyone following this method had at least a suggestion at that time and price that the stock was worth some special research attention. As is almost invariably the case at the low, both the news and the outlook were bad.

Even if one scoffs at charts himself, the fact they are being so widely used by performance funds and even by banks argues for paying some attention to them. At times they provide the only clue to the stock market's aberrations.

Chart-induced excesses in the market should be welcomed as providing investment opportunities for those who understand the fundamentals of the situation. It is a lot easier to keep one's faith in temporarily disregarded fundamentals when one knows the technical developments behind unwarranted buying or selling.

Misinterpretation of charts possibly is no more common and no more costly to investors than misinterpretation of such respected fundamental information as profit margins, rates of return, and growth of sales. The greatest danger in charts, to my mind, is the temptation to use them as a guide to trading, thereby losing sight of the greater opportunities in buying right and holding on.

Let's return to United Fruit. Suppose you had had the good fortune to buy the stock at its 1932 low of 10-1/4. For $10,000 you would have acquired 975 shares, later split 3-for-1. Let us assume that you held the stock until the head and shoulders top was confirmed by a sale at 43-1/4, $1 below the June 7, 1949, low of 44-1/4. Had you sold at that price you would have realized $126,506. After commissions and capital gains taxes aggregating 30 percent your net proceeds would have been $91,555. Then let us assume you reinvested your money in United Fruit at the low of 14-7/8 on December 5, 1960. You would then have had 6,154 shares.

Suppose further that by some magic you sold the entire block at the 1968 high of 88. You might have arrived at that figure by subtracting the date December 5 (12-5) at the preceding low from the date February 13 (2-13) at the preceding high—213 minus 125 = 88. Your gross proceeds would have been $541,552 and your net proceeds after commissions and capital gains taxes $406,553.

By perfect timing on those major swings you would have increased your starting capital fortyfold. Meantime hundreds of stocks had risen more than one hundredfold. Were you aiming at the right target?

"Wait a minute," you may be thinking. "How fanciful can you be—getting a price objective by subtracting a starting date from an ending date! What nonsense!"

I did not dream up the idea. I observed that the advance from 44-1/4 to 73-5/8 began on June 7 (6-7) and ended on February 13 (2-13). Subtracting 67 from 213 gave me 146 compared with 14-7/8, the actual low on the next decline.

"If subtracting the date at the start of an advance in price from the date at the end of that advance 'signals' the price at the bottom of the next decline," I thought, "maybe subtracting the date at the end of that decline (12-5) from the date at its start (2-13) will 'signal' the price at the top of the next advance."

It did, exactly.

Random walks, like bird walks, are more fun if you keep your eyes open.

CHAPTER XIII

Experience Sometimes a Poor Teacher

We used to have a boxer dog named Prince. He was dumb but not stupid. In cold weather he found it much more comfortable to lie on the living room sofa than on the floor. This was not good for the sofa. To discourage Prince we set mousetraps there. When he lay down on them they would go off, pinching what Sir Winston Churchill would call Prince's soft underbelly. Yelping in pain Prince would get off the sofa and stay off until the memory faded. Sometimes that would be a week or two.

Now if Prince had been more intelligent he would have associated the pain with the mousetraps rather with the sofa. When mousetraps were there he would have stayed away. When the sofa was clear he would have made himself comfortable on it.

Not being that smart, Prince confused memory with reasoning, and acted on memory.

In the stock market many people seem to do that too. They do now what hindsight shows would have been profitable if they had done it ten days, ten months, or ten years earlier, under quite different conditions. They shoot where the rabbit was. I have done it myself. Having come to Wall Street as an impressionable young man in 1927, my first great experience was the long and savage decline in stock prices from September 1929 to July 1932.

To show how deeply that decline was branded on my subconscious, let me cite one specific instance. Not many months before the 1929 bull market reached its peak, I bought Southern Railway common stock at $140 a share. In just a few weeks I

132

sold my stock at $160 a share, having doubled my money on the $20 margins then permitted. I began to have a fraternal feeling for J. P. Morgan. You know the bewhiskered story. When asked how much it cost to run his yacht, the "Corsair," Mr. Morgan replied, "If it matters, you can't afford it." I wished I had said that and intended to as soon as I got my yacht.

Some of us on the *Wall Street Journal* saw a decline coming, and I was short of several stocks at the start of the great toboggan. As the decline became more severe, and politicians in Washington began to snipe at Wall Street, our publisher banned all short selling by members of the news staff. Under that edict I covered Curtis Publishing (bought back the stock I had sold short) at $90 a share. By 1932 it was selling at $7 a share.

If newsmen on the *Wall Street Journal* could not sell short we could at least stay out of the market. I did until the Southern Railway stock I had sold at $160 got down to $8. That was the annual dividend Southern Railway had been paying at the time I sold the stock in 1929.

It seemed brilliant to buy back the stock for just the dividend it had been paying when I sold it. I bought all I could at $8 a share on 50 percent margin. Within a few months Southern Railway common had declined to $2.50 a share and I was wiped out.

I did not lose much then because I did not have much to lose. But the "lesson" I learned cost me millions. All the rest of my life I have risked too little and sold too soon. Even though in 1935 I heard President Roosevelt himself expound his doctrine of planned reflation, even though I was covering the United States Supreme Court the day the gold clause was invalidated, my memory was stronger than my reason. I continued to act as though the old rules were still in effect. So did millions of other people.

One college endowment fund with which I did business as a broker was managed for years on a plan of selling stocks on a scale up to 200 in the Dow-Jones Industrial Average and buying them on a scale down to 100. By hindsight a great deal of money could have been made via that plan between 1934 and 1946. But for the period from 1946 to 1966, in which the Dow rose from 160 to 1,000, the plan was disastrous. Once again its sponsors paid the price of "doing now" what hindsight showed they should have done ten years earlier.

My first personal experience with 100-to-one stocks began in April 1932, when I bought 100 Aluminium Ltd. D warrants in odd lots at prices ranging from 3-3/4 to 1-1/8. By the time the warrants expired Aluminium (now Alcan) was selling above $50 a share. Without putting up any more money I had my broker exercise my warrants at $30 a share. In March of 1937, I sold my last ten shares at a profit of more than $100 a share. Eight months later the stock was selling below $60. Clearly it seemed as though I had been wise or lucky to take my profit. Yet if I had held the stock until now the ten shares I sold would be 300 shares with a 1971 market value nearly 700 times my original investment. Had I held on, I would have paid no capital gains taxes or brokers' commissions, but would have been paying interest on my $300 margin.

A trade like that, following my earlier experience with Southern Railway common stock, convinced me that the road to wealth was marked by signs reading "buy 'em low" and "sell 'em high." I could not have been more wrong. Catching swings in the market, even when one is reasonably successful at it, makes pennies compared with the dollars garnered by those who buy right and hold on.

CHAPTER XIV

Why Computers Won't Run the World

We have heard and read a lot in recent years about computers running the world. Yet our prehistoric forefathers survived millions of years without language, logic, or mathematics. Some of us are here today because one of our more recent ancestors started running when the birds stopped singing, instead of waiting until he could count the Indians. Could it be that we moderns are going overboard in our reliance on juggling figures to find the answers to all problems?

Try these three basic economic principles on your computer:

1. *All market value is in the mind.* Nothing is worth anything unless someone wants it. No matter how hard it is to find, no matter how much it costs to make, anything is worth what someone will give for it, not more.

There are many ways to estimate the market for any item or service. They are all based on how badly someone wants it and how hard it is for him to get it. Economists call this demand and supply.

Most of us want to live. Hence demand for what we must have to live is fairly constant. The market for air to breathe, water to drink, and food to eat is assured. The only uncertainty is on the supply side. If there were just enough air to go around —say in a plastic-domed colony on the moon—everyone there who wanted to go on living would give his all for it, if he had no other choice.

If the supply of air became so plentiful that everyone could have all he wanted for nothing, as on earth, it would cease to have market value because no one would give anything for it unless it was compressed enough to inflate a tire or chilled enough to cool a room or make dry ice. And even then what really would be marketed would be not the air but the energy expressed in the compressed, chilled, or solidified air.

If the supply of water became so plentiful that no one wanted any more, as is believed to have been the case at the time of Noah's Ark, it too would cease to have value as such, though ice, steam, and falling water might still find buyers for their energy content. If the supply of water, even though abundant, became so polluted that it was unpleasant or unsafe to drink, pure water would acquire market value as it already has in too many places. It is a horrible thought, but if the world continues on its present trends some of us may live to see the day when the more fortunate members of society buy pure air for release in their homes and offices, the way they now buy pure water.

The same principles apply to food except that as food in general becomes more plentiful we can have larger portions of the foods we like and perhaps stop eating some other kinds of foods altogether. At that point those other kinds of foods cease to have market value—or would if we could not find ways to turn them into something else we did still want. Feeding ensilage to cattle is an example. A man would have to be very hungry to eat cornstocks, even fresh ones, but steers fed on them can be quite good to eat.

The point to keep in mind is that how much it costs to produce anything means little or nothing unless you know what people will pay for it now and in the future. In business, it is bad luck to tell people what they should want instead of trying to give them what they do want. That is what we mean when we say the customer is king. There has never been a successful revolution against him.

2. *All laws made by men can be changed by men, and will be as soon as enough people decide that they would be better off if the laws were changed.* This goes for the Constitution, the Magna Carta, the United Nations, and the zoning ordinance in Podunk.

3. *No one's title or right to any property is worth any more than the ability and willingness of his fellow creatures to defend*

it. I have cited this law before, but it cannot be overemphasized. Those other human beings may be his fellow citizens, or they may be the citizens of the so-called Great Powers saying "Hands off" to the rest of the world while small nations determine things for themselves.

Just as public opinion and law are to each other as water and ice—different forms of the same thing—so are politics to property rights. Those rights are not part of natural law like gravity. Rather they are derived from our social contract with each other. More than half the human race today has little or no property rights. The superior development of those parts of the world that do have property rights seems to argue that they provide an important incentive. But they are not immutable.

What this third law means is that no one has a really good title to any property being used to the detriment of the people making the laws on which that title depends. Even if he is using it for the common good, a man may have title to so much property that people will take away part of it, as we do in this country through progressive income and inheritance taxes. Whether this is right or wrong is as immaterial to one who would understand the psychology of investment as is a moral judgment on a wren eating a bug to a biologist. Mankind has lurched all the way from no one owning anything—even our Pilgrim forefathers tried that—to one owning everything *(L'état c'est moi),* and back again, at many times and in many places. Both extremes have been found uncomfortable. The search for the happy medium still goes on, and always will. The game is no fun—no one tries very hard—if the winner can keep none of the marbles. It cannot go on if the winner gets them all. That is true because, if for no other reason, the losers are understandably slow to rally to the defense of such a status quo, and the sole winner cannot defend it alone.

You do not need to be a mathematician to understand any of these three basic laws of economics. The figuring comes later. But when you see a company operating in ignorance or defiance of these three principles, don't stop to figure. Run, do not walk, to sell your stock, and don't be tempted to buy it back at any price

CHAPTER XV

Profits in Ethics

Earlier, I said there were two approaches to investing, one, the psychological and, two, the statistical. Actually there are three. And in the long run the third is the most important. It is what might be called the ethical or even spiritual approach.

He profits most who serves best. In the long run that is just as true of corporations as of individuals. Beware of cynics in high places. Avoid the fast buck artists, the something-for-nothing shysters. Remember that a man who will steal for you will steal from you. Ask yourself whether the company in which you contemplate investing is contributing to making this a better world. If the answer is no, avoid it like the plague.

The quest for capital gains pits anyone who engages in it against the distilled essence of the best brains in the world. Only a fool thinks he is clever enough to outsmart all others by trading in phony merchandise.

"Never do business with a man you do not trust," is a rule that would have saved many a fortune and many a heartache. No matter how tempting the prospect, how alluring the chance for a quick profit, stay away from men, companies, and ventures based on defrauding rather than helping their customers

If you have ever looked down the railroad tracks in flat country, you will recall how the rails on either side of you seem to meet near the horizon. In the same way, when one takes the long view, there is little to choose between what is right and what is most profitable. Half a century of reporting of one kind and another has convinced me beyond all argument that chiselers are not so much selfish as myopic, not so much greedy as stupid.

If this sounds like impractical idealism look at the $35 million fortune left by James Cash Penney who was such a square that he ran his business by the Golden Rule. Look at the fortune built by Henry Ford. Contrast their enduring success with the meteoric careers of some of the conglomerate manipulators who sought by financial sleight-of-hand to make $2 grow where $1 grew before.

Thirty-five years ago as the editor of *Barron's* I called on a high official of an automobile manufacturer. Having just come from the impressive research facilities at General Motors, I asked what this other company was doing in research. His reply was this classic:

"When better cars are built, we'll copy them." (Buick then was advertising "When better cars are built Buick will build them.")

Doubtless he was joking. Perhaps I should have laughed and forgotten it. But in the years since then, measured from either the lows or the highs of 1936 to the highs of 1971, General Motors stock has risen more than three times as much as the stock of this other company. To the investor such a difference is no laughing matter.

Bernard Kilgore, under whose presidency the Dow-Jones organization achieved its greatest growth, was fond of saying, "It is very hard to cheat an honest man." His point, of course, is that when one approaches any problem with larceny in his soul he becomes vulnerable to even sharper thieves. The individual who operates a business or makes his personal investments with a view to benefiting his fellow men is much less susceptible to trickery. The suckerbait in many of the oldest and most successful frauds is "something for nothing."

Integrity in news was the solid foundation on which the great financial success of the *Wall Street Journal* was built. Kenneth C. (Casey) Hogate was in charge when both Barney Kilgore and I were hired. I can think of no higher tribute to Casey and the Dow-Jones organization he headed than that in eleven years in the course of which I was chief of the politically sensitive Washington bureau and later editor of *Barron's* I was never once told how to angle a story.

There are, of course, many ways of serving mankind. Man

does not live by bread alone. See how many of the companies that have appreciated one hundredfold in the last forty years gratify people's deep urge to make fairy stories come true.

The great success of leaders in the cosmetics industry springs from our hopes for eternal youth. What is television but a magic mirror enabling us to see and hear what is going on hundreds or thousands of miles away? The almost universal longing for a pill to cure all ills underlies the success of the drug companies. Mankind's yearning for a magic carpet has underwritten every fortune made from improved methods of transportation from the Model T to the Boeing 747. The computer provides seven-league boots for man's mind. It can do nothing that the human brain cannot do, but it can do it almost immeasurably faster.

There are three primary reasons for stressing the ethical or spiritual aspects of investing. The first is that corporations are analogous to human bodies in a highly important way.

Suppose you meet today an old friend whom you have not seen for fifteen years. Biologists tell us that there is probably not a single cell in either of you that was there when you last met. Yet you have no trouble recognizing each other and recalling matters which interested you both when you last met. This is possible only because each dying cell is so faithfully replaced by a like cell.

So it is with corporations. No matter how broad-minded we are, how dedicated to equal opportunity, we tend to hire and promote "our kind of people."

When morally derelict men get to the top of great corporations and stay there for a period of years, the evil they do does indeed live after them. Inevitably they bring into the organization and promote to higher levels men like themselves. The moral cancer thus introduced cannot be extirpated simply by removing the evil genius at the top. It may take a generation under a good management to purge the organization of the unprincipled sharp-shooters brought in by a bad management. Hence it is unwise to look for a quick turnaround in any organization whose management has demonstrated a lack of moral principle.

The converse is equally true. B. Brewster Jennings was chief executive of what is now Mobil Oil Corporation during most of the eleven years that I was there. At a time when the public relations department reported to me, the company became involved in a serious dispute. All I remember about it now was that I prepared a public statement demolishing the opposition. When I submitted it to Mr. Jennings, to be issued over his name, he read it carefully, then put it down saying, "This is technically correct. I think it would stand up in court. But the most knowledgeable people in the oil industry would know that that is not quite the way things are. I don't ever want to say anything that those who know the most can question. Let's try a different approach." He did not say it to impress anyone. No one else was in the room with us. And until now I have never told the story publicly. But it set a standard of integrity in high places that has long outlived him.

A second reason why it is advisable to avoid investments in any organization whose management is even suspected of moral obtuseness is that there are so many ways of making the worse appear the better reason, of putting a false face on corporate actions and results. The accounting profession is in the throes of self-examination because of widely varying methods of reporting earnings from the same operations. If professional accountants find it hard to agree on what is right, how can the investor, lacking the qualifications of a certified public accountant, hope to penetrate the devious maze that can be created by a morally bankrupt though legally circumspect corporate management?

Man is the creature most difficult to keep in jail because man makes the jail. What one man can make another man can unmake. No matter what laws are passed, no matter how big the SEC, there will always be men able to hoodwink and defraud others. The best defense against them is to run away from them as fast as possible at the first hint of sharp practice. With more than 50,000 different stocks available to investors in this country, it is not only unnecessary but downright stupid to buy into a company run by men of doubtful integrity.

A third benefit of ethical investing is that when we do it we avoid the trap of buying stocks with the hope and intention of selling them to someone else not quite as brilliant as we are (at a substantially higher price, of course). Basically this is the bigger fool theory of investing. Anyone who adopts it runs the risk of not being able to find a bigger fool.

"Buy stocks as if you knew all markets would be closed for the next ten years," I used to urge my staff. Back in the days when performance was the name of the game such a comment may have convicted me of senility. I still think the idea has merit. If we buy stocks because we believe in them, expecting to hold them for the rest of our lives, the chances are good that others will come to appreciate them too. Then, if some day we do decide to sell them, they will appeal to the wisest buyers—a market that is always liquid.

Please remember that in all these comments I am talking about investing to make money. Trading is fun. Like playing bridge or poker for high stakes, it can take your mind off your more intransigent troubles. But for most people it is a blind alley leading off the way to wealth.

Since most of us want the material good things of life, it seems obvious that to get a great deal more than the average share of them we must somehow put ourselves beyond competition of those who will settle for the average. This is as true for corporations as for individuals. As in racing, the difference between first prize and second or third place is wide.

Know-how is a competition reducer. The longer it takes to learn how to do what your company is doing, the fewer competitors will be around to do it for less. Diligence is another competition reducer. So is integrity, and in fact most of the copybook virtues, provided always that what we have learned so arduously to do so well is something other people really want us to do for them.

Will your investment be a success? Ask yourself how the supply of firms who can do what yours can do compares with the demand. If many want your company's products or services and only your company can supply them, you are made. The only unregulated monopoly which is in the public interest is the possession of unequaled knowledge, talent, or skills. To become that kind of a monopolist can be everyone's goal. The beauty of it is that one does not have to reach the goal to win. Marked progress toward it will be counted success in most communities.

To make the biggest gains, to find your 100-to-one investment, don't buy companies whose sole goal is to make money. In life the straight line is not the shortest distance between two points. For whosoever will save his life shall lose it: but whosoever will lose his life for my sake, the same shall save it.

Bet on men and organizations fired by zeal to meet human wants and needs, imbued with enthusiasm over solving mankind's problems. Good intentions are not enough, but when combined with energy and intelligence the results make it unnecessary to seek profits. They come as a serendipity dividend on a well-managed quest for a better world.

CHAPTER XVI

The Almighty Ego vs. the Almighty Dollar

Egonomics is the art of judging every issue, making eacn decision, on the basis of what it will do for your ego. Sure, it is human nature to be selfish, but the true egonomist is never unselfish. Even when he appears to be, he has calculated the public relations or advertising value of his seeming generosity and sensed a bargain. To him objectivity is heresy. All that matters is his place in the business and social pecking order—his ego.

The story of the school boy illustrates how an egonomist's mind works.

"What's two plus two?" his teacher asked.

"Am I buying or selling?" the pupil replied.

What has egonomics to do with investing? A very great deal. I don't like it and I wish it were not so. But as my realistic former partner, Hardwick Stires, puts it, "This is the way things are. If you can't abide it, you can shoot yourself."

Let us start at the top, with the men who manage the corporations in which we invest. Do they put egonomics ahead of economics? How can we tell?

The last thing to do is to ask them. It might be your last chance to ask them anything. Anyway, what they do speaks so loudly we can't hear what they say—not if we are thoughtful observers.

The corporate egonomist thinks more of making his company bigger than of making it profitable. He spends the stockholders' money to make himself loom larger in the industry, rather than to increase the company's earning power. When you see a company year after year earning a low rate of return

144

on its invested capital *and* still increasing its capital expenditures "to improve its competitive position," the chances are there's an egonomist high in the corporate woodpile. When you see a company paying more attention to its corporate headquarters than to its sales and profit margins, holler or sell out. Egonomist termites are at work.

Already I can hear growls from those who believe corporations must assume a larger social responsibility. So do I. But I want my companies to do it *in addition to* making money, *not instead of.*

In a free society those who direct the investment of the people's money into ventures showing far below average rates of return on the capital required are sabotaging our economy, whether they know it or not. Under our economic system, profit margins and rates of return on invested capital should act as thermostats, calling for more investment when profit margins are high and less, or none at all, when they are low. To persist in plowing new money into an industry with a long-term record of low profit margins and subnormal rates of return on invested capital is to misdirect the use of materials and manpower. Some companies ought to quit, and some managements ought to let them quit. Few ever have quit before they had to. So long as the executive suite is warm, why go out into the cold? If the stockholder is dissatisfied, let him get out.

And get out you should when you see your company reinvesting its retained earnings year after year less profitably than you could use the money yourself. You want an example? For good hunting try the steel industry.

Here are the figures on U.S. Steel, the industry leader, for the last ten years:

	Return on Invested Capital	Return on Equity
1970	4.2%	4.1%
1969	5.4	6.1
1968	6.0	7.3
1967	4.6	5.2

	Return on Invested Capital	Return on Equity
1966	6.1	7.6
1965	6.5	7.3
1964	5.8	6.5
1963	5.1	5.6
1962	4.2	4.5
1961	4.7	5.3
1960	8.0	9.1

Return on invested capital in 1970 would have been twice as high if the money could have been invested in bonds.

I am no expert on the steel industry. As a layman I am not unsympathetic with the problems arising out of a high labor factor, strong unions, and imports of steel made abroad. But hope deferred maketh the heart sick. The challenge to management is to improve those figures promptly or to stop investing more of the shareholders' money in the business.

More than thirty-five years ago Scudder, Stevens & Clark issued a brochure entitled "Monuments Rarely Pay Dividends."

"When a business begins to get stately," it said, "wise investors quietly get out from under. For monuments rarely pay dividends.

"Almost every great railroad has erected at least one vast and ridiculous mausoleum to the memory of departed earnings. Gloomy bank directors brood over past glories in auditoriums of noble architecture and kingly appointments. Just before it collapsed, an empire in textiles was completing a million-dollar golf course and a model village of baby palaces for executives. Splendid administration buildings of industrial plants commemorate the passing of dividends.

"A young business is always a risk. Nine out of ten disappear in less than six years. It offers no assurance that its product can make headway against competition and win for itself a lasting popular acceptance; that its financial structure will stand the shocks of dull years and unforeseen difficulties; or that its management will develop qualities of leadership. To invest money in such a concern is pure speculation.

"But now and then a business demonstrates that it has the

power to live. It is a terror to competition, not a prey. It has mastered its market. Its production is guided by one of those rare geniuses able and determined to stay out in front—a man like Kettering. It is headed by a fighting man of courage, imagination and decision. A realist handles the money. It has a great organization of spirited youngsters who have tasted blood and liked it. It is in a new field unexhausted and promising many years of opportunity.

"To invest money in a business like that at the right time and right price is the way to accumulate wealth.

"But this building period of a business—this period of audacity, big ideas, swift attacks and great rewards—is too often followed by complacent lethargy The fighting leader becomes old, tired and arrogant. The inventive genius, as his vision dulls, grows intolerant of new ideas. The realist becomes greedy or mean and chokes further progress. The organization becomes softened by success and torn by the intrigues of middle-aged men ambitious for personal prestige and rewards.

"The last human emotion to die is pride. A man who has made something of his life, and whose creative days are past, seems to develop an urge to build something tangible, lasting and fine which will be evidence of his achievements. And a noble urge it is.

"So it is natural that an organization which has held together for years, dominated an industry and made money, should in time grow proud in the same way, and try to express its leadership and might in some physical thing that will endure.

"But that is just what a business cannot afford to do. Business is not an established thing—it is a movement, a progress. Its past means nothing—tomorrow is all that counts. It must not be anchored to old ideas, convictions or standards—or to pride.

"The biggest problem in business is not to grow old.

"A concern that is quick on its feet and resourceful can always whip one with stiff knees, no matter how powerful the latter may be.

"An old business is inclined to rely on precedent and tradition. It is impatient of change and often ignores ever-shifting popular taste. Its prestige becomes tarnished. The fine product

becomes old fashioned. Dealers are less loyal and are attracted
to livelier concerns. New generations come along to whom the
old institution means nothing. Movement is slowed down to
the static dignity of a monument and monuments rarely pay
dividends.

"The investment of wealth can never rise above the level of
guess work and hunches until there is an understanding of
these hidden values of business. The investor should be in-
fluenced by only one factor—assurance that the company
has the power to earn profits for a good many years. Financial
statements give little indication of earning power. Piles of
brick and stone mean nothing. Profits are the reward of human
spirit and high endeavor—of great leadership."

But there is more investor danger in egonomics than just
profitless pomposity.

I once worked with two high executives in a great corporation. Both were able. But their treatment of associates and
subordinates could hardly have differed more.

Bring an idea to the first man and he would improve on
whatever good he saw in it and credit you for it.

Bring an idea to the second man and he would enlarge on
whatever bad he saw in it and belittle you for it.

Naturally the first man received many more suggestions
than the second man whose primary concern was demonstrating
his intellectual superiority over his associates and subordinates.
It would be hard to overestimate the cost of the second man
to the company's esprit de corps.

Investment men have their special problems with egonomics.
One is unwillingness to accept ideas other than their own.
Another is to salve their own egos by reiterating the errors of
others.

One of the secrets of the success of Hamilton M. Chase, for
many years chief executive of the Scudder Special Fund with
one of the best long-term records in the business, was his
kindness. Never in the thirty years I have known him have I
seen him remind an informant of a previous error in investment judgment.

If integrity is the investor's first non-statistical prerequisite for management (see *Profits in Ethics,* Chapter XV), I nominate psychological equanimity as the second.

How can an investor appraise management's psychological equanimity?

What I have in mind does not require the help of a psychiatrist and couch. There are many ways for a close reader of the financial press to detect managements motivated more by egonomics than by economics. One relates to depth of management. Is there more than one able man in the executive suite? Or does the head man hog the corporate spotlight? If so he may be straining not only to keep ahead of rivals but to reassure himself that he is as great as his six-figure salary suggests he should be. Beware of the one-man company. It is only a heartbeat away from deep trouble. The corporate spotlight hog hurts his company in another insidious way. His best men leave him because they know they will never get recognition for any achievements as long as he is around. He may have no difficulty filling their shoes with more servile types but some of the spark goes out of the organization.

Years ago I called on the chief executive of a company long since absorbed by another. In his huge but dimly lighted office he sat with his back to a window facing south, with the result that he could see me as though I were in a police lineup while I could make out only the outline of the figure before me. It did not matter. It did not take me thirty seconds to decide against investing money in a business whose chief executive felt he needed that kind of an advantage to cope with his fellow men, be they employes or outsiders. My judgment was right. The stock never proved cheap at any price.

An example of the opposite sort is that of John W. Hill, now eighty-one, founder and principal shareholder of Hill and Knowlton, Inc., the world's largest public relations firm. In a fiercely competitive business in which brains are nearly the sole asset, Mr. Hill for years has put his associates forward with corporate titles, client relationships, and public appearances. His aim, as he puts it, has been to surround himself with men more able than he, an aim that shows such managerial sagacity as to cast doubt on his ability to achieve it.

Some of my comments on egonomics may seem petty. But to the alert, a whiff of smoke can be louder than a fire alarm.

Clarence W. Barron, who owned the *Wall Street Journal* when I went to work there in 1927, relied heavily on his analysis of a man's actions. Sometimes, when interviewing a job applicant, Mr. Barron would ask the young man to clip a story out of that day's newspaper. If the applicant hacked out the clipping so clumsily that it had to be retrimmed before being filed, he got no further. In Mr. Barron's view the man was not only careless and wasteful, but unobservant and unintelligent . . . if he had learned to keep his eyes on where the two scissor blades came together instead of on their points, he could have split the column rule on either side of the desired clipping, leaving adjoining stories intact.

CHAPTER XVII

No Inflation-Control Pill

MONEY

In the Orient I have often had to take off my shoes before entering holy places. In the Occident the presumption that no one—or at least no more than a dozen pundits—understands money suggests that the rest of us take off our heads before venturing into the subject.

Now that so many democratic governments have assumed or accepted responsibility for the economic climate, the need for more widespread understanding of money is vital and urgent. For investors it has always been essential. An investment may increase in monetary value per se, as a lamb does when it grows into a sheep. Or an investment that does not itself change at all may increase in monetary value because the unit of measurement has shrunk.

To invest sensibly, we must try, however humbly, to answer these practical questions:

What gives money its value?

What changes it?

What can be done about it?

What is being done?

Without pretending to be one of the twelve who understand money, but with the audacity of a cat looking at a king, I venture these answers:

The value of money comes primarily from one or more of these three factors:

1. Inherent value
2. Taxes
3. Fiat, or price and wage controls.

Inherent value is the oldest.

151

The first money was valued for itself. This was true of gold, salt (from which comes our word salary), wampum, ivory, and the great hollow stones once used for money on the Island of Yap. Exchange of goods and services for such money was barter, but barter with a common denominator.

An essential characteristic of any money which depends for its worth on its inherent value is that it should take about as much work to produce an additional unit of that money as the additional unit will buy. The value of such money thus is sustained by the fact that additions to the supply cost as much as they are worth. There is no temptation to inflate because there is no profit in inflating—no chance to get something for nothing.

In the United States, inherent worth no longer plays any direct part in determining the value of our money. A five-dollar bill *is* five dollars. It doesn't promise anything. It is not redeemable in anything. Some of the older bills say "The United States will pay to the bearer on demand five dollars" but that promise can be met by handing the same bill back to you because it *is* five dollars.

Until recently only foreign central banks could get gold for their dollars. As they now know, even they could get it only so long as we felt like giving it to them. They used to get an ounce of gold for about $21. Until payments were suspended in 1971 they got an ounce of gold for $35—unless of course we chose to give them some of the newly created International Monetary Fund "paper gold." Under President Franklin D. Roosevelt our government changed the price of gold without getting anybody's permission and can do so again. So can any other sovereign, as so many of them have. Never forget that a sovereign government and a minor child are unable to make contracts binding on themselves.

It can be argued that what determines the value of money is what you can buy with it. But we are trying to understand what determines what you can buy with it. The buying power of money is a measure of its value, not a determinant of that value.

It can be argued that what determines the value of money is

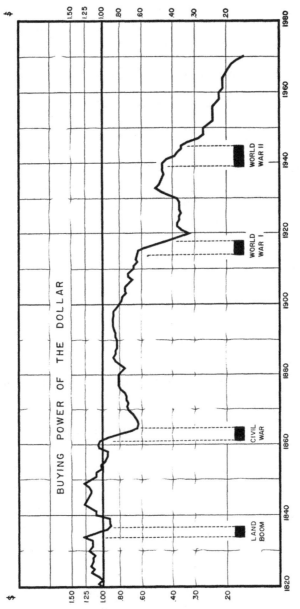

BUYING POWER OF THE DOLLAR

YOUR MONEY WON'T BUY AS MUCH AS IT USED TO

the supply of money relative to the demand for money. But we are trying to understand what determines the supply of money, and what determines the demand for money. It may help if we consider how our money looks to a German or a Japanese. It doesn't matter to them that a five dollar bill has no inherent value, and cannot be exchanged for anything with inherent value, that is, it doesn't matter *if* they can buy something with it that they want and can't get—or can't get cheaper—somewhere else. They do not want and will not accept unlimited amounts of our money—only as much as they need to buy whatever they want to buy from us, including investments, of course. But it is the price and quality of our goods and services that determine how much of them other nations want to buy from us. To understand money we must try to understand what determines the price and quality of our goods and services.

This brings me to a second determinant of the value of money. That is taxes, or more accurately taxes relative to governmental spending. We could make four-leaf clovers pass for money if we could compel our countrymen to pay their taxes with four-leaf clovers. We could raise or lower the value of four-leaf clovers by increasing or decreasing the taxes payable in four-leaf clovers relative to the supply of four-leaf clovers. Even if someone found a way to double the supply of four-leaf clovers, we could still keep the price steady if we raised taxes proportionately.

The point I am trying to make is that taxes can put value into an inherently worthless currency, even one without exchange value, if the tax take is large enough relative to the amount of the otherwise worthless currency issued.

In the 1920s I saw this demonstrated in the Congo. The Belgian franc, while good money in western eyes, was worthless to the natives. They needed little or no clothing. Their women tended their gardens and flocks. Bananas grew wild. Why should a man go down a dark hole to sweat for money he didn't want or need? The problem was solved by a combination of taxes and induced exchange value. A poll tax was imposed for the privilege of breathing the fine air in the Congo. At the same time men were invited to bring their families to rent-free company compounds (villages) complete with company general merchandise stores. It wasn't long before some men were trading pigs to other men in exchange for money to pay their poll tax. Then came the pressure from the ladies for the finery on sale at the company store. Soon taxes were the least of the native man's financial problems, and the Belgian franc was as good as salt. I sometimes wonder if advertising doesn't do to us and for us what the company store did to and for those Congolese.

A third determinant of the value of money is fiat. What do I mean by that? Let me give you an example. Suppose I came unknown to any of you with a mask over my face and a sub-machine gun under my arm. Suppose I announced that I was buying watches and would pay a dollar for each of yours. And suppose I added that anyone who did not trade his watch for one of my dollars would be shot. If you thought I meant business, or if you even feared that I might mean business, some of you would sell me your watches. The difference between *selling* your watch *for a dollar* and surrendering it in a holdup *for nothing* is one of degree, not of principle. So is every other arrangement that compels us to part with goods or services for less than we think they are worth.

Fiat money is worth what we say it is because we are big enough and strong enough to make what we say stick. Price and wage controls are resorts to fiat money. Under such controls people are compelled to accept bargains which they would reject in a free society. Initially those who rebel are seldom shot. They are taken to court. Historically, the shooting has come later, to put down revolt against the inequities of the system.

When a government abandons inherent value for its money, when that money's buying power plummets and the government lacks the will or the votes to impose enough taxes to check the decline, that government publicly confesses its political impotence and moral bankruptcy by imposing controls. The more bipartisan the decision to do so the sadder the state of the nation.

In wartime, controls may be condoned. If men can be drafted, why not money? In peace, controls are beyond the pale except as a temporary, emergency measure to cope with the runaway consequences of many years of governmental irresponsibility.

In one sense fiat is a factor even in the absence of controls. On every piece of paper money in your pocket are two phrases. One is "In God we trust." The other, sadly much more significant these days, says "This note is legal tender for all debts, public and private." What that means is that the creditor *must* accept payment in such notes whether he likes to or not. A creditor who lent dollars payable in gold of specified weight and fineness might otherwise refuse payment in notes redeemable in nothing.

Habit, or the rigidity of our social system, slows down changes in the purchasing power of money but does not determine its value. If by some magic you could cut the value of all money in half overnight, not all prices could double the next day because it would take time to adjust to the new price level. Until wages and prices were raised many people simply would be unable to pay twice as much as before for rent and food. Others, for a while, would accept money at the old value by force of habit. Ultimately the basic factors would prevail.

Internationally, so long as our Government continued able and willing to meet all central bank demands for gold—or its IMF equivalent—at $35 to the ounce, the inherent value of our money was assured. But foreign claims on our gold so far exceeded our reserves that maintenance of a reasonable balance of payments was imperative. This meant both that we must not price our exports out of foreign markets, nor unduly indulge our tastes for foreign goods and foreign travel. When for the first time since 1893 our imports for 1971 threatened to exceed our exports, the jig was up.

The Nixon Administration sought to stabilize the buying power of the dollar by balancing the budget and slowing down the money printing press. Interest rates and unemployment increased sharply. And prices continued to rise. To lower interest rates the Federal Reserve bought government securities—with printing press money. That was inflationary. To combat unemployment the Administration budgeted a huge deficit and proposed tax cuts. Those moves too were inflationary. To counter those effects the President invoked the wage and price freeze.

The situation recalls Victor Hugo's story. You may remember, the Good Lord created a mouse.

"What ho!" he cried. "I've made a mistake." So he created a cat to correct it. President Nixon's freeze is the cat. We can all join in praying that it does not grow into a man-eating tiger.

Basically the problem arises out of our desire as a people to do inflationary things without having inflation. So far no one has invented a pill to make that possible.

INFLATION

What causes and cures inflation?

Inflation is cheating.

It results solely from efforts to get something for nothing.

If the government did something for the poor—or for our military forces in Vietnam—by taking something equal from you and me, no inflation would result. The poor or the military would have more. You and I would have less. The balance between supply and demand would be unchanged.

When the government gives money to anyone for nothing without taking it from someone else for nothing, demand is increased relative to supply. Higher prices—what we call inflation—follow as night the day.

The problem and the remedy could not be simpler. If we stop trying to get something for nothing, we stop inflation.

Every dollar Congress votes to spend is a cheat unless Congress votes to raise that dollar by taxes, or our government borrows it from you and me. Good programs financed with printing press money simply rob Peter to pay Paul.

This does not mean that taxes should be increased to pay for every good program, or that the national debt can rise without limit. Taxes hurt. They hurt you and me who have to pay them. They reduce our ability to make productive investments, our ability to educate our children, our ability to provide for our old age. Borrowing money merely postpones taxes, and ultimately increases them.

Thus the benefits of each good program must be weighed against the harm inevitably done by the taxes required to pay for it. But the all important point is to weigh benefits against the tax cost at the time the benefits are voted. Otherwise the inescapable tax is collected in the form of higher prices.

Inflation *is* the cruelest tax.

Not every effort to get something for nothing is inflationary. If I demand twice what I am being paid, the result may be simply that I am out of work. Even bank robbers and swindlers are not guilty of inflation. They transfer money from your account and mine to theirs. The total money supply is not affected by their nefarious activities.

But how about this cost-push inflation we hear so much about? Is organized labor guilty of inflation when it gets pay increases in excess of increases in productivity? Or are the employers the guilty parties for raising prices to cover the higher wages and then some?

The answer, of course, is that neither is to blame. If labor unions ask too much, their members will be out of work. If employers charge too much, their goods will not sell. That is economic theory, but we are seeing again the tragedy of the murder of a beautiful theory by a gang of brutal facts.

What has gone wrong?

First is the Employment Act of 1946. The stated policy of our government is to keep our people employed *regardless*.

Second is our failure as a self-governing people to distinguish between collective bargaining and coercion. I refer, of course, to some unions' assertion of their right to halt essential public services until they get what they want.

The issue is an old one. Thirty-five years ago, as editor of *Barron's*, I lunched with John L. Lewis, the head of the United Mine Workers. For hours Mr. Lewis tried to get me to see why sitdown strikes were a proper and necessary bargaining weapon for labor. It was nearly 4 P.M. when, still at the luncheon table, ne brought down his fist and declared, "If 100 men in a power plant can pull the switches and paralyze a city, so much the better for their bargaining power. Can't you see that?"

I answered with a question: "What is the difference between that and another 100 men behind machine guns at strategic street corners imposing their will on the city?"

At that Mr. Lewis rose and departed. I never saw him again. My question has never been answered.

The point, of course, is that if one's head is held under water until he agrees, the agreement is extortion, not a bargain. And if the federal government is expected by the Employment Act of 1946 to validate extortionate wage increases by increasing the money supply so that employers can pay the otherwise economically unjustified higher wages, the circle is closed. More inflation is inevitable. How fast it comes depends only on how unrestrained are the demands of workers in crucial places. The wonder is not that they have asked so much. It is that they have not demanded more. All power corrupts. Absolute power corrupts absolutely, whether it is wielded by an employer or an employee.

Inflation, like sin, is likely to be with us a long time. When I asked the great historian, Arnold Toynbee, if he could cite a single instance from his study of all known civilizations wherein the value of a currency had increased over the long term, he replied, "No, that has never happened."

The practical question is not whether we shall have inflation but how much, how fast. What does this mean to common stocks?

The short answer is that inflation makes stocks rise. Yet five years ago, on a visit to the Buenos Aires, Argentina, stock exchange, I was shown charts of the decline in the foreign exchange value of the peso superimposed on the decline in average prices of Argentine stocks. In the four preceding years stock prices had *fallen* faster than the value of Argentine money. But we need not go so far from home to make the point that inflation is not always bullish. On February 9, 1966, the Dow-Jones Industrial Average reached its record intraday high of 1,001. Nearly six years later, at the end of 1971, its intraday high was 895.

The correct answer to the question, "What does inflation mean to common stocks?" is: "Whatever inflation means to their earnings and dividends."

Inflation is most bullish on common stocks when it follows a deep depression and is not generally expected. Rising demand for goods and services can be met by putting idle productive facilities to work. Labor is not yet anticipating further increases in living costs. And by the time more plant capacity is needed, rising construction costs have underwritten the profit margins of existing facilities.

But when inflation persists long enough so that everyone is aware of it, and when the rate of inflation becomes high enough to be a political liability for whoever is in power in Washington, it is no longer automatically beneficial to corporate earnings and may become detrimental to them.

This is where we are in America now. Some companies may still benefit from inflation but more and more will be hurt as controls proliferate. Far from guaranteeing rising profits for all, whether strong or weak, ably or poorly managed, inflation has reached the stage where it presents a challenge only the best can meet. Selectivity seems likely to be much more important in the 1970s than in the 1960s, and it was not unimportant then. I shall have more to say about the kinds of companies to choose in Chapter XXVIII, *Real Growth—How to Spot It and Evaluate It.*

INTEREST

Interest is the price of time. It measures the cost of having or doing now what we hope to be able to pay for later. Thus everything bought with borrowed money costs more than it would if bought for cash. That is true whether the borrower is a man or a woman, a company, a city, a state, or a nation.

The buyer of time takes on an obligation to return the borrowed property at some agreed date in the future, or on demand of the lender. Such obligations we call IOUs, debt, indebtedness, loans, mortgages, debentures, or bonds. They all mean essentially the same thing. For the right to have the money *now,* the borrower agrees to return it later besides paying for using it in the meantime. In principle there is little difference between "renting" money and renting an automobile In each case, you the borrower must promise to return what you borrow and pay the rent too.

There is nothing good or bad about debt and interest per se, despite the Puritanical injunction, "Neither a borrower nor a lender be." Many people have been ruined by debt. Many others have made their fortunes with borrowed money. What makes the difference is simply whether the time bought is used profitably. To my mind it is just as bad a mistake for a businessman *not to borrow* when he could do so profitably as it is for him *to borrow* unprofitably. A businessman, did I say? I mean anyone.

In 1954, to pay a doctor's bill, I sold 150 shares of Polaroid stock for $7,415.97. Here is the confirmation of the sale. Along with it is the confirmation of my purchase thirteen months earlier, and a notice of the receipt of a 50 percent stock dividend. If I had borrowed the money, as I certainly could have, at 8 percent compounded annually from then until now, my 1954 doctor's bill of $7,500 would have amounted to the staggering sum of $27,750 by the end of 1971. Being cautious by nature and upbringing I did not go into debt.

Was I prudent? My 150 shares of Polaroid stock would now be 7,200 shares valued in 1971 at $843,300. It cost me more than $800,000 to stay out of debt that time. Even if I had borrowed the money in 1954 at 30 percent interest compounded annually, the value of my Polaroid stock by 1971 would have been $200,000 more than I owed by then.

As skilled an investor as Bert Tripp (see Chapter XXIV) succumbed to similar conventional wisdom when he sold enough of his Xerox stock to pay for building his new home. He has the dubious satisfaction today of knowing that (1) his home is fully paid for, and (2) in terms of the present value of the Xerox stock he sold, the house cost him a million dollars.

God only knows how many of the early owners of the hundreds of stocks that have risen one hundredfold also sold them

FRANCIS I. DuPONT & Co.

ONE WALL STREET • NEW YORK 5. N. Y.

BOUGHT	SOLD	DESCRIPTION	PRICE	ACCOUNT NO		
	150	POLAROID CORP	49¾	63-7126-13		3 8

AMOUNT	INTEREST OR ODD LOT TAX STATE TAX	COMMISSION	FEDERAL TAX	REGISTRATION FEE ON POSTAGE	NET AMOUNT
7462 50	6 00	40 41	12		7415 97

MR. THOMAS W. PHELPS,
22 LAFAYETTE RD.,
PRINCETON, N. J.

63-7126-13 M

TRADE DATE 12 08 54   PAYMENT DATE 12 14 54

FRANCIS I. DuPONT & Co.

ONE WALL STREET • NEW YORK 5. N. Y.

BOUGHT	SOLD	DESCRIPTION	PRICE	ACCOUNT NO		
100		POLAROID CORP	40¼	63-7126-13		3

AMOUNT	INTEREST OR ODD LOT TAX STATE TAX	COMMISSION	FEDERAL TAX	REGISTRATION FEE OR POSTAGE	NET AMOUNT
4050 00		24 63			4074 63

MR THOMAS W PHELPS
22 LAFAYETTE RD
PRINCETON N J

TRADE DATE 10 27 53   PAYMENT DATE 11 02 53

FORM 4010 REV.

FRANCIS I. DuPONT & Co.

ONE WALL STREET
NEW YORK 5, N. Y.

RECEIVED FROM_____ DATE____3/1/54____

FOR ACCOUNT OF____63 7126____

THE SECURITIES LISTED BELOW HAVE BEEN RECEIVED FOR YOUR ACCOUNT,
AND YOUR ACCOUNT HAS BEEN DEBITED

QUANTITY	SECURITY	AMOUNT
50	POLAROID CORP A/C 50% STOCK DIV	

MR. THOMAS W. PHELPS,
22 LAFAYETTE RD.,
PRINCETON, N. J.

63-7126-13 M

CUSTOMER'S NOTICE

If held for eighteen years the 100 shares of Polaroid bought for $4,074.63 on November 2, 1953, would have increased to 7,200 shares with a market value of $843,300 in 1971. To pay a doctor's bill they were sold for $7,415.97 on December 8, 1954. A 50 percent stock dividend paid in February of 1954 accounts for the extra fifty shares sold.

to keep out of debt. On a quiet evening in the country in mid-summer I can hear them chanting,

"Of all sad words of tongue or pen,
The saddest are these: It might have been."

When any rule, formula, or program becomes a substitute

for thought rather than an aid to thinking, it is dangerous and should be discarded. Too many of us have been raised on the idea that debt is evil, instead of being taught that it is one of the legitimate alternatives open to us in a free society. We have had to learn that the hard way. Debt may lead us to ruin or to riches. It all depends on whether we can make more on the borrowed money than the lender charges for its use.

Going into debt because one lacks the willpower to live within his income has ruined men and women for centuries, and doubtless will continue to do so for centuries to come. The temptation to indulge now, pay later, is almost as insidious as drugs. The basic fallacy of people who make "buy now, pay later" a way of life is that by so doing they actually cannot indulge themselves as much as the stalwarts who pay as they go. Here is how it works:

Two couples each have $500 a year to spend on vacations. The Smiths pay as they go. The Joneses do too, except that they took their first trip a year before they had the money. The second year, when they did have the $500 to get away from it all, paying for the first year's trip took not only the $500 but $100 more for "finance charges." Since the Joneses had only $500 for a vacation, all of which had been spent on the first year's vacation, to go away the second year they had to borrow not only the $500 cost of the second vacation but also $100 unbudgeted finance charges on their first trip.

The third year, when the strait-laced Smiths were taking only their second $500 vacation the Joneses went on their third $500 outing. To do so they had to borrow the $500 again plus $220 to cover unbudgeted finance charges on their first two trips.

The fourth year the Joneses took their fourth $500 vacation, again borrowing the $500. In addition they owed $364 for finance charges on the first three trips.

By the end of the fourth year, when the Joneses were ready for their fifth $500 vacation, they found they owed not only $500 for their fourth trip but also $536.80 finance charges on their first four trips. The Smiths had had three $500 vacations and owed nothing.

At this point the Joneses got out of debt by staying home

through the next *two* years, while the parsimonious Smiths continued to travel as usual. The self-indulgent Joneses thus ended up the sixth year with one less vacation trip than the self-denying Smiths, though both the Smiths and the Joneses had spent the same amount of money on their vacations.

By starting a year earlier than they can afford to, the Joneses of this world get four of everything for the price of five.

What each borrower should do is ask himself whether the time he is buying is worth the money. For a young person to borrow, if necessary, to get an education is usually very good business. So is purchase of needed tools by trained workmen. Loans make it feasible for each generation to start where its predecessor leaves off, by borrowing needed equipment instead of waiting the years required to save enough to buy it.

Inflation introduces some important additional factors into the matter of interest and debt.

Manufacturers who expect or fear that prices of needed equipment will be 20 percent higher a year from now will not hesitate to buy today even if they have to borrow money at 10 percent to do it. At the same time lenders demand compensation for anticipated declines in the purchasing power of their money. If you lend quarts and are paid back pints, you must have 100 percent interest just to stay even.

In general, the higher the rate of inflation the greater the cost of buying time—in other words, the higher the interest rate. One of the most pathetic delusions of our day is the politically popular idea that the government can make interest rates low in a free society while continuing to inflate the money supply. Neither lenders nor borrowers are stupid enough to let that happen. Lenders would sense a loss, borrowers a bargain. Lenders would charge more. Borrowers would gladly pay it. As Lincoln said, you can't fool all the people all the time.

Carried to its ultimate extreme, as it was in Germany in the 1920s, inflation makes everyone try to become a borrower in self-defense. Only by buying now and paying later can the individual protect himself against the swift erosion of the purchasing power of money. The resulting rush of would-be borrowers aggravates the demand for money at the same time lenders are raising their rates to protect themselves against the expected further decline in its value. Under such conditions there is no theoretical limit to how high interest rates can go. Governmental efforts to hold down the cost of borrowed money by printing more of it are as futile as trying to drown a fire with gasoline.

The lesson of history is clear: Interest rates mirror inflation So long as there is any value left in a rotting currency, interest rates will reflect the expectations of both borrowers and lenders as to its further fall. Nothing can set aside the bloodless verdict of the market.

Not until money has become worthless do we see debtors pursuing their creditors and paying them off without mercy, as they did in Germany in the 1920s. Then comes a new currency.

Logically there is no more reason to think that interest rates are on a permanently high plateau now than there was reason in the 1940s to believe that interest rates then were on a permanently low plateau. (Actually many people did believe twenty-five years ago that interest rates would be permanently low. Why else would they have bought long-term bonds to yield 2-1/2 percent or less?)

As the accompanying chart shows, yields on call-protected, long-term, high-grade corporate bonds declined for twenty-five years from a 1921 high of nearly 6 percent to a 1946 low of less than 2-1/2 percent. After such a prolonged decline people who confuse memory with reasoning, as most of us do, are sure interest rates never will rise again.

But, as you can see, interest rates did rise from that point for more than twenty-four years to their May 1970 high when prime corporate bonds yielded about 8-1/2 percent. After such a prolonged rise people who confuse memory with reasoning, as most of us do, are sure interest rates never will fall again.

Actually the cost of borrowing money declines when interest rates relative to the assumed advantage of buying now rather than later dictate decisions to postpone spending. Accordingly,

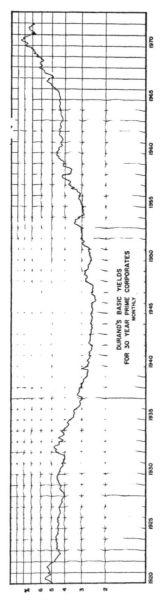

DURAND'S BASIC YIELDS
FOR 30 YEAR PRIME CORPORATES
MONTHLY

THE PRICE OF INTEREST

interest rates can come down for either of two reasons: (1) Because they have reached a level which overdiscounts the assumed advantage of buying now rather than later, or (2) Because the advantage of buying now rather than later has been reduced by a reduction in the rate of inflation, or by deteriora- 'ion in the outlook for profits, or both.

 - To say that interest rates are on a permanently high plateau amounts to saying that the advantage of buying now rather than later is going to be high permanently. Such a statement assumes: (1) A continued high rate of inflation, or (2) A permanently higher rate of return on invested capital than American industry has had in the past, or (3) Both.

Obviously if the rate of inflation can be slowed, the advantage of buying now rather than later is reduced, and hence the decision to postpone spending is made easier. Likewise obviously, if the outlook for profits deteriorates, whether because of foreign competition, overcapacity, taxes, or cost-price squeeze, the incentive to borrow to enter new businesses or expand existing ones will be reduced, and with it the demand for money.

Our needs for capital are great. But needs are not the same thing as effective demand. If we attempt to supply them with printing press money, there is danger the rate of inflation will accelerate. And it already has reached a level that clouds rather than brightens prospects for corporate profits. Levying taxes to meet these needs will simply transfer purchasing power from some people and some industries to other people and other industries. It provides no basis for assuming increased profitability for capital investment taken as a whole.

One of the worst occupational hazards of the investment business arises out of our extraordinary ability to rationalize whatever is, and our common inability to foresee what will be. Mere modesty should make us cautious about accepting as permanent a level of interest rates few were wise enough to see coming. It is easy to make assumptions that support expectations of permanently high interest rates. It is not so easy to support those assumptions.

BONDS VERSUS STOCKS

If you own stock in a company, you are a partner in the business. If you own a company's bonds, you are one of its creditors.

As a shareholder you own a piece of the business. As an owner you are entitled to your share of whatever it makes whenever the directors vote to distribute it. You are promised nothing.

As a creditor you are entitled to be paid whether the company makes any money or not. No one as yet has found a way to get blood out of a stone, however so a prudent bond buyer examines not only his rights but the issuing company's ability to live up to its bargain.

Paraphrasing Kipling's "East is East, and West is West, and never the twain shall meet," it used to be said before the great depression of 1929–32 that a bond man was a bond man, and a stock man was a stock man, and neither could operate successfully in the other's field. Actually it is about as unsound for a bond man not to know stocks as it is for an eye doctor to be totally ignorant of the rest of the human body. In a sense stocks are the buffers which protect bonds from the slings and arrows of outrageous fortune. A bond man who is sensitive to anemia in those buffers seldom is caught holding an issue that defaults. He sees trouble coming long before it affects payments on the senior securities. (Bonds are senior because their claims must be met before the stockholders can get anything.)

No matter how much a company prospers, all that its bondholders receive is the agreed interest and repayment of their principal when due. Since the bondholder thus is barred from sharing prosperity he would be foolish indeed to run the risk of sharing adversity. Weak companies ofttimes entice the unwary bond buyer by offering a higher interest rate than is obtainable on the best bonds. My own experience argues for buying nothing but the best bonds or the worst bonds, and avoiding all that lies in between. That may sound paradoxical, I know. But let me explain. The best bonds have such strong coverage of earnings and such substantial backing of assets as to make a default almost out of the question. As I recall it there were three bonds rated AAA in 1929 that were in default by 1932. But those were the exceptions that test the rule. They probably amounted to a tiny fraction of one per cent of all of the triple A bonds outstanding in 1929. Another depression like 1929–32 is highly improbable in any case. The world has changed since then.

The worst bonds are those in default, of course. Very often, as was the case with the Richfield Oil and Pan American Petroleum bonds mentioned earlier, defaulted bonds are given all or most of the company in the eventual reorganization. Thus when I buy bonds in default I am buying what I hope and expect will be the equity in the reorganized company. I am really buying a "stock" called a bond at what I think is a bargain price for the "stock."

A worm, it has been said, is the only creature than cannot fall down. Defaulted bonds have that characteristic in common with worms. The worst has happened. They may stay in default for years pending reorganization or the issuing company may be liquidated but the holder of defaulted bonds rarely need fear than his morning newspaper will bring him bad tidings. Since the news about his holdings can hardly get worse he has what history has shown time and again to be an almost riskless speculation with substantial chance for eventual appreciation.

How about convertible bonds? These are bonds that may be exchanged for stock of the issuing company, usually at a price above the market at the time the bonds were issued. If the stock has a prolonged and substantial advance in price, the convertible bondholder profits by it. On the other hand if the company gets into trouble and its stock declines, the convertible bondholder usually continues to collect his interest and enjoys a somewhat protected position. The fact remains, however, that if the stock advances, the stockholder makes more money than the owner of the convertible bonds. And all too often, if the stock goes into a severe decline, the convertible bond declines substantially more than do the highest grade "straight" bonds, and sometimes it defaults.

Convertible bonds are useful for institutions restricted as to common stock purchases, and especially so wnen those institutions are advised by experts at spotting "out of line" prices. For the individual, convertible bonds sometimes permit avoiaance of a decision as to whether to buy stocks or bonds Such escapism often is expensive in comparison with what could have been achieved by correct decision.

Why should anyone buy bonds when the country is suffering from inflation? The answer is that interest rates are the result of supply and demand. Lenders charge, and borrowers pay, rates which reflect not only the rental value of money but also anticipated rates of decline in its purchasing power. Theoretically, if the rental value of money is 4 percent and if inflation is expected to continue at the rate of 4 percent a year, interest rates will be around 8 percent. When bonds of the highest quality afford yields that cover both the rental value of money and the anticipated rate of inflation the buyer stands to profit if the actual rate of inflation proves to be less than expected.

In the last two or three years, some bond buyers have been motivated by a belief that a 5 percent or 6 percent annual decline in the purchasing power of the dollar is about as high a rate of inflation as America's social structure can and will tolerate. Hence when the best fully taxable bonds were selling to yield 9 percent and more, and the best tax-exempt bonds were selling to yield 7 percent and more, those people bought in the expectation that something—they knew not what—would be done to check inflation before it got much worse. Whethe1 the Nixon "freeze" proves successful or not, it at least justified those bond buyers' expectation that America would not take continued 6 percent inflation lying down.

Bond prices for the highest grade issues simply reflect changing interest rates. For example, a 6 percent bond due in twenty years will sell at par ($1,000) when the general level of interest rates is 6 percent. Should the general level of interest rates rise to 8 percent that same bond will sell at about 80 ($800 a bond), at which price the buyer gets a current yield of 7-1/2 percent and a yield to maturity of just over 8 percent. Yield to maturity is the yield calculated by allowing year by year for the present value of the $200 "extra" to be received twenty years hence. Remember we are talking about the highest grade issues. With them the buyer assumes that at maturity he will receive not just the $800 he has paid but the $1,000 face amount of the bond.

If interest rates should drop to 4 percent in the next five years that same top grade 6 percent bond which sold at $80 in an 8 percent money market could be expected to sell at $122 ($1,220 a bond), a price advance of more than 50 percent. From 1971 levels, depending on the assumptions you make as to the unknowable future, bonds could show greater capital gains than the average stock.

One thing to watch out for, of course, is call protection. Companies issuing bonds naturally and properly seek to have their cake and eat it too. Hence they offer bonds with high interest rates to attract buyers when everyone else is paying high interest rates, yet they reserve the right to pay off the bonds and issue new ones in case interest rates decline. You may own a bond paying 9 percent and due in 1990, but if it is callable in three years, don't count on it any longer than that. If interest rates generally should drop to 6 percent by 1975—certainly not an impossibility though this is not a forecast—your 9 percent bond probably will be called (paid off) and you will have to reinvest the money at the then "going rate" of 6 percent. Many bonds are not callable for long periods—ten-year call protection is not uncommon, and even longer call protection is available at times. A rule to bear in mind is that callable bonds will be called if it is to your disadvantage.

How can we compare stocks with bonds? Suppose we buy for $50 a stock earning $1 a share and growing at the rate of 20 percent a year. Suppose it pays only stock dividends, reinvesting all earnings in the business. Suppose at the time of our purchase we could have bought call-protected, prime corporate bonds to yield 8 percent.

How long will it be before our stock is earning 8 percent on our purchase price? The answer is between seven and eight years, if growth continues at 20 percent a year.

But even if we are confident that growth will continue that

long at that rate, we face other unanswered questions before we can be confident the stock is the better buy.

One of those questions is: "What will prime bonds be yielding seven or eight years from now?" If yields have dropped to 4 percent and if the bond we could have bought to yield 8 percent is callable or matures in ten years, our bond alternative becomes much less attractive than before.

Another question we must answer before deciding whether we should buy the stock at fifty times earnings is how many times earnings we expect the stock to sell seven or eight years from now. If our stock's earnings quadruple as we expect, but the stock then sells 12-1/2 times earnings, our investment will have produced neither capital gain nor income. Clearly the 8 percent bonds would have been the better buy.

If our stock's earnings quadruple and the stock then sells at twenty-five times earnings, our stock will have doubled in price. A doubling in price in seven or eight years is equivalent to a yield of 10 percent compounded annually. On this assumption, the stock would be a better buy than the bond yielding 8 percent.

If the price-earnings ratio holds at 50, the stock will sell for four times our purchase price to show a gain of 20 percent a year. Those are crucial "ifs".

Taxes and income requirements also enter into the calculations. An individual in the 50 percent federal income tax bracket would surrender half of his 8 percent bond yield to the tax collector. A pension fund could keep and reinvest all of it.

An individual in the 50 percent tax bracket needing 4 percent a year income for current expenses would thus spend and pay in taxes his entire yield from the 8 percent bond. If he bought the growth stock and sold enough to give him 4 percent of his *cost* each year, after capital gains taxes, how he made out would depend on the market price of the stock at the time of each sale. There is no way to tell in advance what that might be. We do know, however, that fixed annual drafts on principal are dollar averaging in reverse. This means selling the most stock when prices are low and the least when prices are high.

If these examples seem tedious and complicated, I can assure you they are simple compared with the actual investment problems encountered every day. All I am trying to show is the impossibility of proving in advance, mathematically, how any investment will work out. The bigger your computer, the more sophisticated your program, the more varied the assumptions you can evaluate. But when all is said and done, the future is still unknown, and always will be. That is why making assumptions and figuring the odds are crucial to investment success.

CHAPTER XVIII

Picking the Right One

It is one thing to discover that the way to wealth is to buy right and hold on. It is quite another to do it.

How does one buy right?

An Aesop fable brought up to date has the grasshopper going to the ant for advice at the end of the summer. "You are sitting pretty," said the grasshopper to the ant. "You have built yourself a house for the winter and stocked it with provisions. I've had a good time but now that the nights are getting cold I'm worried. What should I do?"

"Easy," replied the ant. "Change yourself into a cockroach and go into the house where you will find food and warmth for the winter."

"Thanks," said the grasshopper. Then, as an afterthought, "How do I change myself into a cockroach?"

"I've given you the master plan," the ant said. "It's up to you to work out the details."

The master plan is to buy right and hold on. Some of us, left to work out the details for ourselves, may end up sleeping in the cold with the grasshopper.

I don't know which is harder, buying right or knowing enough to hold on. Mathematically, if you just stick pins into the quotation page, you have not one chance in a hundred of hitting a stock that will give you one hundredfold appreciation, even if the future is as good as the past, which is no certainty. And after you have bought your stock, some of the best brains in Wall Street will be trying to persuade you to sell it and buy something else. Lots of times they will be right, at least for the short term. Every time they are right will make it harder for

174

you not to heed their advice the next time. And the next time they may be advising you to sell your 100-to-one stock after it has gone from one to two. They did that to Mr. Garrett.

But since we have divided the problem of making a fortune from a $10,000 investment into two parts, let us consider first the problem of picking the right one.

To make a sensible choice we investors must make or accept some assumptions about the future. Otherwise we may find ourselves backing losers like the man who bet on a horse before learning that the purse was for the entry producing the most milk.

To make intelligent assumptions about the future, we must try to perceive the tendency of events. That involves us in consideration of money, interest, inflation, bonds versus stocks, and the political situation generally, before we even begin to compare the values available in various kinds of securities.

It all boils down to practical imagination—the ability to see what is not there but will be soon enough to matter to you.

CHAPTER XIX

Where to Look for the Big Winners

John Westcott, one of the best market analysts I ever knew, told me once about a talk he had with Bernard M. Baruch. Mr. Westcott casually referred to a recent purchase of some blue chip stock. He thinks it was either American Telephone or General Motors.

"I don't know how you can afford to buy stocks at that price," said Mr. Baruch. "I can't."

Mr. Baruch was voicing the widespread belief that big profit potentials are to be found only in low-priced stocks. Somehow it seems easier for a penny to grow into a dollar than for a dollar to grow into $100. As Table III shows, however, over the last forty years there have been many opportunities to make 100-for-one in higher priced stocks.

Low-priced stocks, like the poor, are always with us. Many low-priced stocks have advanced spectacularly. I have found nothing to indicate, however, that a stock selling at $1 or less is more likely to advance one hundredfold than a stock selling at $10 or more. It may seem that way simply because there are so many more low-priced stocks than higher-priced ones. Price alone is a poor guide for the investor seeking maximum capital gains.

Another popular impression is that really great opportunities in the stock market are more likely to be found in the Over-the-Counter market than on the New York Stock Exchange or the American Stock Exchange. Those holding this view assume that the stocks on the New York Stock Exchange are subject to more examination by professional security analysts than the much more numerous issues in the Over-the-Counter market.

176

Hence it is felt there is less chance of an outstanding value being overlooked on the New York Stock Exchange than elsewhere. Again the record fails to bear this out. Of the more than 365 stocks that have advanced more than one hundredfold in the last forty years, more were found on the New York Stock Exchange at the beginning of their great advance than anywhere else. (See Table I.) The explanation seems to be that since all any investor can buy anywhere is the unknown future, the chances of that unknown future proving very much better than expected are as good on the New York Stock Exchange as anywhere else.

Most emphatically this does not mean that I believe the investor would do as well to shut his eyes and stick pins in the quotation page of the *Wall Street Journal* as he could do by any other method. For one thing not all stocks that advance one hundredfold have afforded the investor equally favorable odds. The risk of total loss in one may have been many times greater than in another. Money won at Russian roulette may buy as much groceries as money earned any other way, but as a means of earning a livelihood Russian roulette has a well-deserved place at the bottom of the totem pole.

Then where does one look for 100-to-one stocks? The record of the last forty years suggests these hunting grounds:

1. Inventions which enable us to do things we have always wanted to do but could never do before. The automobile, the airplane, and television are examples.

2. New methods or new equipment for doing things we long have had to do but doing them easier, faster, or at less cost than before. Computers and earth-moving machinery are examples from the past.

3. Processes or equipment to improve or maintain the quality of a service while reducing or eliminating the labor required to provide it. Examples are disposable syringes and sheets in hospitals, frozen foods, and the whole family of copiers headed by Xerox.

4. New and cheaper sources of energy such as kerosene replacing whale oil, fuel oil replacing coal, and electricity generated by atomic power replacing them all.

5. New methods of doing essential old jobs with less or no ecological damage. An example is the use of sterilized insects to wipe out a pest rather than employing chemicals harmful to many desirable forms of life.

6. Improved methods or equipment for recycling the materials, including water, required by civilized man instead of making mountains of waste and oceans of sewage.

7. New methods or equipment for delivering the morning newspaper to the home without carriers or waste, yet having it instantly available for review at later dates. Few items have less value for most of us than yesterday's newspaper, but millions of them are printed daily in a form that can be bound and preserved for many years by that tiny fraction of subscribers who want a permanent record. For that we chew up forests.

8. New methods or equipment for transporting people and goods on land without wheels. Fire and the wheel have long been regarded as the two inventions that did most to lift man up from the abyss of savagery. I sometimes wonder if we have not paid homage to the wheel too long. Its inherent contradiction is that the faster it moves the greater the centrifigal force it generates. To achieve supersonic speeds in the air man had to find a way to leave the wheel behind. Someday it will be done on land perhaps with air cushions, perhaps with magnetic forces, probably with ideas, methods, and equipment not yet dreamed of.

To paraphrase Edith Cavell who told her executioners in the first World War, "Patriotism is not enough," neither is invention enough. Financial history is strewn with wrecks of bright ideas incompetently administered. Great fortunes have been made in the automobile industry but I sometimes wonder whether the investor who bought every automobile stock available between 1900 and 1920 would have had a return on his total investment equal to what the savings bank would have given him. In the same vein it would be interesting to know the total return on all of the money spent in drilling for oil. We do not even record the wildcatters' losses. The controversial depletion allowance and expensing of intangible drilling costs imply some recognition by Congress of a need to improve the odds, notwithstanding the fortunes made by those who find oil. Like the winners in a lottery, those who strike it rich in the hunt for oil are not representative of all who participate.

Without making a complete survey, we have pointed out more than 365 stocks which have increased one hundredfold in market value in the last forty years. Many did it in forty years, some did it in thirty-five, some in thirty, quite a few in twenty-five, twenty or more in twenty years, and five in ten years or less. Even those that took the full forty years to multiply in value by 100 far outdistanced the increase in earnings or assets of any professionally managed fund on record in the same period.

In general there seem to be four categories of stocks that have turned in the 100-to-one performance records. I was about to say there *are* rather than there *seem to be*. What stopped me was recalling the story of the show-off who said to the great etymologist: "Have you ever noticed that sugar is the only word in the English language in which 'su' is pronounced 'sh'? The etymologist's reply was: "Are you sure?"

The four categories I see are these:

1. Advance primarily due to recovery from extremely depressed prices at bottom of greatest bear market in American history. Special panic or distress situations at other times belong in this group too.

2. Advance primarily due to change in supply-demand ratio for a basic commodity, reflected in a sharply higher commodity price.

3. Advance primarily due to great leverage in capital structure in long periods of expanding business and inflation.

4. Advance primarily due to the arithmetical result of reinvesting earnings at substantially higher than average rates of return on invested capital.

Individual companies become available from time to time at what appear to be distress prices due to troubles peculiar to a company or its industry. But to have palpable bargains going begging as they did in 1932 and 1933 before the bank holiday, there must be a recurrence of the worldwide deflation and unemployment of that period. Such a recurrence probably is politically impossible. Throughout the Western world it seems clear that if they must choose, people will opt for inflation with or without wage and price controls rather than suffer another great depression. Hence it seems unrealistic to expect to find many 100-to-one profit opportunities in this first category now—at least not until mankind has relearned the fallacy of inflation as an economic cure-all. That may take many, many years.

Clearly a big discovery of oil or minerals can multiply a stock's value many times in short order. Poseidon stock rose to more than 100 times its low in a single year following a sensational nickel ore discovery in Australia. (The stock subsequently lost most of that spectacular gain.) Such discoveries almost by definition are unforeseeable. The investor who makes a fortune by such means is lucky.

Not that I belittle luck. One does not have to be smart to make a fortune. All he has to know and do is what it takes. Ofttimes that is so simple as to be beneath the notice of anyone but an obvious Adams. Oldtimers may recall he was a fictional character who never did anything smart but made more money than his clever rivals by doing the obvious—such as coming in when it started to rain.

Gambling on a big natural resource discovery is like playing the daily double at the races. You may go a lifetime without hitting the winning combination. But there are other natural resource situations where the existence of the resource in the ground is known but where a change in price is required to make mining profitable. Such was the situation with Mesabi Iron's vast taconite reserves. Such likewise was the situation with some of the coal companies whose stocks have appreciated more than one hundredfold since the depression of the 1930s. Such could some day be the situation with regard to uranium ore bodies, oil shale and tar sands, and standing timber.

Leverage opportunities may result from situations where the senior claims on a company's earnings and assets equal or exceed those earnings or assets, leaving no present value for the equity. When such a situation persists for many years with no visible prospect of change the equity may sell at a nominal price. This was the situation in the 1940s with Tri-Continental common stock and warrants. What might be called sales leverage also results sometimes from a prolonged depression of earnings of a large business, even without senior securities. When, for example, one can buy $10.00 or even $20.00 of company sales for each $1 of current equity market price, it is simple arithmetic that if profit margins should improve to the point where 5 percent of those sales came down to the common stockholders, the return on their investment would be handsome indeed.

Opportunities for profiting by capital leverage are easy to find. What is hard is deciding whether the added profit potential outweighs the added risk. The principle is that of the margin account. If you buy a stock on 50 percent margin and it doubles in price, you make nearly twice as much money on your own investment as you would have if you had bought the stock outright.

If it goes down 50 percent you have lost your equity. The kind of situation to watch for is a severe but temporary slump in the business and profits of a large company with a very high proportion of senior securities in its capital structure. Obviously if one can buy the equity for five or ten percent of the value of the total enterprise, a doubling of the value of the total enterprise may result in a ten to twenty fold increase in the market price of the equity.

A relatively new leverage investment, not yet tested in a real depression, is the so-called dual purpose fund, pioneered in America by George S. Johnston, now chief executive of Scudder, Stevens & Clark. Typically such a fund was organized with half the capital provided by those seeking a high and growing income on their investment while the other half was provided by those interested solely in capital gains potential. Accordingly the first group of investors were promised all of the income from the combined funds and were even guaranteed a minimum income at the expense of the second group, if such minimum income should not be available otherwise.

The second group, on the other hand, are entitled to all of the capital gains on the combined funds after the first group have received the agreed income and repayment of their investment.

In effect the capital gains shareholders of these dual purpose funds have a margin account of 50 percent or more. In other words they stand to gain by any advance in the price of securities worth twice or more what they pay for their capital shares. These capital gains shareholders receive no dividends or interest on their investment, but neither do they have to pay any interest on their "debit balance," that is, on the portion of the fund's assets in excess of the cost of the capital shares. For instance, if such a fund has assets valued at $10 for the income shares and $10 for the capital gains shares, and if the income shares are entitled to just $10, the capital gains shares' appreciation potential is about the same as that of an account on 50 percent margin, without the risk of having to put up more margin or be sold out. For anyone who is convinced that the stock market is going to rise, purchase of these capital gains shares is analogous to doubling in a bridge game.

At times in the past year it has been possible to buy the capital gains shares of such dual purpose funds for a third or less of the total value of the assets applicable to the shares held by both groups. For example, assume the assets applicable to the income shares amount to $10 a share and that the assets applicable to the capital shares amount to $6 a share. Assume further that the capital shares sell on the New York Stock Exchange for $5 a share. We have seen such a relationship within the year 1971. If the stock market should advance to five times its current average price as it did in the fifteen years between 1949 and 1964, and if the assets of the dual purpose fund merely kept pace with the market average, those assets in 1986 would amount to five times sixteen or $80 for each unit of one income share and one capital gains share. Since the income shares still would be entitled only to $10, the remaining $70 would be the asset value of the capital gains shares. The buyer of such shares at $5 thus would have fourteen fold his original investment.

Even such a gain is still a long way from the 100-to-one gains we have seen in the last forty years and are seeking now. But suppose war, or threats of war, or a totally unforeseen depression dropped the market price of the capital shares down not just to $5 but to $1 or even 50 cents. From such a level a surprise turnaround in the economic and political situation could provide the 100-to-one investment odds we are seeking. So could outstanding performance by the portfolio of a dual purpose fund, even without such a prior severe decline in the price of its capital shares.

My fourth category of stocks showing one hundredfold appreciation is that of companies reporting a far above-average rate of return on invested capital for many consecutive years. In such issues the investor has simple arithmetic and Father Time on his side. Even in this category, however, there is no free lunch, no "sure thing." First there is the danger that the high rate of return on invested capital may attract too many competitors. No business is so good that it cannot be spoiled if too many get into it. It is vitally important that the high rate of return be protected by a "gate" making entry into the business difficult if not impossible. Such gates may be patents, incessant innovation based on superior research and invention, ownership of uniquely advantageous sources of raw material, exceptionally well-established brand names—you can fill in others as you choose. Just be sure the "gate" is strong and high. Most of us want pretty much the same material things in life—good food, good clothes, a home on the right side of the railroad tracks, good schools for our children. To get more than the average we must be able to do more than the average, or do what we do better than the average. If all we can do is take in washing there will always be someone down the street ready to take it in for two cents a pound less than our price.

Thousands of investors have owned one or another of these 100-to-one "high-gate" stocks at sometime or other in the last forty years. Probably not one in a thousand has held his winner until it increased one hundredfold in value.

All of course wish they had done so. Yet it would be just as great a mistake to assume that what has been will continue to be forever and ever. Or to pay now for all the growth that can be foreseen.

To increase one hundredfold in value in forty years a stock's price must advance at the compounded annual rate of 12.2 percent. The rates of increase required to multiply a stock's value by 100 in fewer years than forty are these:

35 years - 14 percent
30 years - 16.6 percent
25 years - 20 percent
20 years - 26 percent
15 years - 36 percent

It is mathematically impossible for any company to continue to grow endlessly even at the smallest of those rates. The practical problem is to try to estimate, first, how long those rates of growth seem likely to continue and, second, how long they must continue to justify even the present price of the stock.

First, to end all argument as to the possibility of even the smallest of those growth rates continuing endlessly, how much do you think $1 invested at 5 percent 1971 years ago would amount to today with interest compounded annually? When Scudder, Stevens & Clark's Economics Vice President, Dr. Louise Curley, initially gave me the answer, in 1965, it was a sum so vast that to pay it in gold, at $35 to the ounce, would require a solid ball of gold reaching almost from the earth to the sun 90 million miles away. Dr. Curley got her doctorate in economics at Massachusetts Institute of Technology, so I trust her arithmetic. When I asked her to bring the answer up to date, to 1971, she reported it would now take a solid ball of gold more than 100 million miles thick.

But let's be practical. None of us is investing for the next 1971 years. Our problem has a much nearer horizon. First, if we are looking for stocks that might multiply in value by 100 in the next fifteen to forty years, we must estimate the chances that their earnings can and will continue to grow at compound annual rates of 12 percent to 36 percent. Long-term capital growth is tied to long-term earnings growth. The only way an investor can get more growth than that is to catch swings in stock market sentiment from optimism to pessimism and back again. If he misjudges those swings he may get a great deal less in capital growth than in earnings growth.

This line of thought may be helpful in appraising the growth prospects of such giant companies as General Motors and International Business Machines. If General Motors earnings were to increase one hundredfold from their record high of 1965, General Motors would report net income of well over $200 billion. Even if the corporation netted 10 percent of sales this would still mean $2 trillion in sales. It does not denigrate General Motors products or management to suggest that the corporation is unlikely to be doing even forty years from now a volume of business double America's present gross national product.

Similarly multiplying 1969 record earnings of International Business Machines by 100 would make them more than $11 billion annually. Even if the company managed to maintain its 1969 high ratio of net income to sales, IBM would have to do more than $700 billion of business annually to make such profits.

Those bullish on IBM may contend that I am arguing by *reductio ad absurdum.* At last report, IBM was still No. 1 on the list of stocks most popular with mutual funds and it was the favorite stock for 1972 in an *Institutional Investor* survey of money managers and security analysts. They should know what they are doing. Perhaps they plan to hold the stock just until it doubles again. Even that would be a nice profit if it could be realized in the next five years. If it is, IBM stock will be selling above $700 per present share. To do that its earnings must double, or its price-earnings ratio must increase along with its earnings. For IBM's earnings to double in the next five years they must increase at the compound annual rate of 15 percent. They have done even better than that in the past. But for the stock market to put a higher value on each dollar of IBM's 1975 earnings than it is now putting on IBM's 1970 earnings would presuppose either that the outlook for further growth *from the 1975 level* will be even better than it is now, or that interest rates will be lower, or both. See the relative price chart of IBM from 1919 to 1971. As is dramatically apparent, onward and upward has been the stock's course for more than half a century. By now almost everyone must be aware of it.

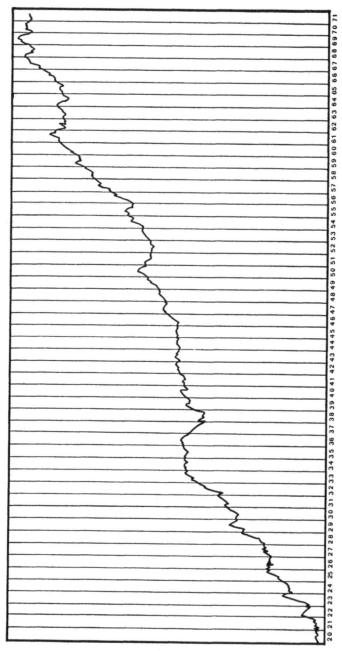

IBM

Table II
PRICE LIST OF FORTUNE-MAKER STOCKS
365 that could have been bought for as little as 4¢ or as
much as $137.50 in 30 different years for 100-fold rise

Contrary to popular impression, unlisted penny stocks are not the only ones that can turn $10,000 into $1,000,000. Shown in CAPITAL LETTERS in the following table is a list of more than 365 securities that could have been bought at the prices and in the years cited for advances by 1971 to at least 100 times each cost. Note that the first twelve on the list were priced at $50 or higher. If any security on the list was renamed or exchanged for issues bearing another name, the 1971 designation is shown immediately following, in parentheses.

	Cost	Year Bought
OLD BEN COAL FIRST GOLD 6s 1944		
(Standard Oil of Ohio)	$137.50	1935
INTERNATIONAL BUSINESS MACHINES	125.50	1948
ANHEUSER-BUSCH	98.00	1935
AVON PRODUCTS	83.00	1955
MINNESOTA MINING &		
MANUFACTURING	60.00	1945
MINNEAPOLIS HONEYWELL		
(Honeywell)	58.00	1935
NEW PROCESS	58.00	1955
PRENTICE-HALL	51.00	1945
ASSOCIATED TELEPHONE UTILITIES		
SERIES C 5½% CONVERTIBLE BONDS		
(General Telephone)	50.00	1933
LAWYERS TITLE INSURANCE		
(Richmond Corp.)	50.00	1936
PORTER (H.K.) 1st 6s 1946	50.00	1932
RICHFIELD OIL OF CALIFORNIA		
1st CONVERTIBLE 6s 1944		
(CERTIFICATES OF DEPOSIT)		
(Atlantic Richfield)	50.00	1932
HALOID XEROX (Xerox)	47.50	1958
EASTMAN KODAK	46.00	1933
GENERAL AMERICA CORP.		
(Safeco)	44.00	1946
JOHNSON & JOHNSON	46.00	1938
EMPIRE TRUST (Dome Petroleum Ltd.)	43.50	1943
MERCK & CO.	43.00	1940

	Cost	Year Bought
POLAROID	42.88	1955
FIDELITY UNION LIFE INSURANCE	42.00	1949
CONTINENTAL ASSURANCE		
(CNA Financial)	40.50	1943
ABBOTT LABORATORIES	40.00	1934
MINNESOTA & ONTARIO PAPER 6s		
SERIES A 1931–45 (Boise Cascade)	40.00	1932
PAN-AMERICAN PETROLEUM (OF CAL.)		
CONVERTIBLE 6s 1940 (CERTIFICATES		
OF DEPOSIT) (Atlantic Richfield)	40.00	1932
GOVERNMENT EMPLOYES INSURANCE	38.00	1951
GRANITEVILLE MANUFACTURING		
(Graniteville)	34.00	1935
AMERICAN HOME PRODUCTS	30.75	1938
OLD BEN COAL 7½% DEBS 1934		
(Standard Oil of Ohio)	30.00	1932
PFIZER (CHAS.) & CO. (Pfizer, Inc.)	29.00	1943
LINCOLN NATIONAL LIFE INSURANCE		
(Lincoln National Corp.)	28.50	1943
CONNECTICUT GENERAL LIFE		
INSURANCE (Connecticut General		
Insurance)	27.63	1943
GLOBE & RUTGERS FIRE INSURANCE		
(American International Group)	27.00	1949
CLOROX	24.00	1942
GENERAL TIRE	23.00	1933
AMEREX HOLDING CORP. (American		
Express)	21.50	1948
DOW CHEMICAL	21.13	1932
MERCANTILE STORES	21.00	1943
U.S. BOBBIN & SHUTTLE PFD.		
(Baker Industries)	20.00	1940
EASTERN GAS & FUEL 6% PFD.	19.75	1943
ZENITH RADIO	19.75	1948
AMERADA CORP. (Amerada Hess)	18.50	1933
BABCOCK & WILCOX	18.50	1934
WINN & LOVETT GROCERY (Winn-Dixie		
Stores Class B Conv.)	18.00	1942
CARNATION COMPANY	17.88	1938
AMERICAN HIDE & LEATHER 7%		
PREFERRED (Tandy common)	17.75	1934
McDONNELL AIRCRAFT (McDonnell		
Douglas)	17.00	1950

	Cost	Year Bought
MOORE CORP. LTD.	17.00	1935
SQUARE D CLASS B COMMON	17.00	1935
BLACK & DECKER	16.50	1944
TAMPAX	16.50	1949
DR. PEPPER	16.00	1935
AETNA CASUALTY & SURETY (Aetna Life & Casualty)	15.00	1932
CLARK EQUIPMENT	15.00	1939
KIRSCH CO. PFD. (Kirsch Company common)	14.00	1946
VIRGINIA IRON COAL & COKE 5% PREF. (Bates Mfg.)	14.00	1942
AMERICAN HIDE & LEATHER 7% PREFERRED (Tandy common)	13.50	1933
CHICAGO FLEXIBLE SHAFT (Sunbeam)	13.50	1935
PLOUGH (Schering-Plough)	13.25	1945
PANHANDLE PRODUCING & REFINING 8% PREFERRED (American Petrofina Class A)	13.00	1940
J. C. PENNEY CO.	13.00	1932
ABITIBI POWER & PAPER CO., LTD. 7% PFD. ($100 PAR) (Abitibi Paper Common)	12.50	1943
SEARS, ROEBUCK & CO.	12.50	1933
AMERICAN HIDE & LEATHER 6% CONV PREFERRED (Tandy common)	12.00	1938
DIEBOLD, INC.	11.63	1950
EDDY PAPER CORP. (Weyerhaeuser)	11.50	1940
NEWMONT MINING	11.50	1933
PHILIP MORRIS	11.50	1934
SHARP & DOHME $3.50 CONV. PFD. A (Merck common)	11.50	1932
BAXTER LABORATORIES	11.25	1956
MOTOROLA	11.25	1948
INTERNATIONAL COMBUSTION ENGINEERING CV. PFD. CTFS. (Combustion Engineering Inc.)	11.00	1933
UNIVERSAL WINDING (Leesona)	11.00	1934
OUTBOARD MOTORS CLASS A (Outboard Marine)	11.00	1936
SKYLINE HOMES (Skyline Corp.)	11.00	1963
GENERAL FIRE EXTINGUISHER (International Telephone & Telegraph)	10.63	1943

	Cost	Year Bought
FOOD MACHINERY (FMC)	10.50	1934
MONROE AUTO EQUIPMENT	10.50	1959
GOODYEAR TIRE & RUBBER	10.25	1942
AMERICAN POWER & LIGHT $6 PFD.	10.13	1935
HART SCHAFFNER & MARX	10.00	1939
HOBART MANUFACTURING .	10.00	1933
REECE BUTTON HOLE MACHINE (Reece Corp.)	10.00	1934
SIGNODE STEEL STRAPPING (Signode Corp.)	9.75	1942
FEDDERS	9.50	1945
NOBILITT-SPARKS INDUSTRIES (Arvin Industries)	9.50	1933
GEORGIA-PACIFIC	9.25	1953
DODGE MANUFACTURING (Reliance Electric)	9.13	1942
ALOE (A.S.) CO. (Brunswick)	9.00	1934
MILTON BRADLEY	9.00	1957
NATOMAS CO.	9.00	1932
PACIFIC WESTERN OIL (Getty Oil)	9.00	1943
MELVILLE SHOE	8.75	1933
SHARP & DOHME (Merck)	8.63	1943
EMERSON ELECTRIC	8.50	1949
McGRAW-HILL	8.50	1943
LANE BRYANT	8.38	1942
AETNA LIFE (Aetna Life & Casualty)	8.25	1932
HOLIDAY INNS	8.13	1958
MASONITE	8.25	1933
NATIONAL CONTAINER $2 CONV. PFD. (Owens-Illinois-Glass)	8.13	1932
THOMPSON PRODUCTS (TRW)	8.13	1938
AMERICAN AIRLINES	8.00	1938
DELTA AIR LINES	8.00	1942
EDISON BROS. STORES	8.00	1934
TRANE	8.00	1943
CROWN CORK & SEAL	7.88	1932
EMERY AIR FREIGHT	7.88	1955
HENRY HOLT & CO. (Columbia Broadcasting System)	7.88	1953
FEDERATED DEPARTMENT STORES	7.50	1933
GARDNER-DENVER	7.50	1933
BRIGGS & STRATTON	7.25	1933
NATIONAL STANDARD	7.25	1932

	Cost	Year Bought
AMERICAN HOME FIRE ASSURANCE (American International Group)	7.00	1949
AUTOMATIC DATA PROCESSING	7.00	1965
ELECTRIC POWER & LIGHT $7 SECOND PREFERRED (Middle South Utilities and Pennzoil)	7.00	1943
NATIONAL HOMES	6.75	1945
GENERAL AMERICAN OIL	6.50	1937
HOLOPHANE (Johns-Manville)	6.50	1936
KENDALL CO.	6.50	1942
SKELLY OIL	6.50	1935
APEX ELECTRICAL MANUFACTURING (White Consolidated Inc.)	6.25	1941
MASCO SCREW PRODUCTS (Masco Corp.)	6.25	1961
VAN DORN IRON WORKS (Van Dorn Co.)	6.25	1950
CONTAINER CORP. (Marcor)	6.13	1934
PHILLIPS-JONES (Phillips-Van Heusen)	6.13	1942
AMERICAN CONSTITUTION FIRE INSURANCE (American International Group)	6.00	1932
ELECTRIC SHOVEL COAL PREFERRED (American Metal Climax)	6.00	1942
PACIFIC MILLS (Burlington Industries)	6.00	1933
INDUSTRIAL ACCEPTANCE	5.90	1942
BURLINGTON MILLS (Burlington Industries)	5.75	1937
DEERE & COMPANY	5.75	1933
HUNT BROS. PACKING (Norton-Simon)	5.75	1944
BRUNSWICK-BALKE-COLLENDER (Brunswick Corp.)	5.50	1938
CATERPILLAR TRACTOR	5.50	1933
SIGNAL OIL & GAS CLASS A (Signal Cos.)	5.50	1935
UNION BAG & PAPER (Union Camp)	5.50	1933
GREYHOUND CORP.	5.25	1934
MARION STEAM SHOVEL 7% PFD. (Merritt-Chapman & Scott)	5.25	1932
LOUISIANA LAND	5.13	1943
WEST VIRGINIA COAL & COKE (Eastern Gas & Fuel)	5.13	1944
WESTERN AUTO SUPPLY CLASS A (Beneficial Corp.)	5.13	1932
AMERICAN METER (Singer)	5.00	1933

	Cost	Year Bought
CHICAGO, ROCK ISLAND & PACIFIC CONVERTIBLE 4⅛s, 1960 (Union Pacific)	5.00	1940
CONTINENTAL CASUALTY (CNA Financial)	5.00	1933
DOUGLAS AIRCRAFT (McDonnell Douglas)	5.00	1932
EMPORIUM CAPWELL (Broadway-Hale Stores)	5.00	1934
GENERAL ALLIANCE (General Reinsurance)	5.00	1933
GOVERNMENT EMPLOYES LIFE INSURANCE	5.00	1949
KIRSCH CO. COMMON B (Kirsch Co. common)	5.00	1946
MAGNAVOX	5.00	1949
NINETEEN HUNDRED (Whirlpool)	5.00	1942
SIMPLICITY PATTERN	4.88	1954
GILLETTE	4.75	1943
HONOLULU OIL	4.75	1932
PYRENE MFG. (Baker Industries)	4.75	1940
CONTINENTAL BAKING (International Telephone)	4.50	1935
NEW ENGLAND LIME (Pfizer Inc.)	4.50	1948
NOXZEMA CHEMICAL (Noxell)	4.50	1944
INTERSTATE CO. (Host International)	4.38	1955
MILLER WHOLESALE DRUG (American Home Products)	4.38	1940
ASSOCIATED DRY GOODS	4.25	1942
MAGMA COPPER (Newmont Mining)	4.25	1932
NEHI (Royal Crown Cola)	4.25	1936
REALTY OPERATORS (Southdown)	4.25	1944
ARMSTRONG CORK	4.13	1933
AYSHIRE PATOKA COLLIERIES (American Metal Climax)	4.00	1942
COLUMBIA RIVER PACKERS (Castle & Cooke)	4.00	1939
GENERAL CABLE CLASS A (General Cable common)	4.00	1935
LERNER STORES	4.00	1933
PHILADELPHIA LIFE INSURANCE	4.00	1945

	Cost	Year Bought
NORTH AMERICAN CAR (Flying Tiger Line)	3.88	1942
(Stone & Webster) (Gulf States Utilities) STONE & WEBSTER (El Paso Electric) (Virginia Electric & Power) (Sierra Pacific Power)	3.76	1935
BIRTMAN ELECTRIC (Whirlpool)	3.75	1933
BRACH (E. J) & SONS (American Home Products)	3.75	1933
CESSNA AIRCRAFT	3.75	1941
EX-CELL-O	3.75	1934
HANCOCK OIL (Signal Cos.)	3.75	1933
INTERNATIONAL UTILITIES CLASS A (common)	3.75	1943
MC GRAW ELECTRIC (McGraw-Edison)	3.75	1934
SLOSS-SHEFFIELD STEEL & IRON (A-T-O Inc.)	3.75	1932
BROADWAY DEPARTMENT STORE (Broadway-Hale Stores)	3.63	1941
DISNEY (WALT) PRODUCTIONS INC.	3.63	1954
LINE MATERIAL (McGraw-Edison)	3.63	1935
AMERICAN MANUFACTURING	3.50	1935
ARMOUR & CO. (ILLINOIS) PREFERRED (Greyhound)	3.50	1932
CLIFFS CORP. (Cleveland Cliffs)	3.50	1933
COOPER INDUSTRIES	3.50	1937
CUTLER-HAMMER	3.50	1932
LION OIL (Monsanto)	3.50	1935
U.S. FREIGHT	3.50	1932
WALKER (HIRAM) GOODERHAM & WORTS	3.50	1933
WESTON ELECTRICAL INSTRUMENT (Schlumberger)	3.50	1932
BORG-WARNER	3.38	1932
UNITED CHEMICALS (FMC)	3.25	1939
U.S. STORES $7 FIRST PREFERRED (Thorofare Markets)	3.25	1941
(Virginia Electric & Power) ENGINEERS PUBLIC SERVICE (El Paso Electric) (Gulf States Utilities)	3.15	1934

	Cost	Year Bought
AMERICAN METAL CLIMAX	3.13	1933
EATON MANUFACTURING (Eaton Yale & Towne)	3.13	1933
INTERNATIONAL VITAMIN (American Home Products)	3.13	1941
KERLYN OIL CLASS A (Kerr-McGee)	3.13	1943
SWEETS CO. OF AMERICA (Tootsie Roll Industries)	3.13	1942
TENNESSEE CORP. (Cities Service)	3.13	1934
AMERICAN INVESTMENT CO. OF ILLINOIS	3.00	1933
CHICAGO RIVET & MACHINE	3.00	1932
COLLINS & AIKMAN	3.00	1933
ELECTRIC POWER & LIGHT $7 PFD. (Middle South Utilities and Pennzoil)	3.00	1935
FEDERAL-MOGUL	3.00	1934
GOODRICH (B.F.) COMPANY	3.00	1933
INTERCONTINENTAL RUBBER (Texas Instruments)	3.00	1952
STARRETT (L.S.)	3.00	1932
WESTVACO CHEMICAL (FMC)	3.00	1932
BALDWIN (D.H.) CO.	2.88	1939
GENERAL AMERICA CORP. (Safeco)	2.75	1934
PACIFIC PORTLAND CEMENT (Ideal Basic Industries)	2.75	1944
RAYTHEON	2.75	1943
WARNER BROS. PICTURES, INC. (Kinney National Service)	2.75	1941
U.S. FOIL B (Reynolds Metals)	2.63	1943
WHITE SEWING MACHINE (White Consolidated Industries)	2.63	1943
CARRIER CORP.	2.50	1932
DOBECKMAN (Dow Chemical)	2.50	1941
ELECTRIC POWER & LIGHT $6 PFD. (Middle South Utilities and Pennzoil)	2.50	1935
MAYTAG	2.50	1943
PARKER PEN	2.50	1932
REMINGTON RAND (Sperry Rand)	2.50	1933
SHELL UNION OIL (Shell Oil)	2.50	1932
TEXAS PACIFIC COAL & OIL	2.50	1934
RAPID ELECTROTYPE (Rapid-American)	2.38	1943
EVERSHARP (Warner-Lambert)	2.25	1942
HOUSTON OIL	2.25	1942

	Cost	Year Bought
SAVAGE ARMS (Emhart)	2.25	1933
CHICAGO PNEUMATIC TOOL	2.13	1933
CITIES SERVICE	2.13	1942
S. R. DRESSER MANUFACTURING CLASS B (Dresser Industries)	2.13	1933
GIMBEL BROTHERS	2.13	1935
MC LELLAN STORES PREFERRED (McCrory Corp. common)	2.13	1933
SPERRY (Sperry Rand)	2.13	1933
ABITIBI POWER & PAPER CO., LTD. 6% PFD. ($100 PAR) (Abitibi Paper common)	2.00	1940
CHICAGO & SOUTHERN AIR LINES (Delta Air Lines)	2.00	1942
FAIRCHILD AVIATION (Fairchild Camera)	2.00	1938
LEHIGH VALLEY COAL CORP. 6% ($50 PAR) CONVERTIBLE PFD. (Lehigh Valley Industries)	2.00	1940
MIDLAND STEEL PRODUCTS (Midland-Ross)	2.00	1932
PHILLIPS PETROLEUM	2.00	1932
PITNEY-BOWES	2.00	1933
PLACER DEVELOPMENT	2.00	1937
TEXAS GULF PRODUCING	2.00	1942
THATCHER MANUFACTURING (Dart Industries)	2.00	1932
UNION GAS OF CANADA	2.00	1934
INTERTYPE (Harris-Intertype)	1.88	1933
KINNEY (G.R.) & CO. (Brown Shoe)	1.88	1943
LINDSAY CHEMICAL (Kerr-McGee)	1.88	1939
UNITED PIECE DYE WORKS 6½% PREFERRED (United Piece Dye Works common)	1.88	1943
WHITMAN & BARNES (TRW, Inc.)	1.88	1934
NEW YORK DOCK (Questor)	1.75	1939
PITTSTON CO.	1.75	1943
AMERICAN CHAIN & CABLE	1.63	1933
AMERICAN CYANAMID	1.63	1932
UNITED-CARR FASTENER (TRW, Inc.)	1.63	1933
VAN RAALTE CO. (Cluett, Peabody & Co.)	1.63	1933
VENTURES (Falconbridge Nickel)	1.57*	1940

*U. S. Funds

	Cost	Year Bought
INDIANA STEEL PRODUCTS (Electronic Memories & Magnetics)	1.50	1940
INTERNATIONAL TELEPHONE & TELEGRAPH	1.50	1942
SETON LEATHER (Seton Co.)	1.50	1933
SUNSTRAND MACHINE TOOL (Sunstrand Corp.)	1.50	1933
FALCONBRIDGE NICKEL	1.43#	1940
YELLOW TRUCK & COACH (General Motors)	1.38	1932
AUSTIN, NICHOLS & CO. (Liggett & Myers)	1.25	1942
BEECH AIRCRAFT	1.25	1938
CELANESE CORP.	1.25	1932
ELECTRIC POWER & LIGHT COMMON (Middle South Utilities and Pennzoil)	1.25	1943
GENERAL CABLE COMMON	1.25	1933
MC CORD RADIATOR & MANUFACTURING (McCord Corp.)	1.25	1943
NATIONAL DEPARTMENT STORES 7% 1st PFD. (International Mining)	1.25	1933
NORTH AMERICAN AVIATION (North American Rockwell)	1.25	1932
UNITED STATES RUBBER (Uniroyal)	1.25	1932
COPPER RANGE	1.13	1932
HOOVER BALL & BEARING	1.13	1934
INDIAN REFINING (Texaco)	1.13	1933
SMITH (HOWARD) PAPER MILLS (Domtar)	1.13	1933
SOSS MANUFACTURING (SOS Consolidated)	1.13	1941
AIR PRODUCTS & CHEMICALS	1.00	1946
ALLEN INDUSTRIES (Dayco)	1.00	1933
CONSOLIDATED AIRCRAFT (General Dynamics)	1.00	1933
CROWN ZELLERBACH	1.00	1933
DAYTON RUBBER MANUFACTURING CLASS A (Dayco)	1.00	1933
ELECTRIC BOAT (General Dynamics)	1.00	1933
FLYING TIGER LINE	1.00	1949
HOUDAILLE-HERSHEY CLASS B (Houdaille Industries)	1.00	1933

#U. S. Funds

	Cost	Year Bought
HUSSMAN-LIGONIER (Pet Milk)	1.00	1934
LINEN SERVICE CORP. OF TEXAS (National Service Industries)	1.00	1939
MEGEL (Marcor)	1.00	1932
MESABI IRON (Mesabi Trust)	1.00	1943
NATIONAL SHIRT SHOPS (McCrory Corp. common)	1.00	1934
PITTSBURGH RAILWAYS (CITIZENS TRACTION COMMON) (Pittway Corp.)	1.00	1940
SCULLIN STEEL $3 PREFERENCE (Universal Marion)	1.00	1932
SELECTED INDUSTRIES $1.50 CONVERTIBLE STOCK (Tri-Continental)	1.00	1942
SOUTH COAST (Jim Walter)	1.00	1941
SPIEGEL, MAY, STERN (Beneficial Corp.)	1.00	1933
TUBIZE CHATILLON (Celanese)	1.00	1932
TUNG-SOL ELECTRIC (Studebaker-Worthington)	1.00	1932
U.S. BOBBIN & SHUTTLE (Baker Industries)	1.00	1941
VIRGINIA CAROLINA CHEMICAL (Mobil Oil)	1.00	1942
VIRGINIA IRON, COAL & COKE (Bates Manufacturing)	1.00	1943
WILCOX (H.F.) OIL & GAS (Tenneco)	1.00	1935
AIR INVESTORS (American Manufacturing)	.94	1942
(Syntex)		
OGDEN CORP. (Ogden Corp.)	.94	1951
(Bunker Ramo)		
LOCKHEED	.90	1934
AMERICAN SEATING	.88	1933
BULOVA WATCH	.88	1933
ELECTRIC BOND & SHARE (Boise Cascade)	.88	1942
EVANS PRODUCTS	.88	1933
GROCERY STORE PRODUCTS (Clorox)	.88	1942
MIDDLE STATES PETROLEUM CLASS A (Tenneco)	.88	1935
RELIABLE STORES	.88	1933

	Cost	Year Bought
JEANETTE GLASS	.82	1942
AMERICAN LABORATORIES		
(American Medical International)	.75	1964
AMERICAN MACHINE & METALS		
(Ametek, Inc.)	.75	1932
BUTLER BROS. (McCrory Corp.)	.75	1932
INSPIRATION CONSOLIDATED COPPER	.75	1932
LOFT (Pepsico)	.75	1938
RUSTLESS IRON & STEEL (Armco Steel)	.75	1935
ST. LAWRENCE CORP. (Domtar)	.75	1942
SELECTED INDUSTRIES (Tri-Continental		
common & warrants)	.75	1944
SHAMROCK OIL & GAS (Diamond		
Shamrock)	.75	1935
VENEZUELAN PETROLEUM		
(Atlantic Richfield)	.75	1941
VENEZUELAN PETROLEUM		
(Sinclair Oil)	.75	1941
TRI-CONTINENTAL WARRANTS	.69	1944
ARMOUR & CO. (ILLINOIS) CLASS A		
(Greyhound)	.63	1932
ART METAL WORKS (Ronson Corp.)	.63	1933
BLISS (E.W.) (Gulf & Western)	.63	1932
DUNHILL INTERNATIONAL (Questor)	.63	1932
EASTERN STATES CORP.		
(St. Regis Paper)	.63	1944
OUTBOARD MOTORS CLASS B		
(Outboard Marine)	.63	1935
SNIDER PACKING FOODS (General Foods)	.63	1933
TRI-CONTINENTAL COMMON	.63	1941
U.S. HOME & DEVELOPMENT	.63	1967
ABITIBI POWER & PAPER COMMON		
(Abitibi Paper common)	.50	1942
BUTTE COPPER & ZINC		
(Jonathan Logan)	.50	1933
BYRON JACKSON (Borg Warner)	.50	1932
CELOTEX (Jim Walter)	.50	1933
DUVAL TEXAS SULPHUR		
(Pennzoil United)	.50	1933
INTERNATIONAL PAPER & POWER		
CLASS A COMMON (International Paper)	.50	1933
JOHNSON MOTOR (Outboard Marine)	.50	1932
MARCHANT CALCULATING MACHINE		
(SMC)	.50	1933

	Cost	Year Bought
NATIONAL AUTOMOTIVE FIBRES		
(Chris-Craft Industries)	.50	1932
NATIONAL FIREPROOFING		
(Fuqua Industries)	.50	1944
SYMINGTON (Dresser Industries)	.50	1932
UNITED PAPERBOARD		
(United Board & Carton)	.50	1933
OCCIDENTAL PETROLEUM	.45	1956
CHEMICAL RESEARCH		
(General Development)	.41	1941
DEVELOPMENT CORP. OF AMERICA	.38	1967
EASON OIL COMPANY	.38	1942
MC CRORY STORES (McCrory Corp.)	.38	1933
MERRITT-CHAPMAN & SCOTT	.38	1932
WARREN BROTHERS		
(Ashland Oil & Refining)	.38	1941
MICHIGAN BUMPER (Gulf & Western)	.32	1943
PARMELEE TRANSPORTATION		
(Checker Motors)	.32	1942
STARRET CORP. (Recrion)	.32	1943
U.S. & FOREIGN SECURITIES (U.S. &		
International Securities)	.32	1933
AMERICAN BEET SUGAR		
(American Crystal Sugar)	.25	1932
BURRY BISCUIT (Quaker Oats)	.25	1942
FANSTEEL	.25	1932
GODCHAUX SUGARS (Gulf States Land &		
Industries)	.25	1933
MC LELLAN STORES (McCrory Corp.)	.25	1933
NESTLE-LE MUR	.25	1938
SUNRAY OIL (Sun Oil)	.25	1933
TRUAX TRAER COAL		
(Consolidation Coal)	.25	1932
GENERAL SHAREHOLDINGS		
(Tri-Continental)	.19	1942
ALLEGHANY CORP. COMMON	.13	1941
NATIONAL BELLAS HESS CO., Inc. 7%		
PFD. (National Bellas Hess, Inc. common)	.13	1932
REPUBLIC GAS (Republic Natural Gas)	.13	1932
WAHL (Schick)	.13	1932
UNITED PIECE DYE WORKS COMMON	.10	1943
OLD BEN COAL NEW COMMON		
(Standard Oil of Ohio)	.05	1935
INTERNATIONAL UTILITIES CLASS B	.04	1942

CHAPTER XX

Getting Away from It All

Sometimes investment problems seem so insoluble that we are tempted to turn our backs on them by sending our money on a foreign trip. For most people, investing abroad amounts to fleeing from hazards they can see to hazards they cannot see. Too often such capital movements glorify hindsight rather than manifest foresight.

I well remember in the 1930s seeing "sophisticated" investors send money to Argentina and France to escape the perils of the New Deal and dollar devaluation in the United States. While I have no records to prove it—people talk more freely about their winnings than about their losses—I very much doubt that any of them made as much money on their foreign ventures as they could have made by taking advantage of the fabulous bargains right here at home.

In summers spent on Minnesota farms in my teens I learned that cattle in a lush pasture will break down a barbed wire fence to get to grass just beyond. To them the grass on the other side of the fence looks greener. So it does to their owners as well. Distance lends enchantment.

In World War II I learned another reason to beware of foreign investment. Some of my customers were British citizens. At the bottom of the market in 1942 the British Government "sequestered" American securities owned by British citizens and sold them to get dollars to help pay for the war.

My conclusions are:

1. Never invest abroad to escape perils at home *unless you are prepared to go with your money.*

2. Otherwise invest abroad only when the foreign opportunity

200

seems better by a wide margin than anything you can find at home. That "wide margin" is to cover the difference between what you know about conditions in your native country and the most you can hope to know about a country you have perhaps visited occasionally and studied intermittently from afar.

You may be thinking, "How about the White Russians whose investments in France saved them when the Revolution came? How about the German Jews whose foreign investments enabled them to make a new start out of Hitler's reach?" Both profited by foreign investments only because they were willing and able to go with their money.

"But," some may argue, "by the time the need for those foreign investments became clear, it was no longer possible to make them."

That is nothing but a statement of all investment problems. By the time the need or the opportunity is clear, the profit potential is in the price.

Ideally, foreign investing should be done as a consequence of a worldwide search for the best relative values. The resulting insurance thus obtained against ruinous social and political developments at home is thus practically free, and free insurance is always a bargain.

If Great Britain enters the Common Market, as now seems assured, and if an economic and/or political United States of Europe evolves, the new superpower should provide great investment opportunities.

On the opposite side of the world is a continental demonstration that nature abhors a vacuum: Australia.

The Australian stock market has advanced sixtyfold in the last seventy-five years, more than twice as much as the Dow-Jones Industrial Average. Following the worldwide depression of 1929–1932, it took twenty-five years for the American, Canadian, and British stock markets to get back to their 1929 highs. The Australian stock market was in new high ground in five years. Why?

Australia is big. How big, this may help you to appreciate· If Texas, our biggest state before we brought in Alaska, is overlaid in exact scale on Australia's biggest state, West Australia, there is enough room around the edges to throw in Alaska too and still have 100,000 square miles left over.

Australia is not only big. It is relatively empty. The area of Australia approximately equals that of the United States before we took in Alaska and Hawaii. Yet the population of the United States is sixteen times the population of Australia.

Australia is not only big and empty. It is unexploited. It was discovered 150 years after the Pilgrams landed at Plymouth Rock, so we had 150 years start on it. In many ways its development still lags the United States by half a century or more. One example of the extreme underexploration of Australia so far is that 2,000 oil wells have been drilled out there in a country as big as the United States where we've drilled more than 2,000,000. Australia's three million square miles of land area and one million square miles of continental shelf should provide a handsome return on a proportionately larger underground exploration.

Many of the biggest discoveries in Australia so far have thrust themselves upon people rather than resulting from intensive, technologically advanced exploration. That is just beginning.

Australians tell an amusing story about the Gove bauxite deposit just west of the Gulf of Carpentaria. During World War II they built an airstrip there. To make the airstrip, they had to go in with bulldozers and scrape away red stuff. There were 5,000 men there during the war: Australians, British, and Americans. Nobody ever thought to ask what the red stuff was.

A year or two after the war, having heard rumors that there was bauxite on some islands north of Australia, a party of geologists flew up to look for it. The plane developed engine trouble. The pilot remembered this now abandoned airstrip, and just made it back there. His engine was in such bad shape that he said they were going to have to be there four or five hours. The geologists, to stretch their legs, got out and walked around. One of them took a look at what was under their feet and thus they "discovered" 500 million tons of bauxite.

Almost as remarkable for the way it thrust itself upon the discoverer was the discovery of iron ore in West Australia.

Lang Hancock, the man who found it and who gets 2-1/2 percent of the gross on all the iron ore shipped by Hamersley, has the biggest taxable income of anybody in Australia. His story is that he and his wife were flying south from a station (ranch) north of this area at the end of the season when a bad storm came up. He didn't have instruments for blind flying and had to stay close to the ground so as not to lose his way. The storm was so bad he flew between hills. As he was going along dodging hills—it was raining cats and dogs—he saw streaks of rust on the side of one hill. He made a note of the location and returned at his first opportunity to find a mountain that is almost pure iron oxide. The whole mountain is a higher grade of iron oxide than once was fed to blast furnaces in this country.

Australia is not only big, empty, and unexploited, but is a prime beneficiary of advances in science and technology. New technology has made feasible the development of many resources which a comparatively short time ago, even if known, would have been disregarded because they would have been uneconomic with the methods and tools then available.

They clear land with Caterpillar Tractors linked with chains. Instead of cutting down trees one at a time as our forefathers did in Vermont and New Hampshire, and then a year or two later digging out the stumps, they pull trees like weeds and stack them up on the edge of the field for burning. Two men can clear 500 acres a day.

The iron ore up at Hamersley and Mount Newman would have been uneconomic to work until they got the kind of equipment that they have today (shovels that pick up twenty-four tons of ore with each bite, trucks that carry 100 tons with each load—four big bites of these shovels fill a truck, one man runs the shovel, another man runs the truck, dumps it into a crusher from which it falls into a 150-car train run by two men).

Air transport is another good example of how modern technology is opening up areas formerly inaccessible and uneconomic in which to operate. Modern technology has brought Australia closer to New York in travel time than New York was to California twenty-five or thirty years ago.

Still another example of what technology is doing for Australia is the development of underground water. In an area where men died of thirst fifty to 100 years ago, they are now bringing up water from only 300 feet below the surface, and it is good water and flows without pumping.

Air conditioning too is revolutionizing the potential of the country, particularly the northern portion that is in the tropics. Agriculture used to be unfeasible for white men in the tropics because of the hard physical labor involved and because the climate was not good for their women and children. Today, everything is air conditioned, even the cabs on the machines.

Much of this big development in Australia has been financed by the Japanese, notably iron ore, bauxite, and coal developments. A great investment problem of the future is, "What will the Japanese do with all of this cheap Australian raw material they are contracting for?" The Japanese are a very ingenious people. In World War II they went down to Darwin, Australia, with their bombers and sank a whole lot of ships. When the war was over, they came again, bought the wrecks, lifted them, and took them back to Japan for scrap iron.

Nothing is certain in investing, but probabilities seem to favor further swift development of the natural resources of this land Down Under which has easily the largest thinly populated land mass to be found in the temperate zone anywhere in the world. The background of English law and respect for private property rights enhances the prospect.

THE INFERNAL CITY

Money, interest, and inflation all have an important bearing on the investment climate in which your investment favorites will run. But the most significant factor of all is people and their views. What are their hopes, their aims, their beliefs? What kind of a life do they want for their children? What kind of a country? What will they fight for? How many of us are doing what we can to help our planet Earth heal its wounds and its people find better lives?

Before the Second World War some investment men used to inquire into the number of churches and their membership as factors in evaluating a community's bonds. Such thinking may be considered square and corny by some today, but it was definite and positive, not vague and uncertain. Property rights vs. human rights meant little to us then because we could not imagine any significant human rights—not even freedom—without property rights. The distinction between right and wrong seemed crystal clear to most of us. Wrongdoers were punished without much thought that society might be to blame for their derelictions.

Things have gotten blurred since then. Just as air pollution now makes it hard for the visitor arriving by airplane to see the towers of Manhattan through the yellow-brown cloud that rises from the city, so moral pollution makes it difficult to distinguish right from wrong, particularly when the wrong is done by a large number of people acting in concert.

Nowhere is this more evident than in our big cities. A metropolis affords anonymity close to invisibility. This means that citizens can act as they would if they knew no one was looking. If there is a moral breakdown in America, the first place it must manifest itself is in the big cities. Nowhere else is interdependence so great, or the opportunity to chisel undetected so patent. Nowhere else are the advantages of mass production and specialization so negated by the rising costs of ineffective policing and inspecting.

Greed that brought the hapless black man to America as prisoner and slave sowed the seeds of the racial tension that undermines our national unity today. Politics that invites their underprivileged descendants to go on relief the day they reach the big city speeds the exodus of the residential taxpayers as the indigents pour in. In the 1960's New York City lost 617,127 white people and gained 702,903 nonwhites. In the decade ended with November, 1971, the number on relief rose 892,917 to a total of 1,242,785. Figures on the number of whites and nonwhites on relief are "not available."

Let no upholder of the status quo accuse me of decrying help for the poor while I write of making millions in the stock market. What I decry is the uneconomic, heartless encouragement of mass migrations by geographic differences in relief standards and payments. If our relief setup did not provide financial inducements for poor people to move to the big cities, my guess is that they would not flock to Bagdad-on-the-Subway where their children are sitting ducks for drug pushers, and where the parents themselves are so often lacking the education and training for the jobs they need so badly. How long can Congress fail to recognize the national nature of the problem?

Pessimists say big cities are outmoded, doomed no longer needed because of improved communications and transportation. (They should try commuting.) Maybe something better will supersede the big city. Two considerations should give the investor pause, though. One is the evidence that our big cities are not so much dying as being murdered. The second is the history of cities as focal points of civilization in all nations at all times.

In a very real sense great cities have been the heads of bodies politic down through the ages. If the head dies, can the body live?

A problem well defined is half solved. If the crisis of the big cities is as serious as it seems to me, not only for them but for the nation as a whole, people surely will see it soon and begin to do something effective about it. The industrial and commercial consequences could be tremendous, especially for mass transit, housing, education, and health.

Don't sell big cities short. It is always darkest just before dawn.

CHAPTER XXI

It's Not Too Late

How does the outlook for the next ten or twenty or thirty or forty years differ from the past? Now that we have seen by hindsight how easily we could have made a million dollars by buying right and holding on in almost any year from 1932 to 1967, can we still do it? Or have we missed the boat?

Some very important factors have changed. That much is sure. The great advance in stock prices that began on July 8, 1932, with the Dow-Jones Industrial Average at an intra-day low of 40.56 and culminated on February 9, 1966, with the same average at an intra-day high of 1,001 was fueled by:

1. A gigantic shift from depression psychology to boom psychology.

In 1932 the Dow-Jones Industrial Average sold at half its book value. In 1966 it sold at twice its book value.

In 1932 stocks sold to yield twice as much as bonds. At their peak in 1969 they sold to yield about half as much as bonds. When people are pessimistic about the business outlook they prefer bonds to stocks even though bonds yield only half as much, "because bonds are safer." When people are optimistic about the business outlook—and fearful of inflation as well—they prefer stocks even though bonds yield nearly twice as much, "because stock earnings and dividends grow."

The shift in this relationship alone would account for a fourfold advance in the stock market even if nothing else had changed at all from 1932. In the years ahead the stock market cannot benefit from such a shift because it already has benefited from it.

207

2. The Second World War laid waste much of the productive capacity of all the more advanced major powers except the United States.

When the war ended, America had not only to supply deferred demands at home but had to assist in rebuilding the productive facilities of Great Britain, France, Germany, and Japan, to say nothing of our aid to many smaller, less developed countries.

Far from counting on any such stimulus in the years ahead, America now faces and is feeling keenly the competition of the countries we helped to put back on their feet.

3. The war's end found America holding most of the world's monetary gold—more than $26 billion dollars worth—which enabled us to finance huge governmental deficits for years without noticeably weakening the foreign exchange value of the dollar. When our monetary gold stock dwindled to $10 billion we suspended gold payments. We can no longer count on living beyond our international means.

4. International cooperation in removing trade barriers was fostered by our aid programs aggregating $140 billion. People are always cooperative when it is clearly in their immediate self-interest to cooperate. Now that the handouts are slackening, human nature is beginning to reassert itself. The danger of an international trade war is real. Competitive protectionism would mean shrinkage in world trade and general deflation.

We can't have the stock market–stimulating effects of those four factors for the same reason we can't eat our cake and have it too. We have had them.

Then what can we have?

Opening the first Atoms-for-Peace conference in Geneva fifteen years ago, the renowned Indian atomic scientist Homi Bhabha, conference chairman, said there have been three great epochs of man. The first, lasting tens of thousands of years, was based on muscle power. The second, lasting some 300 years, was the epoch of chemical energy. The third, which dawned in Stagg Stadium, Chicago, less than thirty years ago, is the epoch of atomic energy.

Unimaginable as have been the changes brought about by

man's advance from the first epoch into the second, Mr. Bhabha said, they will be dwarfed by the changes resulting from our entry into the third epoch.

Three major lines of development from atomic energy were forecast at the conference.

1. Power—limitless when the fusion reaction is brought under control.

2. New materials—irreversible changes in molecular structures of matter brought about by radiation.

3. New life forms resulting from accelerating evolutionary processes by irradiating plant and animal "seed."

Spaceship Earth, like our submarines, must be atomic-powered ultimately if an expanding "crew" using ever more energy is to have enough oxygen left to sustain and improve the quality of life.

Less publicized but potentially no less significant are the prophesied new materials and new life forms.

Opportunities for 100-to-one investments should be found in all three, as they have been in practically every major new development in the past—electric lights, horseless carriages, airplanes, radio and television, birth control pills.

If, as Henry J. Kaiser puts it, problems are opportunities in work clothes, pollution abatement will provide major investment opportunities for someone. So will the production of ever broader lines of disposable items.

Potentialities of the laser are only beginning to be suspected, even in the military. The history of war argues that today's irresistible offensive power once again will yield to tomorrow's impenetrable defenses, as the offensive has yielded to the defensive in the past. Offensive gunpowder triumphed over defensive castles, moats, and suits of armor. Defensive trenches in World War I checkmated gunpowder. Intercontinental ballistic missiles restored the supremacy of the offensive. But their sun too will set, and in setting will cast a rosy glow over still other 100-to-one investment opportunities in the new defensive capabilities.

Holography enabling us to see persons at great distances in color and in three dimensions may reduce both the need and the desire to travel "to see each other," or to hold business conferences except in "executive weather."

Super-cooled cables transmitting electricity at almost zero power loss already have opened the way, in theory, for a national power grid fed by a few stations of undreamed of power and efficiency.

Machines reading printing and handwriting in all major languages will translate them into electrical impulses our computers can comprehend and digest.

Factory made meals can be better than many a mother used to make with such monstrous toil and inefficiency—can be, and will be. It would be madness to try to give a complete catalogue of what is to be. No one knows. These are just a few of the more obvious prospects.

There is just one catch. The sons and daughters of Adam and Eve have been working their way back to the gates of the Garden of Eden. Therein all may live richly, with no more work than is elected to exercise mind and body. We can lift the bar and re-enter unless we exhaust ourselves fighting to see who goes first!

Visionary, impractical, crystal ball, cloud nine nonsense? Perhaps. But don't forget, ye of little faith and less imagination, what skepticism and cynicism have cost us in the last forty years.

Bet just this once against the end of the world. If you lose, there will be no one around to collect.

The worse the stock market is acting when you read this, the better the advice to buy right and hold on. Why did the Rothschilds buy when the streets were running with blood? Not because they liked red. Simply because when things are that bad they have to get better or nothing will matter. I hope and pray that neither you nor I will be given that kind of investment opportunity. But if we are, let's not run away from it!

CHAPTER XXII

Cheer for the Younger Generation

A hungry wolf met a lamb drinking at a small stream.
"You are muddying my drinking water," snarled the wolf. "For that I shall eat you."

"I can't be muddying your water," replied the lamb. "I am downstream from you."

"You were muddying it yesterday," the wolf said. "For that I shall eat you."

"I could not have muddied it yesterday," the lamb explained. "I was only born this morning."

"Then it was your mother," declared the wolf. "For that I shall eat you." And, according to Aesop, so he did.

I recite the story for the benefit of any reader who may be thinking that he was born too late to be guilty of missing these 100-to-one opportunities in the stock market. I can recall seven such chances in the last ten years. No doubt there have been more.

In life, Fate is the wolf. To get the better of her, we must act, not alibi ourselves.

You and I could have bought Masco Screw Products stock in 1961 and turned every dollar of our investment into $100 by 1971.

We could have done the same thing by buying Skyline Homes in 1963, or American Laboratories in 1964, or Automatic Data Processing in 1965, or Fleetwood Enterprises in 1966, or U.S. Home or Development Corporation of America in 1967. Just $10,000 invested in any one of those seven stocks in the years cited would have grown to more than a million dollars by last year.

211

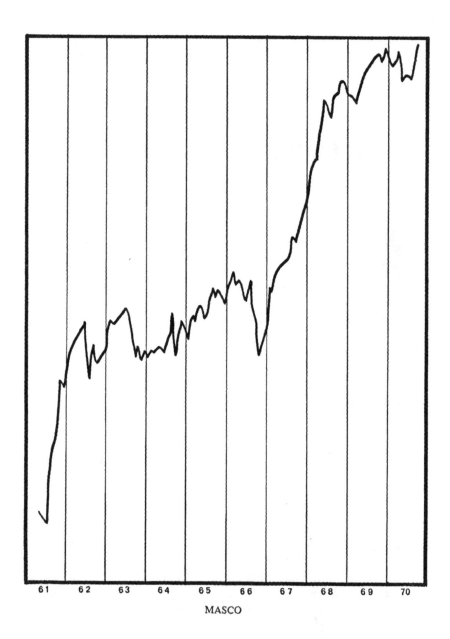

61   62   63   64   65   66   67   68   69   70

MASCO

One of the seven would have had to be bought on the Detroit Stock Exchange, one on the American Stock Exchange, and the other five on the Over-the-Counter market.

How could we have foreseen those opportunities? First let us examine what the seven companies do, and how they looked when they were selling at less than 1 percent of their last year's highs. Perhaps then we may be able to infer a line of thinking that will help us to spot the next 100-to-one chance.

Five of the seven stocks that have risen 100-fold in the 1961–71 decade are in the building industry. The sixth is in the business of automating payrolls and brokerage house record keeping. The seventh, now American Medical International, owns and manages acute care hospitals, and also operates a central medical laboratory, furnishes inhalation therapy equipment, and produces patient counseling motion pictures.

Let us look at them in the chronological sequence in which we would have had to buy them in order to turn $1 into $100:

Masco Screw Products stock could have been bought for $6.25 a share on the Detroit Stock Exchange in February, 1961. Each of those shares would now be 18 shares with a peak market value last year of $729, or 116 times its 1961 cost.

Much more than 100-to-one could have been made in the stock if we had bought it earlier than 1961. Masco has been traded on the Detroit Stock Exchange since 1937. In 1938 and 1939 it sold for as little as 55 cents a share. Anyone who bought it at that price and held it until 1971 would have seen his $1 investment grow to $1,325. Such a gain would turn $10,000 into $13,250,000.

To have held the stock that long would have required extraordinary tenacity, the more so because for 20 years after it made its low of 55 cents a share the highest price it reached was $5 a share in 1946. By 1949 it had lost 75 percent of that price and was selling at $1.25. Here was a stock to tire out almost everyone. What did security analysts have to go on in 1961?

The company's sales had been as high as $9 million in 1953 but had declined by more than half by 1956 and recovered to only $6.4 million in 1960. Per share earnings had peaked at $1.07 in 1952, fallen to 11 cents in 1956, and reached a new high of $1.28 in 1960.

The real tipoff as to better times for Masco was to be found in these figures:

	Invested Capital Per Share	Book Value Per Share	Return on Invested Capital	Return on Book Value	Sales per $ of Invested Capital
1956	$6.16	$6.16	1.7%	1.7%	$1.80
1957	6.32	6.32	6.7	4.7	2.20
1958	6.52	6.80	5.0	4.5	1.60
1959	7.36	7.64	13.2	12.9	2.00
1960	8.72	8.44	15.1	15.1	· 2.00

From 1956 to 1960 book value per share rose 37 percent, invested capital per share rose 41 percent, and per share sales were up from $10.88 to $17.44, or 60 percent. Yet despite that dramatic improvement Masco stock sold in 1960 at prices ranging from 2.7 times earnings for that year to 6.9 times.

In 1961 the big advance was on. The stock sold from a low of 2.9 times its 1961 earnings to a high of 26.9 times. In 1969 Masco sold at more than 38 times earnings.

Here again we see the importance of buying stocks when they are cheap on earnings instead of waiting until they are dear. The advance in Masco's price-earnings ratio (price divided by per share earnings) from 1960 to 1969 would have raised the price of its stock fourteen-fold even if earnings had not increased at all. (Actually earnings rose steeply in that period.) But the point is that if the price of each dollar of earnings rises to 14 times its starting point, the earnings themselves need rise only a little more than seven-fold to produce a stock price advance of one hundredfold (14 times 7 = 98). On the other hand if the price-earnings ratio remains unchanged, earnings have to rise to 100 times their starting figure to produce a 100-fold advance in the price of the stock.

Some analysts prefer to focus on sales and profit margins rather than on invested capital and rates of return. It really makes little difference. Sales times profit margin must equal invested capital times rate of return. They are simply different ways of expressing (and analyzing) the same earnings figures. ($10 sales times 30 percent pre-tax profit margin = $3 times 50 percent tax = $1.50 net profit. $7.50 invested capital times 20 percent rate of return = $1.50.)

The improvement in Masco's figures between 1956 and 1960 would not have produced the dramatic stock market results it did if it had not persisted. Here are some of the same data for the last ten years:

	Return on Invested Capital	Return on Equity	Sales per $ of Invested Capital
1961	20.0%	20.2%	$1.80
1962	26.7	27.5	2.10
1963	27.7	27.6	2.20
1964	29.8	29.8	2.20
1965	28.4	28.3	2.20
1966	26.9	26.2	2.30
1967	21.9	24.4	2.00
1968	22.7	23.5	2.20
1969	12.2	20.7	1.20
1970	11.0	18.5	1.10

"Return on invested capital" measures the earning power of all the money invested in a business, whether that capital shows on the balance sheet as bonds, preferred stocks or common stock and surplus. "Return on equity" measures the earning power of whatever part of the money invested in a business appears on the balance sheet as common stock and surplus.

If a company has issued no bonds and no preferred stocks, its return on invested capital and its return on equity will be the same, of course. When return on equity is higher than return on invested capital, it means that a company is earning more on whatever part of its capital is in the form of bonds and preferred stocks than that senior capital is costing. Such would be the case if a company was paying 5 percent interest on its bonds and 5 percent dividends on its preferred stock, while earning 10 percent on its invested capital. Conversely, when a company pays a higher rate of interest or dividends on its senior securities than it is earning on its invested capital, the return on its equity must be less than the return on its invested capital.

The ratio of sales to invested capital (sales per dollar invested) sometimes gives an early warning of increasing competitive pressures. When a management finds itself obliged to invest large sums "to stay competitive" rather than to increase production, the heat is on.

I have cited the importance of a low initial price-earnings ratio to the seeker after 100-to-one growth. Once a high price-earnings ratio has been achieved, the buyer no longer can profit by the rise in that ratio. Someone else already has had it. Similarly, while a low rate of return on invested capital is not a good sign, an increase in the rate of return from a low figure to a high one can be highly beneficial to a company's earnings. Once a high rate of return has been achieved, the opportunity to profit by improvement from a low rate to a high one is gone, of course.

Figures never tell the whole story of any company. As late as 1959 Masco was described by *Moody's Industrials* as "engaged in the manufacture of screw products for the automobile and other industries." By 1961 faucet sales had become the primary source of revenue. Largely responsible was the success of Masco's Delta single-handle faucet. The company now has a medium priced two handle line as well.

How about the other six big winners of the past decade? Skyline builds mobile homes, travel trailers and tent campers, and also makes sectional homes more suitable for permanent residence. The stock sold at a low of $11 a share in January of 1963, in which year Skyline earned $1.70 a share. The initial price-earnings ratio for this 100-to-one stock thus was less than 6-1/2. One share in 1963 has since become 19.8 shares valued last year at $1,183. At its 1971 high the stock was selling at 31 times its earnings for the year ended May 31, 1971.

What is now American Medical International sold at a low of 75 cents a share in 1964, less than four times earnings subsequently reported for that year. By 1971 each 1964 share had

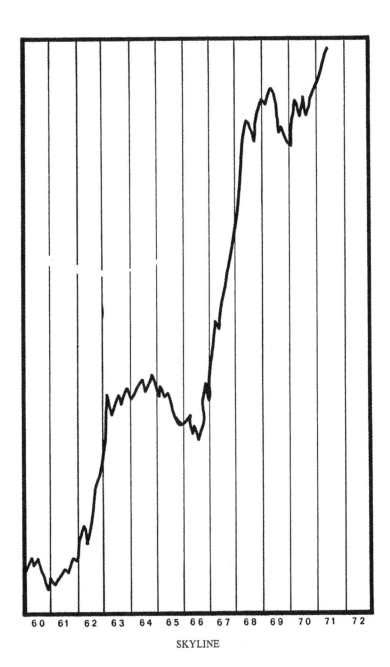

60 61 62 63 64 65 66 67 68 69 70 71 72

SKYLINE

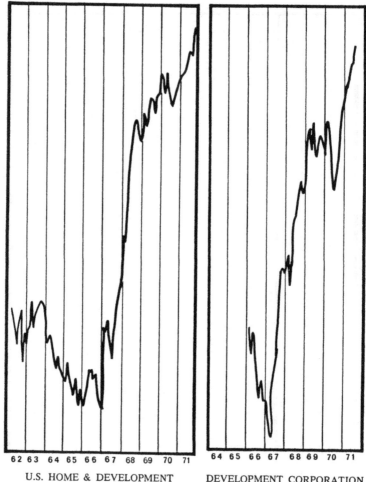

| 62 63 | 64 65 | 66 67 | 68 69 | 70 | 71 | | 64 65 | 66 67 | 68 69 | 70 | 71 |

U.S. HOME & DEVELOPMENT   DEVELOPMENT CORPORATION
                                                        OF AMERICA

become 3.4 shares. In 1971 the stock sold at 44 times latest reported earnings (for 1970). With the 1971 price-earnings ratio 11 times what it had been in 1964, earnings themselves had to rise to only 9 times their 1964 level to produce a 100-to-one advance in the price of the stock. Actually, earnings rose more than that, so the 1971 peak price for the stock was 172 times its 1964 low.

Automatic Data Processing is prominent in payroll processing and computerized handling of brokerage business records.

The stock was quoted at a low of $7 a share bid in tne over-the-counter market in 1965. One share then is nine shares now, valued at last year's high at $704. In 1965 the company earned 56 cents a share, so at $7 the stocks price-earnings ratio was 12-1/2. In 1963 it had sold as low as 1-1/2. At its 1971 high the stock was priced at 90 times its earnings for the year ended June 30, 1971.

Fleetwood Enterprises, another housing stock, makes mobile homes and travel trailers. In 1966 the stock sold just over six times earnings for that year. By the end of 1971 each 1966 share had become 16 shares. They sold 37 times latest reported earnings, roughly four times the 1966 multiplier. Thus the lion's share of this stock's big rise came from higher earnings.

U.S. Home & Development builds single family homes, and apartment buildings, and invests in and develops land in New Jersey and Florida. The over-the-counter low bid for the stock in 1965 was 56-1/4 cents a share, in 1966 50 cents a share and in 1967 62-1/2 cents. Each 1967 share is now two shares with a peak 1971 market value of $78. Earnings in the year ended February 28, 1967, were 20 cents a share, so the price-earnings ratio at that year's low quotation was just over 3.

Development Corporation of America builds single family homes condominiums and communities in New Jersey and Florida and engages in the real estate business. It also makes aluminum windows and doors. The stock was quoted at a low of 38 cents bid in the over-the-counter market in 1967. One share then has grown to 2.2 shares with a market value last year of $74.

Indicative of the limited value of so-called inside information is the report that in 1963 Development Corporation bought back from a former officer 297,582 shares at $1 each. Those shares would now number 654,680 with a peak market value last year of $22,000,000.

At its 1967 low Development Corporation stock was selling just over three times its 1966 earnings and less than twice its 1967 per share net. At its 1971 high it was selling 67 times its 1970 earnings or 50 cents a share, but the company had already reported earnings of $1.07 a share for the first nine months of 1971.

Again the moral is clear: None of the 100-to-one fortune maker stocks of the last ten years were selling at high price-earnings ratios when opportunity beckoned. Their great price advances resulted from a compounding of earnings gains by multiplier gains. Earnings rose and so did the market price of each dollar of those earnings.

(This does not mean that it is impossible to make 100-to-one in a stock bought at a high price-earnings ratio. It simply means that you must foresee much greater earnings growth to warrant a hundredfold price advance when you can count on little or no help from a rising multiplier.)

Was it all luck?

For those who owned any of those seven stocks at less than 1 percent of their 1971 values, and *held on,* it was certainly not all luck. Anyone who can hold on in the face of all the advice and tempations to make sure of a profit demonstrates a quality of mind quite out of the ordinary. But was it just luck to have bought any of those stocks in the first place?

As I look back on the situation it seems to me I should have foreseen the great advance in factory-built home stocks. Archaic building codes and skyrocketing wages for building trades workers had created a situation in which millions of people could not afford to have tailor-made the housing they had to have. The wonder is really not so much that factory-built housing caught on as that it took so long for it to do so.

The surmise is reinforced by the generality of the advance in stocks of factory-built housing companies. National Homes is on the 100-to-one list (see "1945" in Table I). It is the world's largest factory-builder of housing for assembly at homesites. Champion Home Builders, while not in the 100-to-one category, in 1971 sold at 43 times its 1967 low.

A group movement of such magnitude highlights the importance of conceptual as distinguished from statistical investing. By the time you can prove that factory-built housing is the wave of the future, the opportunity to make big money in it is gone.

Every human problem is an investment opportunity if you can anticipate the solution. Except for thieves, who would buy locks?

CHAPTER XXIII

How to Avoid Missing the Boat Next Time

Why with so many fantastic opportunities dangling before us year after year have so few of us taken advantage of them?

The answers are not simple. I can think of half a dozen explanations, and probably there are more.

The basic reason so few of us have ever made $100 on a $1 investment is that we have never tried to do so. In a sense we have been brainwashed into looking for and acting on types of information that have little or nothing to do with multiplying one's investment one hundredfold. We are like small boys in a patch full of ripe melons searching feverishly for a peanut or two. In matters of taste there is no argument. If we enjoy trading profits more than making a fortune, so be it. But there are a lot more financial calories in a ripe melon than in a single peanut or even two or three peanuts.

A great many people, I am sure, have never set out to increase their capital one hundredfold because they had no idea that it could be done. Much investment research is misdirected from the point of view of one wanting to increase his capital rather than "play the market." The responsibility for this fact of life must be shared by many—investors, brokers, financial services, news media, and possibly even our school teachers whose sin, if any, is one of omission.

Brokers live on commissions on transactions. I know because i was a broker for eleven years, and a partner at that. There are two primary ways to generate commission business. One is to give such good service, including investment advice, that more and more people come to that brokerage house to do their buying and selling. The other way to generate commissions is to point out reasons why the clients the firm already has should sell the stocks they own and buy other stocks. I used to try to do both. Taking losses near the year-end to offset for tax purposes profits racked up earlier in the year is a prime example. Much more likely to generate business from a "go-go" fund manager is an early warning that one of his pet growth stocks is about to take one of the pauses that refreshes. Few things make a man feel taller than getting out of 50,000 shares at 50, then seeing the stock at 40 within a month or two. Actually, until he has replaced the stock at a sufficiently lower price to pay the capital gains taxes and commissions incurred, the seller does not really know whether he has gained or lost. As the tortoise remarked to the hare, who is ahead doesn't count until the finish line is crossed. In life the finish line is death, and at that time all potential capital gains tax liability on unrealized gains is forgiven, at least under the law in 1971.

When I said news media share the responsibility for some of the unprofitable overtrading that goes on, I had in mind the way some preen themselves on stories that move the market. The inference, of course, is that if you read the *Daily Clarion* you can make money in the stock market by selling on bad news and buying on good news. Short term such actions often produce the very results good news and bad news are expected to produce. Expecting makes it so.

Much of this news is immaterial to the truly long-term investor. Some news has the opposite of its seemingly obvious significance. Shrewd investors recognize bad news as a chance to acquire good stocks at bargain prices. That is why so often after a savage general market decline we see the best stocks moving up first.

Please understand I do not mean to criticize or denigrate news. In a sense news is the nervous system of civilized society. What I caution against is the delusion that if you have the news you have the investment decision, automatically.

News often provides a reason or an excuse for switching from one stock to another. In theory it is always possible to sell a good stock and buy a better one. What is often overlooked, however, is how much better the new purchase must be to make the switch advantageous. Suppose for example that you buy a stock for $100 and sell it for $1,000. While state taxes vary, it seems fair to assume that federal, state, and possibly city taxes on the capital gain, together with the com missions involved, will take at least 30 percent of the gross profit, leaving you with no more than $730 net. If the stock you sold for $1,000 advances another 50 percent your former holding becomes worth $1,500. To keep pace with that, the stock you buy with the $730 net proceeds of your sale must advance more than 105 percent. In other words the stock into which you switch must do more than twice as well as the stock you sell just to keep you even.

This is not to argue against getting rid of lemons. The point is simply that when you try to substitute a better stock for a good one in which you have a big profit, the substitute stock must be very much better than most people realize if you are to come out ahead.

It is a paradox that the investor seeking to multiply his capital by 100 actually runs less risk than the individual trying to make five points or even double his money. There are at least five reasons why this is so:

1. There is always a market for the best of anything, because people who appreciate quality always seem to have money. That is as true of stocks and bonds as it is of real estate and antiques.

2. Buying for maximum long-term growth avoids the pitfall of underestimating other people. When you buy because you expect the earnings and dividends to increase one hundredfold in the next twenty, thirty, or forty years you are not planning to unload on someone less brilliant than yourself.

3. When you buy a stock with a superior profit margin, an above-average rate of return on invested capital, and sales that are growing faster than the industry's or the country as a whole, you have time on your side. Never bet on a possibility against a certainty. Time marches on, and will continue to march on. That is a certainty. If your stock has no visible ceiling on its indicated growth, time will correct many errors in what you pay for your initial commitment.

4. The old saw about the world beating a path to the door of

the man making better mouse traps may be corn but it is high protein corn. It is sometimes denigrated on the ground that without the help of Madison Avenue the better mouse trap maker would blush unseen. In real life anyone smart enough to make a better mouse trap would not stop there.

5. "Don't marry a man to reform him," a wise mother counselled her daughter. It is seldom profitable to marry a stock to reform it either. Sometimes, as with husbands, the hoped for reform never comes. Even when it does come, it is often sadly delayed. Hope deferred maketh the heart sick. Your turnaround candidate may double in price, but if you have to wait ten years for it to happen your gain is at the compound annual rate of only 7.2 percent.

Perhaps the greatest advantage of all in buying top quality stocks without visible ceilings on their growth is that when we do so we give ourselves the chance to profit by the unforeseeable and the incalculable. Year after year mankind achieves the impossible but persists in underrating what it can and will do in the future. A man from Mars might surmise that having put enough men on the moon to form a club, we humans would be confident we could do anything else we thought necessary or desirable. If he knew our history he would know better. Some bureaucrat advocated closing the patent office a hundred years ago because everything had been invented. Rodgers and Hammerstein put it to music eighty years later: "Everything's up to date in Kansas City. They've gone about as far as they can go."

My old friend, the late Pendleton Dudley, also a *Wall Street Journal* alumnus, delighted in recalling a publicity release he handled for a New York bank about 1905. In a profound analysis of the new horseless carriage industry, the bank's economist concluded that 500,000 automobiles would be all the country could afford, all its roads could accommodate. The story amused me very much when I first heard it. I was confident the automobile industry would not hit its ceiling until we had 30 million or even 40 million cars and trucks in this country. As everyone knows we now have more than 100 million.

Everyday we crisscross the Atlantic Ocean with airplanes of greater tonnage than the "Mayflower." We have proved and put to practical use Einstein's equation that energy equals mass times the velocity of light squared. We have turned the dread sonic barrier—the speed of sound—into a speedometer gauge. We monitor the clouds from space satellites and are steadily increasing our command over the weather. Our progress in identifying and influencing life processes makes Harvey's discovery of the circulation of the blood seem prehistoric. Yet like birds making their first flight the higher we rise the more terrified we seem to be that we shall surely fall.

Maybe we have indeed come to the end of an era. Maybe mankind is biologically exhausted by the unprecedented demand on the human nervous system imposed by the last century's achievements. Maybe a new dark age is required to give us a rest. Certainly it is not the first time we have thought so. As editor of *Barron's* I worked with a Harvard professor on a business index in the mid-1930s. His final conclusion was that the secular trend in America was inclined slightly downward.

About the same time President Roosevelt's committee on social security was estimating our total population by 1980 at 150 million. The committee was composed of Secretaries Perkins, Morgenthau, and Wallace, Attorney General Cummings and Federal Emergency Relief Administrator Hopkins. Here we have already passed 200 million.

The point is not to poke fun at anyone's mistakes. If the Almighty had intended that we humans should be able to see into the future He would have equipped us with another sense. The point is simply that we do not know, never have known, and never can know what the future holds. If perchance it should be very much better than the wisest can foresee there is only one investment policy that can take advantage of it. That is the policy of buying right and holding on.

None of us like to feel that we are to blame for our misfortunes. It helps our ego though not our pocketbook to blame someone else. The research I have done for this book has poured a good deal of salt into my own financial wounds. I have tried hard to reject the idea that I might have done better if I had adopted and followed different principles of investing. One of my friends sought to comfort me by exclaiming: "The whole approach is unrealistic. No one can buy at the bottom. And suppose he does try to buy right and hold on only to find too late that the Stop and Shop he held so happily at $66 a share in 1961 was worth only $28.50 a share at its 1971 high?"

Listening to him made me feel better about myself. But then I became curious. How much chance did I have to buy Stop and Shop even at double its 1941 low of $10 a share? Sadly I found that I could have bought it below 20 in every year from 1938 to 1945. Worse still, the highest price it reached in any of those years was 19.

"But," I consoled myself, "if I had bought the stock at 19 I would not have made 100 for one on my investment even at its historic 1961 high." Further checking showed I was absolutely right about that. If I had paid the highest price in the seven years starting with 1938 my investment at the 1961 peak would have been worth only 65 times what I paid for it. Moreover, I told myself: "To get that profit I would have had to buy determined to hold on. So I would still be holding the stock in 1971 and more than half of my paper profits would have vanished."

"I'm not so dumb, after all," I congratulated myself. "If I had bought the stock at the high of those seven years and held on, my investment at last year's peak would have been worth only . . ."—and here I had to stop to figure again. The answer was 28 times what I paid for it. To get a profit of that size by trading, always taking long-term capital gains, I would have had to buy and sell six different times, slightly more than doubling my money each time. The comparison assumes that I never took a loss, never failed to make at least 100 percent profit.

The arithmetic is inescapable. To turn $10,000 into a million dollars by trading for 100 percent long-term capital gains, you must double your money eight successive times and then make more than 60 percent on your final trade, without ever missing. To increase your investment from $10,000 to $1 million in a single stock you must find one that will double and redouble just over 6-1/2 times. Here are the figures in tabular form:

	Trading Account*	Investment Account
Starting Capital	$ 10,000	$ 10,000
1.	17,000*	20,000
2.	31,000*	40,000
3.	59,000*	80,000
4.	115,000*	160,000
5.	227,000*	320,000
6.	451,000*	640,000
7.	899,000*	1,280,000
8.	1,795,000*	2,560,000

* If paid 30% in taxes on yearly gains, but unlikely would be turning over full portfolio every year

To bring the left-hand column to a million dollars after capital gains taxes and commissions, the ninth trade must show a gross profit of 62 percent. The same percentage increase would bring the right-hand column to $4,147,000. Even after a 30 percent tax at that point, the investment account would stand at nearly $3,000,000.

The figures merely pose a question. Each investor must answer it for himself. If his aim is to make a fortune in the stock market, which way is he more likely to succeed? As the table shows, by trading he needs to double his money on eight successive purchases and make a gross profit of 62 percent on the ninth. If he attempts to buy right and hold on he must find a stock that will double and redouble just over six and a half times. Either course will be difficult. If making money were easy everybody would be rich.

As the record shows, over the last forty years there have been hundreds of opportunities to invest $10,000 in a single stock and have the investment worth more than $1 million in 1971. Doubtless there are traders who have done ás well. Both roads are open. The question each investor must answer for himself is whether it will be easier or harder to make one big decision or nine smaller ones when *all* must be correct if he is to make his million on a $10,000 stake.

The choice is not between plunging and diversifying. The trader could put all of his money on a single stock every time. The investor trying to buy right and hold on could buy as many different stocks as appealed to him. The difference is not in the focussing of investment money but in the intent of the buyer. The trader believes that in a swift-moving, rapidly changing world, with visibility always limited, he can make a series of commitments with better chance of success than trying to decide which companies will do well for the next twenty years. The investor dedicated to buying right and holding on picks managements, products, and processes he thinks able to cope with the unforeseeable as it hoves into view.

By hindsight, buying right and holding on could have made fortunes for investors in more than 365 different stocks starting in any one of more than thirty different years. Trading is more fun—no doubt about that. It certainly is more professional. Buying right and holding on gives the outsider as close to an even break as he will ever get. To say that it is easier misses the point entirely. I have seen men of experience take months to reach a decision on a long-term commitment. But once it is made there is no longer any place for the feverish attention to day-to-day developments which are the trader's life blood.

Even those who decide to trade may be helped if they adopt the rule of never buying anything they would not be happy to hold indefinitely. Parting is such sweet sorrow when one does it at a handsome profit.

One of every man's primary investment objectives should be to make as much money as possible while paying as little taxes as possible under whatever laws are in effect at the time. Back in the 1940's Sir Victor Sassoon gave me this valuable advice: "It will be easy to make money in the years that lie ahead," he said. "But what will prove whether you are smart or not is how much you have left after taxes."

I can think of no more effective tax haven than unrealized appreciation in a long-lived, soundly growing company. Yet not

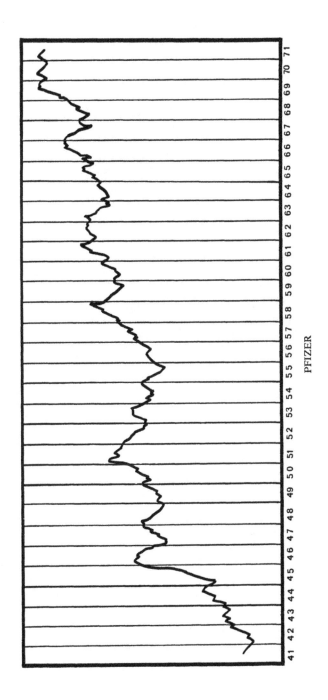

PFIZER

one person in ten thousand identifies this investment goal and sticks to it despite all the temptations to take a profit, get into something better, or simply diversify.

For those who accept this goal and this line of reasoning, there is a simple test of investment efficiency which will be highly unpopular with many brokers. (Please remember I was a partner in a large brokerage firm myself for eleven years.) This test of investment efficiency is to compute the ratio of brokerage commissions to net capital gain, both realized and unrealized. This ratio in the case of Mr. Garrett's fortune in Xerox would be almost zero. The higher the ratio the worse the investment decisions because each sale represents or should represent either a confession of error in the original purchase or the discovery of a better alternative later.

Have I lived by this principle myself? The answer is sadly no. We are too soon old, and too late smart. Good judgment comes from experience. And experience comes from bad judgment. I have had a great deal of experience.

You may be wondering why so few in the financial community advise you to hold fast.

Probably the most important reason is that we won't let them. Investors have been so thoroughly sold on the nonsensical idea of measuring performance quarter by quarter—or even year by year—that many of them would hit the ceiling if an investment advisor or portfolio manager failed to get rid of a stock that acted badly for more than a year or two. Consider Pfizer. This stock lost ground relative to the Dow-Jones Industrial Average from August 1946 to May 1949 and again from August 1951 to September 1956. Performance-minded clients would have chewed the ears off an investment advisor who let them get caught with such a dog. In theory it might have been possible to sell Pfizer in August 1951 and buy it back in September 1956. The fact is, however, that anyone who bought Pfizer in 1942 and held it until now has multiplied the capital involved by 141. There may be traders who have done better than that but if so they are hiding their light under a bushel. Certainly no fund whose record is public has done anywhere nearly that well. The accompanying chart of the relative price of Pfizer stock over the last quarter century tells better than words the courage and patience demanded of the investor who would increase his capital one hundredfold.

What was going on beneath the surface of those Pfizer price waves?

Here are Pfizer earnings, dividends, sales and rates of return on equity for the last twenty years:

	Share Earnings	Dividends	Share Sales	Book Value	Return on Equity
1970	$1.28	.63	$13.68	$7.67	16.6%
1969	1.13	.57	12.73	6.94	16.2
1968	1.03	.50	11.85	6.77	15.6
1967	.96	.48	10.47	6.11	15.6
1966	1.02	.48	10.32	5.49	18.6
1965	.90	.43	9.01	4.89	18.3
1964	.76	.38	8.04	4.48	16.8
1963	.69	.35	7.01	4.29	16.0
1962	.64	.32	6.64	4.16	15.3
1961	.58	.28	5.69	3.56	16.2
1960	.52	.27	5.37	3.34	15.7
1959	.50	.27	5.12	3.03	16.5
1958	.49	25	4.56	2.73	18.0
1957	.47	.23	4.24	2.49	18.8
1956	.37	.19	3.75	2.25	16.5
1955	.33	.17	3.66	1.93	17.1
1954	.33	.15	3.29	1.75	18.8
1953	.30	.14	2.88	1.58	18.9
1952	.24	.13	2.44	1.53	15.7
1951	.27	.18	2.05	1.42	19.0

Would a businessman seeing only those figures have been jumping in and out of the stock? I doubt it. But each investor must judge for himself, primarily because he knows himself better than anyone else does. The secret of success in your quest for 100-to-one stocks is to focus on earning power rather than prices. Can you do it?

How can you get such data for yourself? Most companies report them to you regularly. You simply have to record them year after year. *Moody's* and *Standard & Poor's* manuals provide them. Some brokers will supply them on request.

Share sales are simply total sales divided by the number of shares outstanding. Return on equity is simply share earnings divided by book value. ($1.28 divided by $7.67 = .166 or 16.6 percent.)

Why do so many investors demand quarter by quarter performance?

There are two possible answers. One is that they believe in supermen. Somewhere, they tell themselves, is a man so much smarter than other men that he can pick the stocks that will rise this month and fall next month. This man is so much more clever than other men that he always does the right thing while others are doing the wrong thing. It is simple arithmetic that a portfolio managed by such a superman should outperform all other portfolios in good times or bad. Whenever it fails to do so the remedy is simple: "My superman has lost his touch. Get me a fresh one."

A second reason why some investors insist on judging results quarter by quarter is this: They reason that if their advisor cannot see three months ahead he certainly cannot see five or ten years ahead. It is like arguing that if I can't tell who will win the next point in the tennis match I certainly can't predict who will win the match, even though I know the records of both players. As applied to stocks, the fallacy is that while in the long run price appreciation must reflect rising earnings and dividends, short-run price movements may be the result of wholly extraneous, and often utterly unforeseeable, factors such as distress liquidation of a large portfolio, a strike, or some over-advertised new competition.

I once had a client who had sold his privately owned business for several million dollars and invested the proceeds in the stock market. He came to me in great distress one day, complaining that his holdings were making him so nervous he could not sleep.

"One day I am up $50,000," he said. "The next day I am down

$100,000. The tips I don't take always work out. The ones I do take cost me money. How I wish I could get back to peace of mind I had with all my money in my own business!"

"There was no market for your stock then," I reminded him. "How did you know how you were doing?"

"Easy," he replied. "I watched my monthly sales figures, my expense ratio, and as long as my business was increasing and my profit margin was holding, I slept like a baby."

"We could give you that kind of reports on your portfolio," I said. "It wouldn't do you any good though unless you could promise not to look at the quotation pages in the *Wall Street Journal.*"

Honest even with himself, he replied "I couldn't do that."

Another reason why investors demand activity, even if it is profitable only to their broker, is if they have never learned to distinguish between activity and results. When I was a boy a carpenter working for my father made this sage observation: "A lot of shavings don't make a good workman."

Until investors learn that he also serves who only stands and waits, the market for the counselors who let well enough alone will not be brisk.

Not all of the fault is with investors, of course. An obvious reason why the financial community does not advise and help investors to hold their good stocks is that Wall Street lives on activity. Every transaction carries a commission. Since the customers demand action, and since action pays the rent, why not give them what they want?

Even among the most high-minded in the financial community there is also the problem of never being sure of anything. Investors deal in the unknown future. A decision to ignore what seems like a passing threat could be disastrous. Getting out of a threatened stock until the situation has clarified is not only good for business but may save the customer's shirt as well. If the broker or investment counselor advises a sale he at least shows that he is aware of what is going on in the world. Not to act might well lose the account, especially if the stock acted badly for the next year or two.

In 1949 when I was a broker I lost a multi-million dollar

account by stubbornly insisting that stocks were cheap and should not be sold. Having gone on record in an article entitled "1929 Upside Down" in *Fortune* magazine, I could hardly have done anything else.

"Everyone tells me to get into cash," my client said at our last meeting. "What makes you think you know better?"

All I needed to do to get his order to sell thousands of shares was to fall into line. When I refused to do so my client left me and never came back.

My case was like that of the man who died in a traffic accident where he had the green light: "He was right, absolutely right, but just as dead as though he had been wrong."

And the next time I might be wrong.

CHAPTER XXIV

"Buy Right and Hold On" in Practice

Apart from a few individuals such as Paul Garrett, Mr. Darrell's unnamed client, and some of my old associates on the *Wall Street Journal,* I cannot cite any "track records" to prove the profitability of buying right and holding on. The management of any publicly owned fund that tried to operate that way would be fired for sleeping on the job. Only the most exceptional individuals have the will power to adopt such a course and hold to it through the bad years that punctuate almost every great stock price rise.

One fund manager who has come close to buying right and holding on is Hulbert W. Tripp, who retired last spring from the chairmanship of the investment committee of the University of Rochester.

While not subscribing wholly to the idea that buying right and holding on is the way to wealth, Mr. Tripp's actions speak louder than words. The 1970 annual investment report of the University of Rochester listed twenty-seven common stock holdings. More than half of them—fourteen of the twenty-seven—were the same companies that appeared in the University's 1966 investment report. At that time the portfolio held twenty-nine different stocks.

The small number of issues held reflects Mr. Tripp's belief that excessive diversification dodges rather than solves the investment problem. His emphasis on selection becomes clearer when the number of stocks held is related to the 1970 year-end value of the stock portfolio. The University's average investment per common stock was close to ten million dollars.

How has the policy paid off? Income for the fiscal year

ended June 30, 1970, as percentage of historical book value of endowment, was 11.12 percent. The comparable figure twenty years earlier was 4.31 percent. Historical book value of endowment increased 59.5 percent in that period, and actual income received rose 327.3 percent, the investment committee reported.

As of the start of 1951 less than 45 percent of the University's endowment fund investments was in common stocks. Twenty years later more than 72 percent of the market value of the portfolio was in equities.

Not until 1954 did the market value of the University's investments top $100 million. By the end of 1969 it was $415 million, and at the close of 1970, $376 million.

By his own method of "share accounting" to reflect investment performance, Mr. Tripp's score was a gain from $1.64 at the end of 1957 to $4.46 at the end of 1970. The figures are adjusted for new money bequests and grants.

Some all-common-stock funds have done much better. Scudder, Stevens & Clark's Special Fund, for example, rose from $10.33 to $76.29 in the same period. Value of shares received as capital gains distributions is included without allowance for capital gains taxes because the University of Rochester is tax exempt. But among balanced funds, and balanced institutional portfolios, the University of Rochester's "buying right and holding on" has produced outstanding results.

Mr. Tripp would not rely 100 percent on selection and retention, nor would I. "Beware the one-answer man!" is one of the soundest rules in the infinitely complex business of investing in the unknown and unknowable future. But one need not go overboard on the idea of buying right and holding on to benefit from it. Just a slight change in a golfer's grip and stance may improve his game. So a little more emphasis on buying for keeps, a little more determination not to be tempted to sell your winners just because they have gone up in price, may fatten your portfolio. It could cost you—as it has cost me—much less to try it than not to try it.

CHAPTER XXV

Do It Yourself?

Lawyers have a saying that anyone who tries to be his own lawyer has a fool for a client. But why should anyone who simply wants to buy right and hold on require professional assistance? Paul Garrett made a fortune on his own. Why can't you?

Maybe you can. Here are some of the questions you should ask yourself before you decide to do it yourself:

1. Do my education, training, and contacts in finance and industry equip me to do an above average job of investing my own money, or would I be playing the other fellow's game?

Life is infinitely complex. In civilized society there are countless ways to make money. Some people are lucky enough to make it without any special qualifications—their number is drawn in a lottery. But most of the time money is made by people who know more, work harder, think better than their rivals and competitors. Having such an advantage in one business, they stick to it rather than run the risks of competing in other activities where they have no edge.

About 5 P.M. one Saturday afternoon in the 1940s I had a question about Amerada Petroleum. Knowing that Amerada's president, Alfred Jacobsen, was a hard worker, I phoned the company headquarters on the chance someone might still be around. The Amerada switchboard was closed but Mr. Jacobsen answered the phone himself. Without even pausing to refer to any papers he replied to my questions about developments in the Williston basin, even giving me the depths of several wells currently being drilled, and the thickness of sands encountered. The incident helped me to understand why Amerada so often held strategically located acreage in new oil plays.

237

Paul Garrett could answer my first question affirmatively. Can you?

2. Am I prepared to do the vast amount of screening necessary to find a stock with 100-to-one potential? Mr. Garrett did not shut his eyes, stick a pin in the quotation page of *The New York Times* and hit Haloid. Friends in finance helped him winnow fifty stocks out of more than 50,000. Then he tirelessly reviewed and analyzed those fifty until he had narrowed his list to three. And finally he studied those three intensively until he chose Haloid, now Xerox. Am I ready and able to do that much work to get started? Or do I want to concentrate on my business, profession, or hobby and let someone else pick and choose investments for me?

3. Am I strong enough, financially and emotionally, to risk a major investment in one, or even two or three, stocks I have chosen myself? Or will I lose faith in my judgment the first time the market goes down, as it often does even in the case of stocks which ultimately advance 100 for one?

Polaroid declined from above 50 in 1946 to below 20 in 1949, giving rise to the saying, "Only the brave deserve the fare."

The old Packard automobile advertising slogan, "Ask the man who owns one," had a sound psychological basis. Most of us need the reassurance of company in new ventures we undertake. Successful "do it yourself" investors almost by definition have to go it alone. If the stock is popular the opportunity in it is certain to be reduced and may be gone. If it is being accumulated by a few farsighted professional investors you can be sure they are not going to encourage you—a non-client—to buy it in competition with them.

Ask yourself again: Can I walk alone when the going is rough?

4. What if despite all my efforts to buy right I end up buying wrong? Have I the facilities and the knowhow to watch the stock, or stocks, of my choice, and its competitors, closely enough to discover my error before all is lost?

Mr. Garrett's Haloid went his way almost from the first day. But many 100-to-one stocks have sorely tried the courage and patience of their owners before the big advance got under way. And many might-have-been 100-to-one stocks never made good at all.

Stubbornness is no substitute for savvy in investing.

Ask yourself: Do I know the difference between the courage of conviction and mulish balking at admitting and correcting errors?

Unless you can answer these questions in the affirmative, you should seek professional guidance. Where should you look for it?

How do you decide on your lawyer or your doctor? Your friends like him. They have gone to him for years with good results. Very good, for a starter.

How do you decide whether to stay with him? What should he do for you?

One of the simplest tests is "advantage-disadvantage," based not just on market prices but on earnings and dividends or interest. The only justifiable reason for making any change in your investments is to make you richer. Keep track of what is sold. Compare what you would have had if it had not been sold with what you do have after the sale. But don't do this for at least a year. It often takes that long, and sometimes two or three years, or even more, for good investment decisions to prove themselves. Finally, compare your overall results over several years with good general market averages such as those of Dow-Jones or *Standard & Poor's*. But don't compare bond investment results with a stock average, or stock investment performance with a bond average!

If after some such period you find that your purchases have gone up less than the stocks you sold ask your financial doctor to explain. He may be able to show you that you have gained in earnings and dividends even though the market has not yet recognized the improvement.

You have a right to expect that in toto changes effected in your security holdings will benefit you over a reasonable time span. If they do not, you should ask yourself whether you have been rocking the boat by ill-advised suggestions or demands. If you can honestly say you have not done so, you may very well conclude that you need another financial advisor.

A good way to check up on your financial doctor is to relate what he is making *on you* to what he is making *for you.* The West Coast widow who lost half her fortune while her broker-adviser was reaping a harvest in commissions on her account might have been saved at least a part of her suffering if she had used both "advantage-disadvantage" and "on you–for you" to appraise her financial doctor.

A third index of advisory efficiency, previously cited, is turnover. As we have seen, the stock market harbors hundreds of opportunities to make $1 grow into $100 by buying right and holding on. Many other stocks have missed 100 for one by less than a dollar. Hundreds more have risen 50 for one, and an even longer list has advanced twenty-five fold.

If your goal is to achieve maximum capital gain over the next ten or twenty years, every purchase should be made with the intention of holding on. Every sale should be recognized as a confession of error—a lost opportunity. There will be many such errors, of course. Making money is not easy and never will be. But it is helpful in trying to make money to have the right target, to keep one's thinking straight.

As a minimum, if you are to buy a stock that will increase 100 times in value in forty years, you must buy one that will go up at the compounded annual rate of 12.2 percent a year. If it falls short of that rate in one year it must make it up in another year.

Even if you are to buy a stock that will increase fiftyfold in value in forty years you must find one that will rise at the annual rate of 10-1/4 percent.

CHAPTER XXVI

A Sense of Values

All successful investing is based on foresight, but foresight alone is not enough. The other essential ingredient is a sense of values. Many a man is on relief because he paid too much for what he correctly foresaw. What does it profit a man to foresee that a stock will treble its earnings, if he pays four times as much for it as it is worth on its present earnings? Answer: Nothing, unless he can find someone else to sell it to for more than it is worth when the expected has come to pass.

Time is an often overlooked element in value. A dollar you will get five years from now is worth something like 78 cents today. A dollar you will get ten years from now may be worth 61 cents today. Neither figure allows for inflation. They are simply the amounts you would have to invest at 5 percent compounded annually, net after taxes, to have $1 five years or ten years from now. Discounted at 9 percent instead of 5 percent, a dollar you will get five years from now is worth 65 cents instead of 78 cents. A dollar due in ten years is worth only 42 cents now, instead of 61 cents. No wonder stocks selling on the basis of earnings expected five or ten years in the future declined in price as long-term interest rates rose in 1970!

Being right too soon is just as painful as being wrong. In fact it is one of the many ways to be wrong in investing.

Much money has been made by investors in the telephone television, and companies working on devices to translate the spoken word into print electronically. But much could have been lost, and doubtless some was lost, by being too soon. The ideas for all three developments are more than ninety years old. In a little book published in 1878, Professor A. E. Dolbear of Tufts College said:

"Mechanism is all that stands between us and aerial navigation; all that is necessary to reproduce human speech in writing; and all that is needed to realize completely the prophetic picture of the 'graphic,' of the orator who shall at the same instant address an audience in every city in the world."

The most important questions in investing are these:

1. How much will what I expect to happen increase the status quo value of the property I am thinking of buying?

2. How long will this take?

3. What is the present worth of the increase I expect?

4. How much of the expected value increase is already in the price I shall have to pay?

5. Is there enough difference between the value increase I expect and the expected increase I have to pay for now to give me a profit if I am right and a margin for error if I am wrong?

Status quo value means the value you would put on the property if things stayed the way they are. Anything you pay over that means that you are cutting the seller in on your flock of chickens before your eggs have hatched, and doing so at the very moment he stops bearing any of the risk. Thus stated, it seems as simple and as obvious as "A bird in the hand is worth two in the bush." Seriously asked and answered, our fifth question should help us avoid the mistake of swapping a bird in the hand for just one bird in the bush. If you think no one could be that foolish, take another look at the stock market. It happens there all the time.

You doubt it? Look at it this way: When you hand the grocer a dollar, he does not ask where you got it. A dollar from one stock or bond is worth exactly as much to him as a dollar from another. Why then do we pay more for dollars from one source than for dollars from another? The only reason that makes sense is that we expect the flow of dollars from the first source to catch up with and surpass the flow of dollars from the second source.

This may be easier to understand if we talk about hens and eggs. One flock of 100 hens lays eighty eggs a day. Another flock of the same size lays forty eggs a day. If we are interested only in getting the most eggs for the least money and if these suppositious hens scrounge for themselves so we need make no allowance for their care, the hens laying the larger number of eggs might seem to be worth twice as much as those laying the smaller number. If they were priced that way, a dollar would buy us as many eggs from one flock as from the other.

But let us suppose the forty-egg flock once laid eighty eggs a day. We might be fearful that the rate would drop some more. To protect ourselves against that possibility, we might offer to pay only a quarter as much for hens from the forty-egg flock as for hens from the eighty-egg flock. At that price, we should still be getting as many eggs for our money from the cheaper hens as from the dearer ones, even if the cheaper ones' rate of laying dropped from forty eggs to twenty a day. If we could buy those forty-egg hens at a fourth of the price of the eighty-egg hens, the seller in effect would be giving us free all the eggs they laid over twenty a day. It would cost us nothing if the forty-egg hens' rate of laying fell by half. If, instead of falling, their rate of laying stayed where it was, we should have twice the eggs we paid for. And if the forty-egg flock should increase its rate of laying to sixty or even eighty eggs a day, we should have three or four times as many eggs as we paid for. In other words, if the rate of laying remained unchanged, our "egg profit" would be 100 percent because we would be getting forty eggs a day when we had paid for only twenty. If we thought the chances of the flock's laying eighty eggs a day were equal to the chances of its stopping laying altogether, our opportunity-risk ratio would be 4-to-1.

Since no one can foretell the future with certainty, it makes sense to try to buy when the seller bears the brunt of possible adverse developments and to sell when the buyer is willing to transmute our hopes for the future into present cash.

In a free society, life is a series of trades. Each of us is continually exchanging whatever we have or can offer for what we can get from others. This is true whether we are ditchdiggers or symphony orchestra conductors, ministers of the gospel or call girls.

In such an exchange how do a few people get so much more than others? You have heard of the man who rode to the county fair bareback on a spavined old horse, and by trading briskly all day was able to drive home that night in a new carriage drawn by a spanking team of dapple grays? Life is like that. The boys who paid Tom Sawyer to let them whitewash the fence Tom had been ordered to paint made a voluntary exchange of their labor and their money for satisfactions that had not occurred to them until Tom pointed them out. That is salesmanship.

Few of us can say truthfully we have never made a bad trade. Almost all of us have paid for the privilege of whitewashing someone else's fences. Why do we do it?

Mostly, I suspect, it is because we do not stop to think. One of the most common ways of making a bad bargain is to buy something because it is cheap. But as John Ruskin said, "There's hardly anything that cannot be made a little worse and sold a little cheaper, and those who buy on price alone are that man's lawful prey." Nothing is cheap or dear except in relation to what we get for our money.

Those who buy on price alone may also be misled by high prices. Someone wrote a popular play years ago about a young man who breathed new life into an ailing soap business by cutting the cakes in half and doubling the price. Enough people inferred that the higher-priced soap must be better for their skins to make them avid victims of his trickery.

Some of us are misled by moving prices. We buy sugar, stocks, or Florida lots because today's price is higher than yesterday's, and hence tomorrow's price must be higher than today's. When we do this we are showing a lower order of intelligence than the poor fish I mentioned earlier. The fish is caught because he strikes at something moving, without stopping to examine it first. But a fish must play percentages. If he stopped to appraise every little thing that moved in his range of vision, he would starve to death. Not so with us. We do not have to bite on everything that moves, to stay out of the red—quite the contrary.

Other reasons why we make bad bargains in life reflect the truth that man does not live by bread alone. We buy things we do not want because of the ofttimes mistaken belief that doing so marks us as people of discernment. In other words we really are trying to bolster our tottering egos when we ape spending patterns of those whom we should like to be. It is almost impossible to make a good trade when we do not know—or admit to ourselves—what we want or why we want it.

Life is, of course, infinitely complex. A trade made to be in style, or to get ahead of the crowd, may be a good bargain in toto even though the goods or services bought may be worth less per se than we pay for them.

Many a seemingly bad bargain is made for the spiritual satisfaction of atonement. The stock market has its masochists as well as its egotists and egonomists. The stock market masochist seems to enjoy the pain of repeated losses, the more savage the better. His theme song is:

> I'm unlucky, the most unlucky man
> Born on Friday afternoon, on the thirteenth day
>   of June.
> If the sky were raining soup, I'd surely have a
>   fork.

The stock market egotists, much more numerous, would rather lose money on their own ideas than make it on anyone else's. I have dealt with the egonomists in the chapter on "The Almighty Ego vs. The Almighty Dollar."

In these, as in so many other ways, stock trading is more a study in psychology than in finance or economics. It sometimes seems to appeal most to those least qualified by temperament to succeed at it.

A true story illustrates what makes a good trader. At luncheon some years ago when Brunswick—a manufacturer of bowling lanes and automatic pinsetters—was a market darling, Peter Falk, investment manager for a big insurance group, remarked that he had just sold his Brunswick stock at $70 a share.

"Why?" I asked. All the news was good.

"Too many bowling alleys catching fire," was his reply.

Four years later Brunswick sold at $6 a share

CHAPTER XXVII

What Makes a Stock Grow

What makes a stock grow? Look for these possibilities:

1. Reinvesting earnings at a constant or rising rate of return on invested capital, above the average of around 9 percent currently. See chart below.

2. Investing borrowed money to earn more than the cost of borrowing.

3. Acquiring other companies by exchange of stock at lower price-earnings ratios for the companies acquired than for the company acquiring them.

4. Increasing sales without having to increase invested capital. The greatest opportunities to do this are found in companies operating far below capacity. New methods, increasing efficiency, may have the same effect.

5. Discoveries of natural resources, such as a great new oil field, gold mine, or nickel deposit.

6. New inventions, processes, or formulas for filling human needs not previously met, or for doing essential old jobs better, faster, and/or cheaper.

7. Contracts to operate facilities for others, usually governments.

8. Rising price-earnings ratios.

It is simple arithmetic that a company with a book value of $10 a share earning 15 percent on its invested capital will have a book value of $11.50 a share at the end of one year if it pays no dividends. At the end of the second year its book value will be $13.22 and at the end of the third year $15.20. In five years the company's book value will have doubled. In ten years it

246

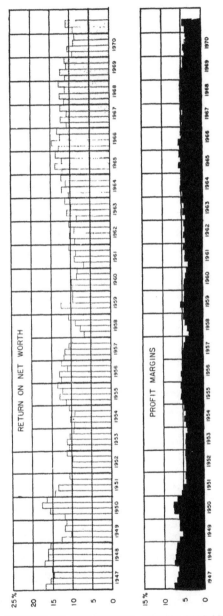

RETURN ON NET WORTH—PROFIT MARGINS
After Federal Income Taxes

will have quadrupled. In thirty-three years it will be up one hundredfold.

If the same company pays out a third of its earnings in dividends, reinvesting earnings at the rate of 10 percent of its book value each year, its book value will quadruple in fifteen years instead of ten. In 33 years it will be up 23.2 times instead of 100.

Obviously, dividends are an expensive luxury for the investor seeking maximum growth. If you must have income, don't expect your financial doctor to match the capital gains that might have been obtainable without dividends. When you buy a cow to milk, don't plan to race her against your neighbor's horse.

To the investor, borrowed money has a threefold significance in gauging a company's growth and prospects.

First let us assume that a company has $100 million book value on which it is earning 10 percent, no debt, and only one class of stock. Suppose the company borrows $50 million at 5 percent and invests the money to earn 10 percent, or $5 million a year. Since only $2.5 million is required for interest on the loan, the other $2.5 million is added to earnings on the stock. Return on book value thus rises to 12-1/2 percent from 10 percent, though the company still is earning at the same rate as before on its assets.

This is the first significance of the addition of borrowed money to a company's capitalization. Earnings may seem to improve without any improvement in the earning power of the assets employed in the business.

The second significance is that the improvement in earnings resulting from the addition of borrowed money to a company's capitalization may be non-recurring—there is a limit to how much any company can borrow at favorable rates. Once that much has been borrowed, no further help to earnings can be expected from borrowing.

The third significance is that all borrowing increases the risk in a business. One risk is that when the debt comes due interest rates may have risen so that the loan first made at 5 percent must be refinanced at 10 percent. Another risk is that the earning power of the assets may decline below the cost of the borrowed money so that the loan is carried at a loss. A third risk—the worst of all—is that the loan may come due at a time when the company is unable to refinance it. Result: Bankruptcy and reorganization, often turning the company over to its creditors.

Clearly rising earnings derived from rising debt are worth less than rising earnings derived from rising book value.

The game of acquiring companies at ten times their earnings by exchanging stock priced at 20 times earnings accounted for some of the glamour surrounding conglomerates a few years ago. To illustrate, suppose Company A with 5,000,000 shares selling 20 times $1 a share earnings on its reputation as a growth company exchanges its stock for all the 2,000,000 shares of Company B selling ten times $2 a share earnings. Assuming the merger is effected on the basis of equivalent market values, Company A has 40 percent more stock outstanding than before while the earnings of the new combination are 80 percent greater than before. Assuming both parts of the merged company continue to earn at unchanged rates, Company A reports a 12.8 percent rise in its per share earnings. Investors who watch earnings alone thus are misled into thinking that their growth stock has continued its growth when as a matter of fact the basic earning power of the constituent companies has shown no gain at all.

The concept of earnings growth resulting from putting idle plants to work is one of the easiest to understand. It is as simple as the statement that hotels make more money when they are fully occupied than they do when half their rooms are vacant. Opportunities to make money by that kind of growth usually are found only when an industry or the economy as a whole is in a depression.

A great deal of luck enters into making money on discoveries of natural resources, but it need not be all luck. As I have said before, companies actively prospecting are better bets than those which are not looking. And just as some hunters and some fishermen consistently do better than others, so some companies' exploration efforts seem to succeed oftener than others. Here as in so many other aspects of life it is good business to back a winner.

It used to be said in Socony-Vacuum (now Mobil Oil) that if we knew in advance that a research project was going to pay out, it was not research but only product development. If companies themselves don't know where their research will take them, how can the investor? Obviously he cannot. Here, as with discoveries of natural resources, making money depends on identifying in advance those organizations with the best records of incessant innovation, in the expectation that they will do it again and again. As for those unforeseeable new inventions, processes, and formulas that a free society is constantly producing, the only way I know for an investor to take advantage of them is to evaluate their potential as promptly as he can as soon as he hears of them. Few individuals are qualified to do that for themselves.

Rising price-earnings ratios often double and may triple or quadruple the stock market impact of rising earnings based on Points 1 to 7. To benefit by this factor the investor must have the good luck or good judgment to buy when a stock's price-earnings ratio is relatively low. A simple guide for the average investor is to watch the price-earnings ratio of the Dow-Jones Industrial Average, published in the *Wall Street Journal* and *Barron's* every Monday. If that is 15, and the stock he is contemplating buying is selling around the same figure or lower, he can assume safely that his enthusiasm for the stock is not widely shared. If his hopes for the stock to increase its earnings are justified, he can expect those earnings to command progressively higher multipliers as years go by. At 15 times earnings of $1 a share a stock will sell at $15. At 45 times earnings of $3 a share the same stock will sell at 135. Earnings triple but the market price rises ninefold.

CHAPTER XXVIII

Real Growth—How to Spot It and Evaluate It

Stocks go up and down for many reasons having nothing to do with changes in their earning power. Even their earnings may go up or down for many reasons having nothing to do with their earning power. Anyone hoping to make 100 for one in the stock market by way of earnings growth must focus on *earning power.*

What is the difference between *earnings* and *earning power?*

Earnings are simply reported profits no matter how obtained. As we have already seen, earnings may rise because of a sudden, non-recurring surge in demand, because of a price advance, because of a change in accounting practices, because of improvement in business generally which permits utilization of what previously was excess productive capacity. None of those reasons reflects earning power any more than the movement of a cork downstream attests its motive power.

Earning power is competitive strength. It is reflected in above-average rates of return on invested capital, above-average profit margins on sales, above-average rates of sales growth. It shows to best advantage in new or expanding markets.

Failure to distinguish between ephemeral earnings fluctuations and basic changes in earning power accounts for much over trading, many lost opportunities to make 100 for one in the stock market.

Too much research in Wall Street is not even directed at making this distinction. Why should it be? The customers all too often would not understand or appreciate it, and, even if they did, such research would generate much less business than focussing on probable earnings fluctuations. Making money by investing in earning power takes time.

How can the individual investor make this distinction between earnings and earning power? This is not a textbook on security analysis. Those who want one should read *Security Analysis* by Graham and Dodd. The rest should watch:

1. Sales growth.
2. Profit margins.
3. Rate of return on book value (equity).
4. Rate of return on invested capital.
5. Ratio of sales to invested capital.
6. Buildup of book value.

By recording these data year by year the understanding investor can alert himself to significant trend changes.

Many will prefer, and should prefer, to ask their financial advisors to focus on earning power for them. "A little learning is a dangerous thing." Like a passenger in a taxicab, the client's role is to say where he wants to go, and leave it to the driver to get there. But he should know when he is being taken the long way around.

If you doubt that your financial advisor is emphasizing competitive strength as much as you wish, you can either ask him to prove it or seek another doctor. The data are readily available from statistical services. Any well-equipped broker, banker, or investment counselor can supply them to answer a specific inquiry if your business warrants the cost of doing so.

Never look at the data for just one year. Trends are important. A ten-year record is desirable, both on an absolute and relative basis—relative to any good stock market average such as Dow-Jones or Standard & Poor's.

Real growth is as simple and certain as arithmetic *if* the book value of a stock is increased by retained earnings while the rate of return on invested capital remains constant. To illustrate, let us assume our company has a book value of $10 a share, with no senior securities, and is earning 15 percent on its invested capital. In this example, book value and invested capital per share are the same. Let us assume further that our company pays no dividends.

At the end of the first year per share book value will be $10 plus 15 percent of $10, or $11.50. At the end of the fifth year book value will be $20, and at the end of the tenth year $40. If our company can continue to earn at the same rate on its invested capital, its earnings in ten years will be four times the starting figure.

If our company pays out a third of its earnings in dividends, the amount plowed back each year will be 10 percent of per share book value. At that rate it will take nearly fifteen years, instead of ten, for book value and earnings to quadruple.

Earning at 15 percent and paying no dividends, our stock would grow one hundredfold in thirty-three years. Earning 15 percent and paying a third of earnings in dividends, our stock would take more than forty-eight years to multiply its assets and earnings by 100.

Tampax is an exceptionally good example of the arithmetic of growth because its figures are not complicated by debt or preferred stocks. Here they are, for the last fifteen years.

	Return on Invested Capital	Book Value per Share	Earnings per Share	Dividends per Share	Reinvested Earnings per Share
1970	36.7%	$17.89	$6.58	$4.10	$2.48
1969	34.6	15.41	5.34	3.55	1.79
1968	35.3	13.62	4.82	3.10	1.72
1967	36.6	11.90	4.36	2.80	1.56
1966	36.8	10.34	3.81	2.50	1.31
1965	37.6	9.03	3.39	2.00	1.39
1964	36.0	7.63	2.15	1.75	.40
1963	34.1	6.63	2.26	1.35	.91
1962	37.4	4.92	1.84	1.18	.66
1961	37.9	4.26	1.61	1.03	.58
1960	38.8	3.67	1.42	.93	.49
1959	37.4	3.35	1.25	.80	.45
1958	37.5	2.90	1.08	.70	.38
1957	39.0	2.52	.97	.63	.34
1956	39.7	2.18	.86	.56	.30

Any such stock will grow as fast as its book value grows IF its rate of return on invested capital holds steady.

Between the end of 1956 and the end of 1970 Tampax's book value increased from $2.18 a share to $17.89 a share, or 8.2 times the starting figure. In the same period earnings rose 7.6 times. The difference was due to a decline in the rate of return from 39.7 percent at the start to 36.7 percent in the last year. Had the rate of return stayed at 39.7 percent, Tampax's 1970 earnings would have been $7.10 a share, instead of $6.58. Earnings of $7.10 would have been 8.2 times 1956 earnings of 86 cents, the same as the increase in book value, of course. (Share earnings figures have been adjusted for the 3-for-1 split in 1962.)

Almost all of the $15.71 increase in book value—$14.46 to be exact—came from retained earnings, the difference between earnings a share and dividends a share. Obviously if Tampax had reduced its dividends each year by enough to increase retained earnings by 50 percent, Tampax's earnings would have grown 50 percent faster than they did—assuming that Tampax could have invested the additional money at the same rates of return.

Tampax is also a good example of the arithmetic of investor psychology. In 1956 Tampax stock sold at a low of 9-1/2 and a high of 11.66. Those prices were 11 and 13-1/2 times 1956 earnings. At 11 times 1970 earnings Tampax's price would have been 76 instead of its actual 1970 low of 146. At 13-1/2 times 1970 earnings, Tampax's price would have been 89 instead of its actual 1970 high of 228. The difference was entirely due to investor willingness to pay for anticipated Tampax growth further into the future than before.

At its 1971 high of 329 Tampax was selling at 50 times its 1970 earnings.

In looking for stocks that might someday sell 100 times your purchase price, the price-earnings ratio at the time you buy is highly important. If you can foresee the price-earnings ratio rising from 10 to 40, your stock's earnings need rise only to 25 times your starting level to give you $100 for $1 on your purchase. If, on the other hand, you buy at 40 times earnings and encounter a decline to 20 times earnings, your starting level of earnings must be multiplied by 200 to give you $100 for $1 on your investment.

It does not denigrate Tampax's business prospects to say that further advances in the price of the stock seem likely to depend on further gains in sales and earnings with comparatively little if any help from further rise in its price-earnings ratio.

Two of the most important questions in buying for great growth are these:

1. How high and strong is the company's "gate" against competition? If others can enter the business easily, the above average rate of return is bound to be whittled down.

2. How good are the prospects for sales growth? No matter how high the rate of return, the company cannot grow by plowing back earnings if it already has enough capacity to supply all foreseeable markets.

Tampax's sales doubled in six years, from 1964 to 1970.

One last lesson from Tampax is that the way to buy high yields is to buy growing stocks. Tampax at its 1956 high yielded 4.8 percent on dividends paid that year. But the buyer who held on had a yield of 35 percent in 1970.

How can you evaluate such a stock?

The mathematically inclined have developed tables which help to quantify assumptions about the unknown future—assumptions regarding interest rates and the earnings of industry generally, assumptions about taxes. Essentially what they do is to divide estimates by guesses and carry the answers out to the fourth decimal place.

Stock traders sometimes proceed on a simpler basis. They predict that a stock's earnings will grow another year at 15 percent. They predict that with a continuance of that growth the price-earnings ratio will hold up, or increase. Having made those two assumptions, they come to the inevitable conclusion that the price of the stock a year hence will be up 15 percent or more.

It is an easy step from making such assumptions for another year to making them for another two years, three years, five years, or even ten years. The logic is irrefutable if you accept the assumptions.

That reminds me of a picture showing a Chinese wise man

in his study looking up from his figures to exclaim, "I have proved it. The Mongols cannot get through the Great Wall." Behind him stands a tight-lipped Mongol warrior, sword upraised, ready to cut off his head.

What mathematics cannot do, common sense often can. In many instances 100-to-one stocks have been available before their great advance at no higher price-earnings ratios than the general market. In more cases, prices of these incipient superstars have discounted no more than the earnings gain that might have been foreseen in the next year or two. To the buyer with vision such opportunities are too great to require mathematical analysis. The spread between what the buyer expects and what the stock market is discounting is large enough to cover any probable error in the buyer's expectations.

Much can never be foreseen or even imagined. The one way to benefit by it is to buy the best stock or stocks you can with no intention of selling them until they turn bad. If history is any guide, some will end up in your high bracket estate.

By a long, circuitous route we have come around to our starting point.

In the last forty years the stock market has harbored hundreds of opportunities to turn $10,000 into a million.

Many other stocks are growing at rates which if continued would produce the same one hundredfold appreciation in the next two, three, or four decades. In a free and research-oriented society such opportunities seem bound to recur again and again.

The two reasons so few of us profit by 100-to-one stocks are first that we do not try to do so and second that even when we are wise or lucky enough to buy one we do not hold on.

To buy right requires vision and courage—faith that is evidence of things not seen, things not susceptible of mathematical proof.

To realize 100 for one requires patience, extraordinary tenacity—the will to hold on.

In *Alice in Wonderland* one had to run fast in order to stand still. In the stock market, the evidence suggests, one who buys right must stand still in order to run fast.

Appendix

During 1971 each of the following securities sold for more than 100 times the price at which it could have been bought in the year indicated. The table is arranged alphabetically according to present names, which are shown in CAPITAL LETTERS.

ABBOTT LABORATORIES
One share 1934 = 50.4 shares 1971
1934 cost $40. 1971 value $4,302

Abitibi Power & Paper Common —ABITIBI PAPER
One share 1942 # = 6 shares 1971*
1942 cost 50 cents. 1971 value $52
    # Abitibi Power & Paper common
    *Abitibi Paper common

Abitibi Power & Paper Co., Ltd. 6% Pfd. ($100 Par)— ABITIBI PAPER
One share 1940# = 40.6 shares 1971*
1940 cost $2. 1971 value $355†
    # Abitibi Power & Paper Co., Ltd. 6% Pfd.

* Abitibi Paper common
† Assumes $100 cash received July 30, 1954, was reinvested in Abitibi common at high of ensuing week.

Abitibi Power & Paper Co. Ltd. 7% Pfd. ($100 Par)— ABITIBI PAPER
One share 1943 # = 183.6 shares 1971 *
1943 cost $12.50. 1971 value $1,606 †
    # Abitibi Power & Paper Co., Ltd. 7% Pfd.
    * Abitibi Paper common
    † Assumes $187.50 cash received August 1, 1949, was reinvested in Abitibi common at $12.25 a share, high for the week ended August 5, 1949.

257

Aetna Casualty & Surety—
AETNA LIFE & CASUALTY
One share 1932 # = 28½
shares 1971 *
1932 cost $15. 1971 value
$1,998
   # Aetna Casualty & Surety
   * Aetna Life & Casualty

Aetna Life—AETNA LIFE &
CASUALTY
One share 1932 # = 13⅓
shares 1971 *
1932 cost $8.25. 1971 value
$934
   # Aetna Life
   * Aetna Life & Casualty

AIR PRODUCTS &
CHEMICALS
One share 1946 = 2.5 shares
1971
1946 cost $1. # 1971 value $144
   # Reynolds & Co., New York,
   offered 150,000 shares at $1 a
   share on May 6, 1946.

ALLEGHANY CORP. common
One share 1941 = one share
1971
1941 cost 13 cents. 1971 value
$18

Amerada Corp.—AMERADA
HESS
One share 1933 # = 36 shares
1971 *
1933 cost $18.50. 1971 value
$2,574
   # Amerada Corp.
   * Amerada Hess

AMERICAN AIRLINES
One share 1938 = 20 shares 1971
1938 cost $8. 1971 value $877

AMERICAN CHAIN & CABLE
One share 1933 = 6.4 shares

1971
1933 cost $1.63. 1971 value $194

American Beet Sugar—
AMERICAN CRYSTAL
SUGAR
One share 1932 # = 3 shares
1971 *
1932 cost 25 cents. 1971 value
$80
   # American Beet Sugar
   * American Crystal Sugar

AMERICAN CYANAMID
One share 1932 # = 8 shares
1971 *
1932 cost $1.63. 1971 value $303
   # Class B
   * Common

Amerex Holding Corp.—
AMERICAN EXPRESS
One share 1948 # = 18 shares
1971 *
1948 cost $21.50. 1971 value
$2,448
   # Amerex Holding Corp.
   * American Express

AMERICAN HOME
PRODUCTS
One share 1938 = 36 shares 1971
1938 cost $30.75. 1971 value
$3,384

Brach (E. J.) & Sons—
AMERICAN HOME
PRODUCTS
One share 1933 # = 8.4 shares
1971 *
1933 cost $3.75. 1971 value
$789
   # Brach (E. J.) & Sons
   * American Home Products

International Vitamin—
AMERICAN HOME
PRODUCTS

One share 1941 # = 4.5 shares
1971 *
1941 cost $3.13. 1971 value $423
  # International Vitamin
  * American Home Products

Miller Wholesale Drug—
AMERICAN HOME
PRODUCTS
One share 1940 # = 7.4 shares
1971 *
1940 cost $4.38. 1971 value $695
  # Miller Wholesale Drug
  * American Home Products

American Constitution Fire
Insurance—AMERICAN
INTERNATIONAL GROUP
One share 1932 #   = 11.4 shares
1971 *
1932 cost $6. 1971 value $1,105
  # American Constitution Fire
  Insurance
  * American International
  Group

American Home Fire Assurance
—AMERICAN
INTERNATIONAL GROUP
One share 1949 # = 10.9 shares
1971 *
1949 cost $7. 1971 value $1,043
  # American Home Fire
  Assurance
  * American International
  Group

Globe & Rutgers Fire Insurance
—AMERICAN
INTERNATIONAL GROUP
One share 1949 # = 32.8 shares
1971 *
1949 cost $27. 1971 value $3,198
  # Globe & Rutgers Fire
  Insurance
  * American International
  Group

AMERICAN INVESTMENT
CO. OF ILLINOIS
One share 1933 = 17.5 shares
1971
1933 cost $3. 1971 value $347

AMERICAN
MANUFACTURING
One share 1935 = 16 shares
1971
1935 cost $3.50. 1971 value $712

Air Investors—AMERICAN
MANUFACTURING
One share 1942 # =2.5 shares
1971 *
1942 cost 94 cents. 1971 value
$111
  # Air Investors
  * American Manufacturing

American Laboratories—
AMERICAN MEDICAL
INTERNATIONAL
One share 1964 # = 3.4 shares
1971*
1964 cost 75 cents. 1971 value
$129
  # American Laboratories
  * American Medical International

AMERICAN METAL CLIMAX
One share 1933 = 8.44 shares
1971
1933 cost $3.13. 1971 value $315

Ayrshire Patoka Collieries—
AMERICAN METAL CLIMAX
One share 1942 # =13.5 shares
1971 *
1942 cost $4. 1971 value $504
  # Ayrshire Patoka Collieries
  * American Metal Climax

Electric Shovel Coal Preferred—
AMERICAN METAL CLIMAX
One share 1942 # =27.1 shares
1971 *

1942 cost $6. 1971 value $1,012
  # Electric Shovel Coal Pre-
  ferred
  * American Metal Climax

Panhandle Producing &
Refining 8% Preferred—
AMERICAN PETROFINA
CLASS A
One share 1940 # = 54.4 shares
1971 *
1940 cost $13. 1971 value
$1,598
  # Panhandle Producing &
  Refining 8% Preferred
  * American Petrofina Class A

AMERICAN POWER &
LIGHT $6 Preferred
One share 1935 = (in 1971)
                        4.9 shares (a)
                        1.2 shares (b)
                        3.7 shares (c)
                        8.9 shares (d)
                        2.3 shares (e)
1935 cost $10.13. 1971 value
$1,160
(a) Florida Power & Light
common
(b) Minnesota Power & Light
common
(c) Montana Power common
(d) Texas Utilities common
(e) Washington Water Power
common

AMERICAN SEATING
One share 1933 = 6.4 shares
1971
1933 cost 88 cents. 1971 value
$138

American Machine & Metals
—AMETEK, INC.
One share 1933 # = 8 shares
1971 *
1933 cost 75 cents. 1971 value

$153
  # American Machine &
  Metals
  * Ametek, Inc.

ANHEUSER-BUSCH
One share 1935 = 236.7 shares
1971
1935 cost $98. 1971 value
  $13,610

Rustless Iron & Steel—
ARMCO STEEL
One share 1935 # = 4.8 shares
1971 *
1935 cost 75 cents. 1971 value
$111
  # Rustless Iron & Steel
  * Armco Steel

ARMSTRONG CORK
One share 1933 = 12 shares
1971
1933 cost $4.13. 1971 value
$550

Noblitt-Sparks Industries—
ARVIN INDUSTRIES
One share 1933 # = 23.3 shares
1971 *
1933 cost $9.50. 1971 value
$955
  # Noblitt-Sparks Industries
  * Arvin Industries

Warren Brothers—ASHLAND
OIL & REFINING
One share 1941 # = 1.3 shares
1971 *
1941 cost 38 cents. 1971 value
$39
  # Warren Brothers
  * Ashland Oil & Refining

ASSOCIATED DRY GOODS
One share 1942 = 9 shares 1971
1942 cost $4.25. 1971 value $535

Pan-American Petroleum (of
Cal.) Cv. 6s 1940 (Certificates
of Deposit)
—ATLANTIC RICHFIELD
One $1,000 bond 1932 # = 147.7
shares 1971*
1932 cost $40. 1971 value
$11,557
  #Pan-American Petroleum
  (of Cal.) Cv. 6s 1940
  *Atlantic Richfield

Richfield Oil of California 1st
Cv. 6s 1944 (Certificates of
Deposit)
—ATLANTIC RICHFIELD
One $1,000 bond 1932 # = 164.9
shares 1971*
1932 cost $50. 1971 value
$12,903
  #Richfield Oil 1st Cv. 6s
  1944
  *Atlantic Richfield

Venezuelan Petroleum—
ATLANTIC RICHFIELD
One share 1941 # = 1$\frac{1}{16}$
shares 1971*
1941 cost 75 cents. 1971 value
$83 †
  #Venezuelan Petroleum
  *Atlantic Richfield
  †Assuming acceptance of
  1967 offer of Atlantic Richfield
  $3 convertible preference.

Sloss-Sheffield Steel & Iron—
A-T-O, INC.
One share 1932 # = 5 shares
1971*
+ $500 A-T-O debenture 6s,
1988
+ 20 A-T-O warrants
1932 cost $3.75. 1971 value
$411 †
  #Sloss-Sheffield Steel & Iron

*A-T-O, Inc.
†Assuming sale of A-T-O
debenture 6s, 1988, at 68 bid,
when received.

AUTOMATIC DATA
PROCESSING
One share 1965 = 9 shares 1971
1965 cost $7. 1971 value $704

AVON PRODUCTS
One share 1955* = 84.2 shares
1971
1955 cost $83. 1971 value
$9,430
  *Before 2-for-1 split

BABCOCK & WILCOX
One share 1934 = 50.1 shares
1971
1934 cost $18.50. 1971 value
$2,135

Pyrene Manufacturing—BAKER
INDUSTRIES
One share 1940 # = 22.9 shares
1971*
1940 cost $4.75. 1971 value $543
  #Pyrene Manufacturing
  *Baker Industries

U.S. Bobbin & Shuttle—BAKER
INDUSTRIES
One share 1941 # = 5.4 shares
1971*
1941 cost $1. 1971 value $128
  #U.S. Bobbin & Shuttle
  *Baker Industries

U.S. Bobbin & Shuttle
Preferred—BAKER
INDUSTRIES
One share 1940 # = 87.3 shares
1971*
1940 cost $20. 1971 value $2,073
  #U.S. Bobbin & Shuttle
  preferred
  *Baker Industries

BALDWIN (D.H.) CO.
One share 1939 = 8.2 shares
1971
1939 cost $2.88. 1971 value
$463

Virginia Iron, Coal & Coke—
BATES MANUFACTURING
One share 1943 # = 7.2 shares
1971 *
1943 cost $1. 1971 value $143
  # Virginia Iron, Coal & Coke
  * Bates Manufacturing

Virginia Iron, Coal & Coke 5%
Pfd.—BATES
MANUFACTURING
One share 1942 # = 101 shares
1971 *
1942 cost $14. 1971 value
$2,007
  # Virginia Iron, Coal & Coke
  5% Pfd.
  * Bates Manufacturing

BAXTER LABORATORIES
One share 1956 = 32 shares
1971
1956 cost $11.25. 1971 value
$1,260

BEECH AIRCRAFT
One share 1938 = 10.7 shares
1971
1938 cost $1.25. 1971 value $231

Spiegel, May, Stern—
BENEFICIAL CORP.
One share 1933 # = 5.9 shares
1971 *
1933 cost $1. 1971 value $402
  # Spiegel, May, Stern
  * Beneficial Corp.

Western Auto Supply Class
A—BENEFICIAL CORP.
One share 1932 # = 13.7 shares
1971 *

1932 cost $5.13. 1971 value $935
  # Western Auto Supply Class
  A
  * Beneficial Corp.

BLACK & DECKER
One share 1944 = 22.7 shares
1971
1944 cost $16.50. 1971 value
$1,835

Electric Bond & Share—BOISE
CASCADE
One share 1942 # = 1.3 shares
1971 * plus nontaxable dividends
in utility common stocks
1942 cost 88 cents. 1971 value
$115
  # Electric Bond & Share
  * Boise Cascade

Minnesota & Ontario Paper 6s
Series A, 1931–45—BOISE
CASCADE
One bond 1932 # = 110.3 shares
1971 *
1932 cost $40. 1971 value
$5,501 †
  # Minnesota & Ontario Paper
  * Boise Cascade
  † $500 5% bonds and $7.50
  cash received in 1941

BORG-WARNER
One share 1932 = 12 shares
1971
1932 cost $3.38. 1971 value
$387

Byron Jackson—BORG-
WARNER
One share 1932 # = 2.2 shares
1971 *
1932 cost 50 cents. 1971 value
$70
  # Byron Jackson
  * Borg-Warner

BRIGGS & STRATTON
One share 1933 = 24 shares 1971
1933 cost $7.25. 1971 value $888

Broadway Department Store—
BROADWAY-HALE STORES
One share 1941 # = 10⅛
shares 1971*
1941 cost $3.63. 1971 value $489
  # Broadway Department
  Store
  * Broadway-Hale Stores

Emporium Capwell—BROAD-
WAY-HALE STORES
One share 1934 # = 10.9 shares
1971*
1934 cost $5. 1971 value $527
  # Emporium Capwell
  * Broadway-Hale Stores

Kinney (G. R.) & Co.—BROWN
SHOE
One share 1943 # = 6.1 shares
1971*
1943 cost $1.88. 1971 value $256
  # Kinney (G. R.) & Co.
  * Brown Shoe

Aloe (A. S.) Co.—BRUNSWICK
One share 1934# = 27.7 shares
1971*
1934 cost $9. 1971 value
$1,073
  # Aloe (A. S.) Co.
  * Brunswick

Brunswick-Balke-Collender—
BRUNSWICK
One share 1938 # = 19.4 shares
971*
1938 cost $5.50. 1971 value $751
  # Brunswick-Balke-Collender
  * Brunswick Corp.

BULOVA WATCH
One share 1933 = 9.9 shares
971

1933 cost 88 cents. 1971 value
$271

Burlington Mills—
BURLINGTON INDUSTRIES
One share 1937 # = 13.2 shares
1971*
1937 cost $5.75. 1971 value $656
  # Burlington Mills
  * Burlington Industries

Pacific Mills—BURLINGTON
INDUSTRIES
One share 1933 # = 14.5 shares
1971*
1933 cost $6. 1971 value $721
  # Pacific Mills
  * Burlington Industries

CARNATION COMPANY
One share 1938 = 18.4 shares
1971
1938 cost $17.88. 1971 value
$1,872

CARRIER CORP.
One share 1932 = 6.6 shares
1971
1932 cost $2.50. 1971 value $320

Columbia River Packers—
CASTLE & COOKE
One share 1939 # = 15.9 shares
1971*
1939 cost $4. 1971 value $429
  # Columbia River Packers
  * Castle & Cooke

CATERPILLAR TRACTOR
One share 1933 = 25.9 shares
1971
1933 cost $5.50. 1971 value
$1,447

CELANESE CORP.
One share 1932 = 2.8 shares
1971
1932 cost $1.25. 1971 value $223

Tubize Chatillon Class A—
CELANESE
One share 1932 # = 6.6 shares
1971 *
1932 cost $1. 1971 value $523
   # Tubize Chatillon Class A
   * Celanese

CESSNA AIRCRAFT
One share 1941 = 14½ shares
1971
1941 cost $3.75. 1971 value
$418

Parmelee Transportation—
CHECKER MOTORS
One share 1942 # = 2.8 shares
1971 *
1942 cost 32 cents. 1971 value
$81
   # Parmelee Transportation
   * Checker Motors

CHICAGO PNEUMATIC
TOOL
One share 1933 = 7.6 shares
1971
1933 cost $2.13. 1971 value $343

CHICAGO RIVET &
MACHINE
One share 1932 = 11¼ shares
1971
1932 cost $3. 1971 value $337

National Automotive Fibres A—
CHRIS-CRAFT INDUSTRIES
One share 1932 # = 5.6 shares
1971 *
1932 cost 50 cents. 1971 value
$55
   # National Automotive Fibres
   * Chris-Craft Industries

CITIES SERVICE
One share 1942 = 5.7 shares
1971
1942 cost $2.13. 1971 value $282

Tennessee Corp.—CITIES

SERVICE
One share 1934 # = 7.5 shares
1971 *
1934 cost $3.13. 1971 value $372
   # Tennessee Corp.
   * Cities Service

CLARK EQUIPMENT
One share 1939 = 33 shares 1971
1939 cost $15. 1971 value
$1,637

Cliffs Corp.—CLEVELAND
CLIFFS
One share 1933 # = 4.5 shares
1971 *
1933 cost $3.50. 1971 value $357
   # Cliffs Corp.
   * Cleveland Cliffs

CLOROX
One share 1942 = 44.3 shares
1971
1942 cost $24.00. 1971 value
$2,696

Grocery Store Products—
CLOROX
One share 1942 # = 2.5 shares
1971 *
1942 cost 88 cents. 1971 value
$145
   # Grocery Store Products
   * Clorox

Van Raalte Co.—CLUETT,
PEABODY & CO.
One share 1933 # = 7.3 shares
1971 *
1933 cost $1.63. 1971 value $198
   # Van Raalte Co.
   * Cluett, Peabody & Co.

Continental Assurance—CNA
FINANCIAL
One share 1943 # = 172.7 shares
1971 *
1943 cost $40.50. 1971 value
$4,403

#Continental Assurance
* CNA Financial

Continental Casualty—CNA
FINANCIAL
One share 1933 # = 29.6 shares
1971 *
1933 cost $5. 1971 value $754
  # Continental Casualty
  * CNA Financial

COLLINS & AIKMAN
One share 1933 = 12 shares 1971
1933 cost $3. 1971 value $372

Henry Holt & Co.—COLUMBIA
BROADCASTING SYSTEM
One share 1953 # = 15.8 shares
1971 *
1953 cost $7.88. 1971 value $835†
  # Henry Holt & Co.
  * Columbia Broadcasting
  System
  † Including Viacom Interna-
  tional distribution.

International Combustion
Engineering Cv. Pfd. Ctfs.—
COMBUSTION ENGINEER-
ING INC.
10 shares plus $1 in 1933 # =
18.9 shares 1971 *
1933 cost $11. 1971 value
$1,332
  # International Combustion
  Engineering Cv. Pfd. Ctfs.
  * Combustion Engineering Inc.

Connecticut General Life
Insurance—CONNECTICUT
GENERAL INSURANCE
One share 1943 # = 48 shares
1971 *
1943 cost $27.63. 1971 value
$3,756
  # Connecticut General Life
  Insurance
  * Connecticut General
  Insurance

Truax Traer Coal—
CONSOLIDATION COAL
One share 1932 # = 2.4 shares
1971 *
1932 cost 25 cents. 1971 value
$61 †
  # Traux Traer Coal
  * Consolidation Coal
  † Taking 1966 liquidating
  distributions at then market
  values, plus five years interest
  compounded annually at 5
  percent.

COOPER INDUSTRIES
One share 1937 = 10 shares 1971
1937 cost $3.50. 1971 value $375

COPPER RANGE
One share 1932 = 3.3 shares
1971
1932 cost $1.13. 1971 value $139

CROWN CORK & SEAL
One share 1932 = 40 shares 1971
1932 cost $7.88. 1971 value $935

CROWN ZELLERBACH
One share 1933 = 4.9 shares
1971
1933 cost $1. 1971 value $186

Crum & Forster Insurance
Shares—
CRUM & FORSTER
One share 1932 # = 12.1 shares
1971*
  1932 cost $3. 1971 value $428
  # Crum & Forster Insurance
  Shares
  * Crum & Forster

CUTLER-HAMMER
One share 1932 = 8 shares 1971
1932 cost $3.50. 1971 value $362

Thatcher Manufacturing—
DART INDUSTRIES
One share 1932 # = 5.2 shares
1971 *

1932 cost $2. 1971 value $252
  #Thatcher Manufacturing
  *Dart Industries

Allen Industries—DAYCO
One share 1933 # = 16.4 shares
1971*
1933 cost $1. 1971 value $358
  #Allen Industries
  *Dayco

Dayton Rubber Manufacturing
Class A—DAYCO
One share 1933 # = 5½ shares
1971*
1933 cost $1. 1971 value $119
  #Dayton Rubber Manufactur-
  ing Class A
  *Dayco

DEERE & COMPANY
One share 1933 = 12.3 shares
1971
1933 cost $5.75. 1971 value $668

DELTA AIR LINES
One share 1942 = 28.1 shares
1971
1942 cost $8. 1971 value $1,443

Chicago & Southern Air Lines
—DELTA AIR LINES
One share 1942 # = 11.2 shares
1971*
1942 cost $2. 1971 value $575
  #Chicago & Southern Air
  Lines
  *Delta Air Lines

DEVELOPMENT CORP. OF
AMERICA
One share 1967 = 2.2 shares
1971
1967 cost 38 cents. 1971 value
$74

Shamrock Oil & Gas—
DIAMOND SHAMROCK
One share 1935 # = 4.5 shares

1971*
1935 cost 75 cents. 1971 value
$113
  #Shamrock Oil & Gas
  *Diamond Shamrock

DIEBOLD, INC.
One share 1950 = 28.1 shares
1971
1950 cost $11.63. 1971 value
$1,594

DISNEY (WALT)
PRODUCTIONS INC.
One share 1954 = 11.4 shares
1971
1954 cost $3.63. 1971 value
$1,630

DR. PEPPER
One share 1935 = 48 shares
1971
1935 cost $16. 1971 value $1,938

Empire Trust Co.—DOME
PETROLEUM, LTD.
One share 1943 = 99.1 shares
1971*
1943 cost $43.50. 1971 value
$4,681
  #Empire Trust Co.
  *Dome Petroleum, Ltd.

Smith (Howard) Paper Mills—
DOMTAR
One share 1933 # = 14 shares
1971*
1933 cost $1.13. 1971 value $218
  #Smith (Howard) Paper Mills
  *Domtar—Exchange of shares
  not open to U.S. residents

St. Lawrence Corp.—DOMTAR
One share 1942 # = 5.5 shares
1971*
1942 cost 75 cents. 1971 value
$85
  #St. Lawrence Corp.
  *Domtar

DOW CHEMICAL
One share 1932 = 23.9 shares 1971
1932 cost $21.13. 1971 value $2,854

Dobeckman—DOW CHEMICAL
One share 1941 # = 4 shares 1971*
1941 cost $2.50. 1971 value $313
 #Dobeckman
 *Dow Chemical

S. R. Dresser Manufacturing Class B—DRESSER INDUSTRIES
One share 1933 = 8 shares 1971
1933 cost $2.13. 1971 value $300

Symington Class A—DRESSER INDUSTRIES
One share 1932 # = 1.4 shares 1971*
1932 cost 50 cents. 1971 value $52
 # Symington Class A
 *Dresser Industries

EASON OIL COMPANY
One share 1942 = 4 shares 1971
1942 cost 38 cents. 1971 value $100.

Eastern Gas & Fuel 6% Pfd.—EASTERN GAS & FUEL
One share 1943 # = 45.2 shares 1971*
1943 cost $19.75. 1971 value $2,322
 #6% Preferred
 *Eastern Gas & Fuel common

West Virginia Coal & Coke—EASTERN GAS & FUEL
One share 1944 # = 9.8 shares 1971*
1944 cost $5.13. 1971 value $503
plus 50 †
$553

#West Virginia Coal & Coke
*Eastern Gas & Fuel
†Aggregate of nontaxable distributions

EASTMAN KODAK
One share 1933 = 64.8 shares 1971
1933 cost $46. 1971 value $6,480

Eaton Manufacturing—EATON YALE & TOWNE
One share 1933 # = 8 shares 1971*
1933 cost $3.13. 1971 value $358
 #Eaton Manufacturing
 *Eaton Yale & Towne

EDISON BROS. STORES
One share 1934 = 27.2 shares 1971
1934 cost $8. 1971 value $1,199

Indiana Steel Products—ELECTRONIC MEMORIES & MAGNETICS
One share 1940 # = 9½ shares 1971*
1940 cost $1.50. 1971 value $166
 #Indiana Steel Products
 *Electronic Memories & Magnetics

EMERSON ELECTRIC
One share 1949 = 11.3 shares 1971
1949 cost $8.50. 1971 value $912

EMERY AIR FREIGHT
One share 1955 = 10.6 shares 1971
1955 cost $7.88. 1971 value $829

Savage Arms—EMHART
One share 1933 # = 6.2 shares 1971*
1933 cost $2.25. 1971 value $275
 #Savage Arms
 *Emhart

Engineers Public Service—
GULF STATES UTILITIES
EL PASO ELECTRIC
VIRGINIA ELECTRIC &
POWER
One share common # plus
.1137375 share
$5 preferred # in 1934 = in 1971:
5 shares Gulf States Utilities
2.55 shares El Paso Electric
8.4 shares Virginia Electric &
Power
$1.04 cash
1934 cost $3.15. 1971 value $387
  #Engineers Public Service

EVANS PRODUCTS
One share 1933 = 13.5 shares
1971
1933 cost 88 cents. 1971 value
 $367

EX-CELL-O
One share 1934 = 15.9 shares
1971
1934 cost $3.75. 1971 value $389

Fairchild Aviation—
FAIRCHILD CAMERA
One share 1938 # = 6.6 shares
1971*
1938 cost $2. 1971 value $320
  #Fairchild Aviation
  *Fairchild Camera

FALCONBRIDGE NICKEL
One share 1940 = one share
1971
1940 cost $1.43.# 1971 value
$153#
  # U.S. funds

Ventures, Ltd.—FALCON-
BRIDGE NICKEL
One share 1940 # = 1.04 shares
1971*
1940 cost $1.57.† 1971 value
$159†

#Ventures, Ltd.
*Falconbridge Nickel
†U.S. funds

FANSTEEL
One share 1932 = 4.2 shares
1971
1932 cost 25 cents. 1971 value
$67

FEDDERS
One share 1945 = 20 shares 1971
1945 cost $9.50. 1971 value
$1,000

FEDERAL-MOGUL
One share 1934 = 11.8 shares
1971
1934 cost $3. 1971 value $377

FEDERATED DEPARTMENT
STORES
One share 1933 = 19.2 shares
1971
1933 cost $7.50. 1971 value
$1,027

FIDELITY UNION LIFE
INSURANCE
One share 1949 = 100 shares
1971
1949 cost $42. 1971 value
$4,425

FLYING TIGER LINE
One share 1949 = 2.5 shares
1971
1949 cost $1. 1971 value $123

North American Car—FLYING
TIGER LINE
One share 1942 # = 6.4 shares
1971* plus 3 warrants
1942 cost $3.88. 1971 value $409
  #North American Car
  *Flying Tiger Line

Food Machinery—FMC
One share 1934 # = 40.2 shares

1971 *
1934 cost $10.50. 1971 value $1,226
  # Food Machinery
  * FMC

United Chemicals—FMC
One share 1939 # = 14.3 shares 1971 *
1939 cost $3.25. 1971 value $436
  # United Chemicals
  * FMC

Westvaco Chemical—FMC
One share 1932 # = 15 shares 1971 *
1932 cost $3. 1971 value $457
  # Westvaco Chemical
  * FMC

National Fireproofing—FUQUA INDUSTRIES
One share 1944 # = 3.1 shares 1971 *
1944 cost 50 cents. 1971 value $82
  # National Fireproofing
  * Fuqua Industries

GARDNER-DENVER
One share 1933 = 20¼ shares 1971
1933 cost $7.50. 1971 value $1,012

GENERAL AMERICAN OIL
One share 1937 = 17.1 shares 1971
1937 cost $6.50. 1971 value $825

GENERAL CABLE
One share 1933 = 5 shares 1971
1933 cost $1.25. 1971 value $131

General Cable Class A—
GENERAL CABLE
One share 1935 # = 20 shares 1971 *

1935 cost $4. 1971 value $525
  # Class A
  * Common

Chemical Research—
GENERAL DEVELOPMENT
One share 1941 # = 1.3 shares 1971 *
1941 cost 41 cents. 1971 value $43
  # Chemical Research
  * General Development

Consolidated Aircraft—
GENERAL DYNAMICS
One share 1933 # = 3.4 shares 1971 *
1933 cost $1. 1971 value $107
  # Consolidated Aircraft
  * General Dynamics

Electric Boat—GENERAL DYNAMICS
One share 1933 # = 3.15 shares 1971 *
1933 cost $1. 1971 value $100
  # Electric Boat
  * General Dynamics

Snider Packing—
GENERAL FOODS
One share 1933 # = 6.4 shares 1971 *
1933 cost 63 cents. 1971 value $279
  # Snider Packing Foods
  * General Foods

Yellow Truck & Coach—
GENERAL MOTORS
One share 1932 # = 2 shares 1971 *
1932 cost $1.38. 1971 value $182
  # Yellow Truck & Coach
  * General Motors

General Alliance—GENERAL REINSURANCE

One share 1933 # = 2 shares
1971 *
1933 cost $5. 1971 value $656
   # General Alliance
   * General Reinsurance

Associated Telephone Utilities
Series C, 5½% convertible
bonds—
GENERAL TELEPHONE
. One bond 1933 # = 142.8 shares
1971*
1933 cost $50. 1971 value $5,087
   # Each bond exchanged for
   21.158 General Telephone
   shares
   * General Telephone

GENERAL TIRE
One share 1933 = 113.6 shares
1971
1933 cost $23. 1971 value $3,209

GEORGIA-PACIFIC
One share 1953 = 15.8 shares
1971
1953 cost $9.25. 1971 value $957

Pacific Western Oil—GETTY
OIL
One share 1943 # = 10½
shares 1971 *
1943 cost $9. 1971 value $1,023
   # Pacific Western Oil
   * Getty Oil

GILLETTE
One share 1943 = 12 shares
1971
1943 cost $4.75. 1971 value $610

GIMBEL BROTHERS
One share 1935 = 8 shares 1971
1935 cost $2.13. 1971 value $364

GOODRICH (B. F.)
COMPANY
One share 1933 = 9 shares 1971
1933 cost $3. 1971 value $315

GOODYEAR TIRE &
RUBBER
One share 1942 = 29.2 shares
1971
1942 cost $10.25. 1971 value
$1,029

GOVERNMENT EMPLOYES
INSURANCE
One share 1951 = 44 shares 1971
1951 cost $38. 1971 value $3,938.

GOVERNMENT EMPLOYES
LIFE INSURANCE
One share 1949 = 14.3 shares
1971
1949 cost $5. 1971 value $670

Graniteville Manufacturing—
GRANITEVILLE
One share 1935 # = 179.5 shares
1971 *
1935 cost $34. 1971 value $6,170
   # Graniteville Manufacturing
   * Graniteville

GREYHOUND CORP.
One share 1934 = 30½ shares
1971
1934 cost $5.25. 1971 value $777

Armour & Co. (Illinois) Class
A—GREYHOUND
One share 1932 # = 4.3 shares
1971 *
1932 cost 63 cents. 1971 value
$109
   # Armour & Co. (Illinois)
   Class A
   * Greyhound

Armour & Co. (Illinois)
Preferred—GREYHOUND
One share 1932 # = 25.9 shares
1971 *
1932 cost $3.50. 1971 value $660
   # Armour & Co. (Illinois)
   Preferred
   * Greyhound

Godchaux Sugars Class B—
GULF STATES LAND &
INDUSTRIES
One share 1933 # = 10 shares
1971 *
1933 cost 25 cents. 1971 value
$62
   # Godchaux Sugars Class B
   * Gulf States Land &
   Industries

Bliss (E.W.)—GULF &
WESTERN
One share 1932 # = 2.6 shares
1971 *
1932 cost 63 cents. 1971 value
$80
   # Bliss (E.W.)
   * Gulf & Western

Michigan Bumper—GULF &
WESTERN
One share 1943 # = 1.5 shares
1971 *
1943 cost 32 cents. 1971 value
$46
   # Michigan Bumper
   * Gulf & Western

Intertype—HARRIS-
INTERTYPE
One share 1933 # = 6.5 shares
1971 *
1933 cost $1.88. 1971 value $450
   # Intertype
   * Harris-Intertype

HART SCHAFFNER & MARX
One share 1939 = 35.1 shares
1971
1939 cost $10. 1971 value
$1,105

HOBART MANUFACTURING
One share 1933 = 25.4 shares
1971
1933 cost $10. 1971 value
$1,651

HOLIDAY INNS
One share 1958 = 16.3 shares
1971
1958 cost $8.13. 1971 value $825

Minneapolis Honeywell—
HONEYWELL
One share 1935 # = 48 shares
1971 *
1935 cost $58. 1971 value $6,660
   # Minneapolis Honeywell
   * Honeywell

HONOLULU OIL
One share 1932 = 4 shares 1971
1932 cost $4.75. 1961 liquidating
distributions on 4 shares = $394
Subsequent liquidating distributions on 4 shares $22.72.
10 years' interest on $394, com-
pounded at 5 percent = $247
1971 total receipts = $663

HOOVER BALL & BEARING
One share 1934 = 6.6 shares
1971
1934 cost $1.13. 1971 value $237

Interstate Co.—
HOST INTERNATIONAL
One share 1955 # = 14.4 shares
1971 *
1955 cost $4.38. 1971 value $561
   # Interstate Co.
   * Host International

Houdaille-Hershey Class B—
HOUDAILLE
One share 1933 # = 9 shares
1971 *
1933 cost $1. 1971 value $142
   # Houdaille-Hershey Class B
   * Houdaille

HOUSTON OIL
One share 1942 = $166.50 cash
1957
1942 cost $2.25. 1971 value

$340 #
  # Cash received in liquidation
  in 1956 and 1957 compounded
  15 years at 5 percent.

Pacific Portland Cement—
IDEAL BASIC INDUSTRIES
One share 1944 # = 19.6 shares
1971*
1944 cost $2.75. 1971 value $374
  # Pacific Portland Cement
  * Ideal Basic Industries

INDUSTRIAL ACCEPTANCE
One share 1942 = 32 shares
1971
1942 cost $5.90 (U.S.). 1971
value $644 (U.S.) #
  # 1942 low on Montreal Stock
  Exchange was $6.50 with
  Canadian dollar at .909.

INSPIRATION
CONSOLIDATED COPPER
One share 1932 = 2 shares 1971
1932 cost 75 cents. 1971 value
$102

INTERNATIONAL BUSINESS
MACHINES
One share 1948 = 38 shares 1971
1948 cost $125.50. 1971 value
$13,898

National Department Stores 7%
first preferred—
INTERNATIONAL MINING
One share 1933 # = 17.6 shares
1971*
1933 cost $1.25. 1971 value $268
  # National Department Stores
  7% first preferred
  * International Mining

International Paper & Power
Class A common—
INTERNATIONAL PAPER
One share 1933 # = 4.2 shares
1971*

1933 cost 50 cents. 1971 value
$170
  # International Paper & Power
  Class A common
  * International Paper

INTERNATIONAL
TELEPHONE & TELEGRAPH
One share 1942 = 4.2 shares
1971
1942 cost $1.50. 1971 value $282

Continental Baking Class A—
INTERNATIONAL
TELEPHONE
One share 1935 # = 7.3 shares
1971*
1935 cost $4.50. 1971 value $491
  # Continental Baking Class A
  * International Telephone

General Fire Extinguisher—
INTERNATIONAL
TELEPHONE &
TELEGRAPH
One share 1943 # = 9.5 shares
1971*
+ 7.9 shares 1971†
1943 cost $10.63. 1971 value
$1,096
  # General Fire Extinguisher
  * International Telephone &
  Telegraph
  † American District Telegraph

INTERNATIONAL UTILITIES
One share 1943 # = 16.8 shares
1971*
1943 cost $3.75. 1971 value $753
  # Class A
  * Common

International Utilities Class B
—INTERNATIONAL
UTILITIES
One share 1942 # = .12 shares
1971*
1942 cost 4 cents. 1971 value

$5.38
  # Class B
  * Common

JEANNETTE GLASS
One share 1942 = 3.4 shares 1971
1942 cost 82 cents. 1971 value $97

Celotex—JIM WALTER
One share 1933 # = 2.1 shares 1971 *
1933 cost 50 cents. 1971 value $97
  # Celotex
  * Jim Walter

South Coast—JIM WALTER
One share 1941 # = 2.7 shares 1971 *
1941 cost $1. 1971 value $124
  # South Coast
  * Jim Walter

Holophane—
JOHNS-MANVILLE
One share 1936 # = 16.3 shares 1971 *
1936 cost $6.50. 1971 value $752
  # Holophane
  * Johns-Manville

JOHNSON & JOHNSON
One share 1946 = 52 shares 1971
1946 cost $44. 1971 value $5,174

Butte Copper & Zinc—
JONATHAN LOGAN
One share 1933 # = 1¼ shares 1971 *
1933 cost 50 cents. 1971 value $81
  # Butte Copper & Zinc
  * Jonathan Logan

Sullivan Machinery—
JOY MANUFACTURING
One share 1932 # = 5 shares

1971 *
1932 cost $3.25. 1971 value $329
  # Sullivan Machinery
  * Joy Manufacturing

KENDALL CO.
One share 1942 = 15 shares 1971
1942 cost $6.50. 1971 value $695

Kerlyn Oil Class A—KERR-MC GEE
One share 1943 # = 17.5 shares 1971 *
1943 cost $3.13. 1971 value $861
  # Kerlyn Oil Class A
  * Kerr McGee

Lindsay Chemical—KERR-MC GEE
One share 1939 # = 5.8 shares 1971 *
1939 cost $1.88. 1971 value $285
  # Lindsay Chemical
  * Kerr-McGee

Warner Bros. Pictures, Inc.—
KINNEY NATIONAL SERVICE
One share 1941 # = 4¼ shares 1971 *
+ 7.7 shares 1971 †
+ Cash and compound interest at 5 percent
1941 cost $2.75. 1971 value $278
  # Warner Bros. Pictures, Inc.
  * Kinney National Service
  † Glen Alden

Kirsch Co. Preferred—KIRSCH COMPANY
One share 1946 # = 38.6 shares 1971 *
1946 cost $14. 1971 value $1,686
  # Kirsch Co. preferred
  * Kirsch Company common

Kirsch Co. Common B—
KIRSCH CO.
One share 1946 # = 15.4 shares

1971 *
1946 cost $5. 1971 value $671
   # Kirsch Co. common B
   * Kirsch Co. common

LANE BRYANT
One share 1942 = 26.4 shares
1971
1942 cost $8.38. 1971 value $970

Universal Winding—LEESONA
One share 1934 # = 60 shares
1971 *
1934 cost $11. 1971 value
$1,275
   # Universal Winding
   * Leesona

Lehigh Valley Coal Corp. 6%
$50 par convertible preferred—
LEHIGH VALLEY
INDUSTRIES
One share 1940 # = 26 shares
1971 *
1940 cost $2. 1971 value $205 †
   # Lehigh Valley Coal 6% cv.
   pfd.
   * Lehigh Valley Industries
   † Including 1946 cash of $7.50
   received in recapitalization and
   compounded at 5 percent.

LERNER STORES
One share 1933 = 24 shares
1971
1933 cost $4. 1971 value $1,233

Austin, Nichols & Co.—
LIGGETT & MYERS
One share 1942 # = 2.3 shares
1971 *
1942 cost $1.25. 1971 value $138
   # Austin, Nichols & Co.
   * Liggett & Myers

Lincoln National Life Insurance
—LINCOLN NATIONAL
CORP.
One share 1943 # = 39.9 shares

1971 *
1943 cost $28.50. 1971 value
$3,630
   # Lincoln National Life
   Insurance
   * Lincoln National Corp.

LOCKHEED
One share 1934 = 6.7 shares
1971
1934 cost 90 cents. 1971 value
$102

LOUISIANA LAND
One share 1943 = 12 shares
1971
1943 cost $5.13. 1971 value $624

MAGNAVOX
One share 1949 = 15.3 shares
1971
1949 cost $5. 1971 value $841

Container Corp. Class A—
MARCOR
One share 1934 # = 20 shares
1971 *
1934 cost $6.13. 1971 value $777
   # Container Corp. Class A
   * Marcor common

Mengel—MARCOR
One share 1932 # = 4 shares
1971 *
1932 cost $1. 1971 value $155
   # Mengel
   * Marcor

Masco Screw Products—
MASCO CORP.
One share 1961 # = 18 shares
1971 *
1961 cost $6.25. 1971 value $729
   # Masco Screw Products
   * Masco Corp.

MASONITE
One share 1933 = 18.4 shares
1971

1933 cost $8.25. 1971 value
$1,214

MAYTAG
One share 1943 = 8 shares 1971
1943 cost $2.50. 1971 value $336

McCord Radiator & Manufacturing—MC CORD CORP.
One share 1943 # = 4.6 shares
1971*
1943 cost $1.25. 1971 value $160
  # McCord Radiator & Manufacturing
  · * McCord Corp.

Butler Brothers—MC CRORY
CORP.
One share 1932# = 3 shares
1971*
+ one share Canal-Randolph
1932 cost 75 cents. 1971 value
$114
  # Butler Brothers
  * McCrory Corp.

McCrory Stores—MC CRORY
CORP.
One share 1933 = 2 shares 1971
1933 cost 38 cents. 1971 value
$63

McLellan Stores—MC CRORY
CORP.
One share 1933 # = 1.2 shares
1971*
1933 cost 25 cents. 1971 value
$37
  # McLellan Stores
  * McCrory Corp.

McLellan Stores Preferred—
MC CRORY CORP.
One share 1933 # = 10.8 shares
1971*
1933 cost $2.13. 1971 value $341
  # McLellan Stores preferred
  * McCrory Corp. common

National Shirt Shops—
MC CRORY CORP.
One share 1934 # = 7.1 shares
1971*
1934 cost $1. 1971 value $224
  # National Shirt Shops
  * McCrory Corp. common

Douglas Aircraft—
MC DONNELL DOUGLAS
One share 1932 # = 13.2 shares
1971*
1932 cost $5. 1971 value $513
  # Douglas Aircraft
  * McDonnell Douglas

McDonnell Aircraft—
MC DONNELL DOUGLAS
One share 1950 # = 48.1 shares
1971*
1950 cost $17. 1971 value $1,924
  # McDonnell Aircraft
  * McDonnell Douglas

Line Material—MC GRAW-
EDISON
One share 1935 # = 12.4 shares
1971*
1935 cost $3.63. 1971 value $536
  # Line Material
  * McGraw-Edison

McGraw Electric—MC GRAW-
EDISON
One share 1934 # = 16 shares
1971*
1934 cost $3.75. 1971 value $692
  # McGraw Electric
  * McGraw-Edison

MC GRAW-HILL
One share 1943 = 36 shares 1971
1943 cost $8.50. 1971 value $868

MELVILLE SHOE
One share 1933 = 18.8 shares
1971
1933 cost $8.75. 1971 value
$1,222

MERCANTILE STORES
One share 1943 = 20 shares 1971
1943 cost $21. 1971 value $2,702

MERCK & CO.
One share 1940 = 54 shares 1971
1940 cost $43. 1971 value $7,087

Sharp & Dohme—MERCK
One share 1943 # = 6¾ shares
1971 *
1943 cost $8.63. 1971 value $885
 # Sharp & Dohme
 * Merck

Sharp & Dohme $3.50 Conv.
Pfd. A—MERCK
One share 1932 # = 13.5 shares
1971 *
1932 cost $11.50. 1971 value
$1,771
 # Sharp & Dohme $3.50 Conv.
 Pfd. A
 * Merck common

Marion Steam Shovel 7% Pfd.
 –MERRITT-CHAPMAN &
SCOTT
One share 1932 # = 19.8 shares
1971 *
1932 cost $5.25. 1971 value $581
 # Marion Steam Shovel 7%
 Pfd.
 * Merritt-Chapman & Scott
Oct. 25, 1965, tender plus 5 per-
cent interest on cash received.

MERRITT-CHAPMAN &
SCOTT
One share 1932 = 2 shares 1971
1932 cost 38 cents. 1971 value
$45 *
 * Aggregate of liquidating
 distributions

Mesabi Iron—MESABI TRUST
One share 1943 # = 11 shares
1971 *
1943 cost $1. 1971 value $121

Mesabi Iron stock
* Mesabi Trust Units of
 beneficial interests

Electric Power & Light common
—MIDDLE SOUTH
UTILITIES, PENNZOIL
One share 1943 # = (in 1971)
1.4 shares *
2.8 shares †
1943 cost $1.25. 1971 value $151
 # Electric Power & Light
 common
 * Middle South Utilities
 † Pennzoil

Electric Power & Light $6
Preferred—MIDDLE SOUTH
UTILITIES, PENNZOIL
One share 1935 # = (in 1971)
16.4 shares *
12.7 shares †
1935 cost $2.50. 1971 value $966
 # Electric Power & Light
 $6 preferred
 * Middle South Utilities
 † Pennzoil

Electric Power & Light $7
Preferred—MIDDLE SOUTH
UTILITIES, PENNZOIL
One share 1935 # = (in 1971)
18 shares *
14 shares †
1935 cost $3. 1971 value $1,062
 # Electric Power & Light $7
 preferred
 * Middle South Utilities
 † Pennzoil

Electric Power & Light $7
Second Preferred—MIDDLE
SOUTH UTILITIES,
PENNZOIL
One share 1943 # = (in 1971)
17.2 shares *
13.5 shares †
1943 cost $7. 1971 value

$1,034 # #
#Electric Power & Light $7
second preferred
*Middle South Utilities
†Pennzoil
#Including $5.25 cash
received in 1949 and
compounded at 5 percent
annually

Midland Steel Products—
MIDLAND-ROSS
One share 1932 # = 8 shares
1971*
1932 cost $2. 1971 value $282
#Midland Steel Products
*Midland-Ross

MILTON BRADLEY
One share 1957 = 22.9 shares
1971
1957 cost $9. 1971 value $1,030

MINNESOTA MINING &
MANUFACTURING
One share 1945 = 48 shares
1971
1945 cost $60. 1971 value
$6,480

Virginia Carolina Chemical
—MOBIL OIL
One share 1942 # = 2.4 shares
1971*
1942 cost $1. 1971 value $144
#Virginia Carolina Chemical
common
*Mobil Oil

MONROE AUTO
EQUIPMENT
One share 1959 = 30 shares 1971
1959 cost $10.50. 1971 value
$1,346

Lion Oil—MONSANTO
One share 1935 # = 7.6 shares
1971*
1935 cost $3.50. 1971 value $400

#Lion Oil
*Monsanto

MOORE CORP., LTD.
One share 1935 = 48 shares
1971
1935 cost $17. 1971 value $1,842

MOTOROLA
One share 1948 = 13.2 shares
1971
1948 cost $11.25. 1971 value
$1,184

National Bellas Hess Co., Inc.
7% Preferred—
NATIONAL BELLAS HESS,
INC. COMMON
One share 1932 #   = 5.3 shares
1971*
1932 cost 13 cents. 1971 value
$28†
#National Bellas Hess Co.
Inc. 7% preferred
*National Bellas Hess, Inc.
common
†Plus $15.53 liquidating
dividends received by end of
1937

NATIONAL HOMES
One share 1945 = 23.9 shares
1971
1945 cost $6.75. 1971 value $917

Linen Service Corp. of Texas—
NATIONAL SERVICE
INDUSTRIES
One share 1939# = 3.9 shares
1971*
1939 cost $1. 1971 value $115
#Linen Service Corp. of Texas
common
*National Service Industries

NATIONAL STANDARD
One share 1932 = 22.5 shares
1971
1932 cost $7.25. 1971 value $978

NATOMAS CO.
One share 1932 = 10 shares 1971
1932 cost $9. 1971 value $1,013

NESTLE-LE MUR
One share 1938 # = 6 shares
1971 *
1938 cost 25 cents. 1971 value
$29
   # Class A
   * Common

NEW PROCESS
One share 1955 = 120 shares
1971
1955 cost $58. 1971 value $7,380

NEWMONT MINING
One share 1933 = 36 shares 1971
1933 cost $11.50. 1971 value
$1,413

Magma Copper—NEWMONT
MINING
One share 1932 # = 11.9 shares
1971 *
1932 cost $4.25. 1971 value
$467
   # Magma Copper
   * Newmont Mining

North American Aviation—
NORTH AMERICAN ROCK-
WELL, SPERRY RAND, TWA
One share 1932 = in 1971:
2.8 shares North American
Rockwell
7.3 shares Sperry Rand
88/1000 share TWA
1932 cost $1.25. 1971 value $371

Hunt Bros. Packing—NORTON
SIMON
One share 1944 # = 16.6 shares
1971 *
1944 cost $5.75. 1971 value
$1,045
   # Hunt Bros. Packing
   * Norton Simon

Noxzema Chemical—NOXELL
One share 1944 = 12 shares 1971
1944 cost $4.50. 1971 value $501

OCCIDENTAL PETROLEUM
One share 1956 = 3.7 shares
1971
1956 cost 45 cents. 1971 value
$84

Johnson Motor—OUTBOARD
MARINE
One share 1932 # = 2.7 shares
1971 *
1932 cost 50 cents. 1971 value
$120
   # Johnson Motor no par
   common
   * Outboard Marine

Outboard Motors Class A-
OUTBOARD MARINE
One share 1936 # = 27 shares
1971 *
1936 cost $11. 1971 value $1,269
   # Outboard Motors Class A
   * Outboard Marine

Outboard Motors Class B—
OUTBOARD MARINE
One share 1935 # = 2.7 shares
1971 *
1935 cost 63 cents. 1971 value
$126
   # Outboard Motors Class B
   * Outboard Marine common

National Container $2 Conv.
Pfd.—OWENS-ILLINOIS-
GLASS
One share 1932 #   = 12.7 shares
1971 *
1932 cost $8.13. 1971 value $841
   # National Container $2
   convertible preferred
   * Owens-Illinois-Glass common

PARKER PEN
One share 1932 = 10.4 shares

1971
1932 cost $2.50. 1971 value $273.

J C. PENNEY CO.
One share 1932 = 18 shares 1971
1932 cost $13. 1971 value $1,395

Duval Texas Sulphur—
PENNZOIL UNITED
One share 1933 # = 7.7 shares
1971 *
1933 cost 50 cents. 1971 value
$300
  # Duval Texas Sulphur
  * Pennzoil United

Loft, Inc.—PEPSICO
One share 1938 # = 6.06 shares
1971 *
1938 cost 75 cents.1971 value $427
  # Loft, Inc.
  * Pepsico

Hussman-Ligonier—PET MILK
One share 1934 # = 3.5 shares
1971 *
1934 cost $1. 1971 value $167
  # Hussman-Ligonier
  * Pet Milk

Pfizer (Chas.) & Co.—PFIZER,
INC.
One share 1943 # = 81 shares
1971 *
1943 cost $29. 1971 value $3,493
  # Pfizer (Chas.) & Co.
  * Pfizer, Inc.

New England Lime—PFIZER
INC.
One share 1948 # = 13.5 shares
1971 *
1948 cost $4.50. 1971 value $582
  # New England Lime
  * Pfizer Inc.

PHILADELPHIA LIFE
INSURANCE
One share 1945 = 37.1 shares

1971
1945 cost $4. 1971 value $714

PHILIP MORRIS
One share 1934 = 18.9 shares
1971
1934 cost $11.50. 1971 value
$1,323

PHILLIPS PETROLEUM
One share 1932 = 8 shares 1971
1932 cost $2. 1971 value $277

Phillips-Jones—PHILLIPS-VAN
HEUSEN
One share 1942 # = 27.6 shares
1971 *
1942 cost $6.13. 1971 value $690
  # Phillips-Jones
  * Phillips-Van Heusen

PITNEY-BOWES
One share 1933 = 6.4 shares 1971
1933 cost $2. 1971 value $215

PITTSTON CO.
One share 1943 = 10.9 shares
1971
1943 cost $1.75. 1971 value $572

Pittsburgh Railways (Citizens
Traction common)—PITTWAY
CORP.
One share 1940 # = 4.2 shares
1971 *
1940 cost $1. 1971 value $161
  # Citizens Traction common
  * Pittway

PLACER DEVELOPMENT
One share 1937 = 6 shares 1971
1937 cost $2. 1971 value $231

POLAROID
One share 1955 = 48 shares 1971
1955 cost $42.88. 1971 value
$5,622

Porter (H.K.) 1st 6s of 1946—
PORTER (H.K.)

One bond 1932 # = 19,101 shares
1971 *
1932 cost $50. 1971 value
$448,873
  # Porter (H.K.) 1st 6s of 1946
  * Porter (H.K.) common

PRENTICE-HALL
One share 1945 = 108.5 shares
1971
1945 cost $51. 1971 value $5,452

Burry Biscuit—QUAKER OATS
One share 1942 # = 1 share
1971 *
1942 cost 25 cents. 1971 value
$50
  # Burry Biscuit
  * Quaker Oats

Dunhill Int'l.—QUESTOR
One share 1932 # = 3.8 shares
1971 *
1932 cost 63 cents. 1971 value
$72
  # Dunhill International
  * Questor

New York Dock—QUESTOR
One share 1939 # = 10 shares
1971 *
1939 cost $1.75. 1971 value $220
  # New York Dock
  * Questor

Rapid Electrotype—RAPID-
AMERICAN
One share 1943 # = 20.4 shares
1971 *
1943 cost $2.38. 1971 value $413
  # Rapid Electrotype
  * Rapid-American

RAYTHEON
One share 1943 = 9.2 shares
1971
1943 cost $2.75. 1971 value $420

Starret Corp.—RECRION
One share 1943 # = 1.3 shares
1971 *
1943 cost 32 cents. 1971 value
$66
  # Starret Corp.
  * Recrion

Reece Button Hole Machine—
REECE CORP.
One share 1934 # = 30 shares
1971 *
1934 cost $10. 1971 value $1,140
  # Reece Button Hole Machine
  * Reece Corp.

RELIABLE STORES
One share 1933 = 8.2 shares
1971
1933 cost 88 cents. 1971 value
$123

Dodge Manufacturing—
RELIANCE ELECTRIC
One share 1942 # = 33.6 shares
1971 *
1942 cost $9.13. 1971 value $953
  # Dodge Manufacturing
  * Reliance Electric

Republic Gas—REPUBLIC
NATURAL GAS
One share 1932 # = 1/2 share
1966 *
1932 cost 13 cents. 1971 value
$26 † plus five to nine years'
interest on liquidating
distributions.
  # Republic Gas
  * Republic Natural Gas
  † Based on liquidating
  distributions of $49.12 a share,
  1962–66.

U.S Foil B—REYNOLDS
METALS
One share 1943 # = 10.3 shares
1971 *

1943 cost $2.63. 1971 value $342
   # U.S. Foil B
   * Reynolds Metals

Lawyers Title Insurance—
RICHMOND CORP.
One share 1936 # = 106 shares
1971 *
1936 cost $50. 1971 value $5,830
   # Lawyers Title Insurance
   * Richmond Corp.

Art Metal Works—RONSON
CORP.
One share 1933 # = 15½
shares 1971 *
1933 cost 63 cents. 1971 value
$149
   # Art Metal Works
   * Ronson Corp.

Nehi—ROYAL CROWN COLA
One share 1936 # = 24.8 shares
1971 *
1936 cost $4.25. 1971 value $861
   # Nehi
   * Royal Crown Cola

General America Corp.—
SAFECO
One share 1938 # = 105.6 shares
1971 *
1938 cost $46. 1971 value $4,686
   # General America Corp.
   * Safeco

Eastern States Corp.—ST.
REGIS PAPER
One share 1944 # = 1.6 shares
1971 *
1944 cost 63 cents. 1971 value
$67
   # Eastern States Corp.
   * St. Regis Paper

Plough—SCHERING-PLOUGH
One share 1945 # = 15.6 shares
1971 *

1945 cost $13.25. 1971 value
$1,402
   # Plough
   * Schering-Plough

Wahl—SCHICK
One share 1932 # = 2.9 shares
1971 *
1932 cost 13 cents. 1971 value
$15
   # Wahl
   * Schick

Weston Electrical Instrument
—SCHLUMBERGER
One share 1933 # = 2¼ shares
1971 *
1932 cost $3.50. 1971 value $350
   # Weston Electrical Instrument
   * Schlumberger

Marchant Calculating Machine—
SCM
One share 1933 # = 4.3 shares
1971 *
1933 cost 50 cents. 1971 value
$100
   # Marchant Calculating
   Machine
   * SCM

SEARS, ROEBUCK & CO.
One share 1933 = 24 shares 1971
1933 cost $12.50. 1971 value
$2,499

Seton Leather—SETON CO.
One share 1933 # = 10 shares
1971 *
1933 cost $1.50. 1971 value $155
   # Seton Leather
   * Seton Co.

Shell Union Oil—SHELL OIL
One share 1932 # = 4.48 shares
1971 *
1932 cost $2.50 1971 value

$251 †
  # Shell Union Oil
  * Shell Oil
  † Including Shell Oil of
  Canada Class A received as
  nontaxable dividend.

Hancock Oil—SIGNAL COS.
One share 1933 # = 19.6 shares
1971 *
1933 cost $3.75. 1971 value $436
  # Hancock Oil
  * Signal Cos.

Signal Oil & Gas Class A—
SIGNAL COS.
One share 1935 # = 32.7 shares
1971 *
1935 cost $5.50. 1971 value $728
  # Signal Oil & Gas Class A
  * Signal Cos.

Signode Steel Strapping—
SIGNODE CORP.
One share 1942 # = 18.1 shares
1971 *
1942 cost $9.75. 1971 value $995
  # Signode Steel Strapping
  * Signode Corp.

SIMPLICITY PATTERN
One share 1954 = 5.2 shares
1971
1954 cost $4.88. 1971 value $772

Venezuelan Petroleum—
S. NCLAIR OIL
)ne share 1941 # = 5/8 share
.971 *
1941 cost 75 cents. 1971 value
$90 †
  # Venezuelan Petroleum
  * Sinclair Oil
  † Assuming acceptance of
  December 1968 offer by
  Atlantic Richfield to purchase
  Sinclair common at $145 a
  share.

American Meter—SINGER
One share 1933 # = 7.4 shares
1971 *
1933 cost $5. 1971 value $573
  # American Meter
  * Singer

SKELLY OIL
One share 1935 = 14.6 shares
1971
1935 cost $6.50. 1971 value $770

Skyline Homes—SKYLINE
CORP.
One share 1963 # = 19.8 shares
1971 *
1963 cost $11. 1971 value $1,183
  # Skyline Homes
  * Skyline Corp.

Soss Manufacturing—SOS
CONSOLIDATED
One share 1941 # = 5.6 shares
1971 *
1941 cost $1.13. 1971 value $133
  # Soss Manufacturing
  * SOS Consolidated

Realty Operators—SOUTH-
DOWN, INC.
One share 1944 # = 13.8 shares
1971 *
1944 cost $4.25. 1971 value $674.
  # Realty Operators
  * Southdown, Inc.

Remington-Rand—
SPERRY RAND
One share 1933 # = 6.9 shares
1971 *
1933 cost $2.50. 1971 value $263
  # Remington-Rand
  * Sperry Rand

Sperry—SPERRY RAND
One share 1933 # = 7.3 shares
1971 *
1933 cost $2.13. 1971 value $278

#Sperry
*Sperry Rand

SQUARE D Class B—SQUARE D
One share 1935 # = 106.3 shares 1971*
1935 cost $17. 1971 value $3,361
 # Square D Class B
 *Square D Common

Old Ben Coal new common—
STANDARD OIL OF OHIO
One share 1935 # = 5 shares 1971*
1935 cost 5 cents. 1971 value $460
 # Old Ben Coal new common
 *Standard Oil of Ohio

Old Ben Coal 7½% debentures 1934—STANDARD OIL OF OHIO
One $1,000 bond 1932 # = 94 shares 1971*
1932 cost $30. 1971 value $10,994†
 # Old Ben Coal 7½% debentures 1934
 *Standard Oil of Ohio
 †Assuming investment of bond redemption in 1946 in Old Ben Coal common at 1946 high of 50 after paying 25 percent capital gains tax on bond profit.

Old Ben Coal first gold 6s 1944 —STANDARD OIL OF OHIO
One $1,000 bond 1935 # = 171 shares 1971*
1935 cost $137.50. 1971 value $15,732†
 # Old Ben Coal first gold 6s 1944
 *Standard Oil of Ohio
 †For tax-exempt fund, assum-

ing reinvestment of 1946 bond redemption proceeds in Old Ben Coal common at 1946 high of 50. Individual paying 25 percent capital gains tax on bond profit would have $13,754 in 1971.

STARRETT (L.S.)
One share 1932 = 16 shares 1971
1932 cost $3. 1971 value $304

Stone & Webster—
 STONE & WEBSTER
 GULF STATES UTILITIES
 EL PASO ELECTRIC
 VIRGINIA ELECTRIC & POWER
 SIERRA PACIFIC
 ENGINEERS PUBLIC SERVICE $5.00 PFD.

One share 1935# = (in 1971)
 2 shares Stone & Webster
 4 shares Gulf States Utilities
 2.04 shares El Paso Electric
 6.72 shares Virginia Electric & Power
 .8 shares Sierra Pacific
 .09 shares Engineers Public Service $5 Preferred
1935 cost $3.76. 1971 value $421
 # Stone & Webster

Tung-Sol Electric—STUDE-BAKER-WORTHINGTON
One share 1932# = 1.4 shares 1971*
1932 cost $1. 1971 value $100
 # Tung-Sol Electric
 *Studebaker-Worthington

Sunray Oil—SUN OIL
One share 1933# = ⁹⁄₁₀ share 1971*
1933 cost 25 cents. 1971 value $52
 # Sunray Oil
 *Sun Oil

Chicago Flexible Shaft—
SUNBEAM
One share 1935# = 51½ shares
1971*
1935 cost $13.50. 1971 value
$1,622
  # Chicago Flexible Shaft
  * Sunbeam

Sunstrand Machine Tool—
SUNSTRAND CORP.
One share 1933# = 7.7 shares
1971*
1933 cost $1.50. 1971 value $233
  # Sunstrand Machine Tool
  * Sunstrand Corp.

Ogden Corp.—SYNTEX
              OGDEN CORP.
              BUNKER-RAMO
One share 1951# = (in 1971) 1½
shares Syntex
  plus 50 cents 1958*
  one share Ogden
  1⅝ shares Bunker-Ramo
1951 cost 44 cents
      plus <u>50 cents</u>
          94 cents. 1971 value
             $174
  # Ogden Corp.
  * To exercise rights to Syntex
stock.

TAMPAX
One share 1949 = 9 shares 1971
1949 cost $16.50. 1971 value
$2,961

American Hide & Leather 7%
Preferred—TANDY common
One share 1934# = 45 shares
1971*
1934 cost $17.75. 1971 value
$1,912
  # American Hide & Leather
  * Tandy

American Hide & Leather 6% cv
preferred—TANDY COMMON
One share 1938# = 29 shares
1971*
1938 cost $12. 1971 value $1,232
  # American Hide & Leather
  6% cv preferred
  * Tandy common

Middle States Petroleum Class
A—TENNECO
One share 1935# = 3.3 shares
1971*
1935 cost 88 cents. 1971 value
$97
  # Middle States Petroleum
  Class A
  * Tenneco

Wilcox (H.F.) Oil & Gas—
TENNECO
One share 1935# = 3.8 shares
1971*
1935 cost $1. 1971 value $112
  # Wilcox (H.F.) Oil & Gas
  * Tenneco

Indian Refining—TEXACO
One share 1933# = 4.5 shares
1971*
1933 cost $1.13. 1971 value $178.
  # Indian Refining
  * Texaco

TEXAS GULF PRODUCING
One share 1942 = 3.7 shares in
liquidation
1942 cost $2. 1964–69 liquidating
payments $239#
  # Not including subsequent
  interest.

Intercontinental Rubber—
TEXAS INSTRUMENTS
One share 1952# = 2½ shares
1971*
1952 cost $3. 1971 value $322

\# Intercontinental Rubber
* Texas Instruments

TEXAS PACIFIC COAL & OIL
One share 1934 = 4 shares 1964
1934 cost $2.50. 1964 liquidating
distributions $274*
  * Seven years' interest at 5
  percent compounded would
  bring 1971 total to $385

U.S. Stores $7 first preferred—
THOROFARE MARKETS
One share 1941# = 44.8 shares
1971*
1941 cost $3.25. 1971 value $683
  \# U.S. Stores $7 first preferred
  * Thorofare Markets

Sweets Co. of America—
TOOTSIE ROLL INDUSTRIES
One share 1942# = 22½ shares
1971*
1942 cost $3.13. 1971 value $444
  \# Sweets Co. of America
  * Tootsie Roll Industries

TRANE
One share 1943 = 15 shares 1971
1943 cost $8. 1971 value $1,125

TRI-CONTINENTAL common
One share 1941 = two shares
1971
1941 cost 63 cents. 1971 value
$64

TRI-CONTINENTAL warrants
One warrant in 1944 = one
warrant in 1971
1944 cost 69 cents. 1971 value
$72

General Shareholdings—TRI-
CONTINENTAL
One share 1942# = 1.1 shares
1971*
1942 cost 19 cents. 1971 value

$35
  \# General Shareholdings
  * Tri-Continental

Selected Industries—TRI-
CONTINENTAL
One share 1944# = ⅒ share
              1971*
              + 1¼ warrant
1944 cost 75 cents. 1971 value
$93
  \# Selected Industries common
  * Tri-Continental

Selected Industries $1.50
convertible stock—TRI-
CONTINENTAL
One share 1942# = 4½ shares
1971*
1942 cost $1. 1971 value $145
  \# Selected Industries $1.50
  convertible stock
  * Tri-Continental

Thompson Products—TRW
One share 1938# = 23.2 shares
1971*
1938 cost $8.13. 1971 value
$1,003
  \# Thompson Products
  * TRW

United-Carr Fastener—TRW
One share 1933# = 8.8 shares
1971*
1933 cost $1.63. 1971 value $380
  \# United-Carr Fastener
  * TRW

Whitman & Barnes—TRW
One share 1934# = 4.4 shares
1971*
1934 cost $1.88. 1971 value
$200†
  \# Whitman & Barnes
  * TRW, Inc.
  † Assuming reinvestment of

50 percent of proceeds of preferred, called Nov. 1, 1958, at the highest price of that month.

Union Bag & Paper—UNION CAMP
One share 1933# = 24 shares 1971*
1933 cost $5.50. 1971 value $1,005
  # Union Bag & Paper
  * Union Camp

UNION GAS OF CANADA
One share 1934 = 15 shares 1971
1934 cost $2. 1971 value $241

Chicago, Rock Island & Pacific convertible 4½s, 1960—UNION PACIFIC
One $1,000 bond 1940# = 8.4 shares 1971*
1940 cost $5. 1971 value $554†
  # Chicago, Rock Island & Pacific convertible 4½s, 1960
  * Union Pacific
  † Not including $12.42 cash received October 17, 1945

United States Rubber—UNIROYAL
One share 1932# = 8.4 shares 1971*
1932 cost $1.25. 1971 value $198
  # United States Rubber
  * Uniroyal

United Paperboard—UNITED BOARD & CARTON
One share 1933# = 5¼ shares 1971*
1933 cost 50 cents. 1971 value $57
  # United Paperboard
  * United Board & Carton

UNITED PIECE DYE WORKS common
One share 1943 = one share 1971
1943 cost 10 cents. 1971 value $51

United Piece Dye Works 6½% preferred—UNITED PIECE DYE WORKS
One share 1943# = 14 shares 1971*
1943 cost $1.88. 1971 value $724
  # United Piece Dye Works 6½% preferred
  * United Piece Dye Works common

U.S. FREIGHT
One share 1932 = 12 shares 1971
1932 cost $3.50. 1971 value $375

U.S. HOME & DEVELOPMENT
One share 1967 = 2 shares 1971
1967 cost 63 cents. 1971 value $78

U.S. & International Securities—U.S. & FOREIGN SECURITIES
One share 1933# = 1½ shares 1971*
1933 cost 32 cents. 1971 value $53.
  # U.S. & International Securities
  * U.S. & Foreign Securities

Scullin Steel $3 preference—UNIVERSAL MARION
One share 1932# = 5.4 shares 1971*
1932 cost $1. 1971 value $124
  # Scullin Steel $3 preference
  * Universal Marion

Van Dorn Iron Works—VAN DORN CO.

One share 1950# = 26.6 shares 1971*
1950 cost $6.25. 1971 value $714
  # Van Dorn Iron Works
  * Van Dorn Co.

Engineers
Public Service—VIRGINIA
               ELECTRIC &
               POWER
               GULF STATES
               UTILITIES
               EL PASO
               ELECTRIC
One share 1934#
plus
.1137375 shares = (in 1971)* 8.4
EPS   shares (a)
$5 Preferred   5.0 shares (b)
              2.55 shares (c)

  # Engineers Public Service
  common
  (a) Virginia Electric & Power
  (b) Gulf States Utilities
  (c) El Paso Electric
  * Plus $1.04 cash distribution

WALKER (HIRAM)
GOODERHAM & WORTS
One share 1933 = 24 shares 1971
1933 cost $3.50. 1971 value
$1 014

Eversharp—WARNER-
LAMBERT
One share 1942# = 3.2 shares
1971*
1942 cost $2.25. 1971 value
$262†
  # Eversharp
  * Warner-Lambert
  † Plus residual value in
  Frawley stock

Eddy Paper Corp.—
WEYERHAEUSER
One share 1940# = 20 shares
1971*
1940 cost $11.50. 1971 value
$1,245
  # Eddy Paper Corp.
  * Weyerhaeuser

Birtman Electric—WHIRLPOOL
One share 1933# = 4.2 shares
1971*
1933 cost $3.75. 1971 value $410
  # Birtman Electric
  * Whirlpool

Nineteen Hundred—
WHIRLPOOL
One share 1942# = 8 shares
1971*
1942 cost $5. 1971 value $799
  # Nineteen Hundred
  * Whirlpool

Apex Electrical Manufacturing—
WHITE CONSOLIDATED
INDUSTRIES
One share 1941# = 22 shares
1971*
1941 cost $6.25. 1971 value $646
  # Apex Electrical
  Manufacturing
  * White Consolidated
  Industries

White Sewing Machine—WHITE
CONSOLIDATED
INDUSTRIES
One share 1943# = 9.8 shares
1971*
1943 cost $2.63. 1971 value $287
  # White Sewing Machine
  * White Consolidated
  Industries

Winn & Lovett Grocery—WINN
DIXIE STORES
One share 1942# = 54 shares
1971*

1942 cost $18. 1971 value $3,105
   # Winn & Lovett Grocery
   * Winn-Dixie Stores

Haloid Xerox—XEROX
One share 1958# = 60 shares
1971*
1958 cost $47.50. 1971 value

$7,605
   # Haloid Xerox
   * Xerox

ZENITH RADIO
One share 1948 = 36 snares 1971
1948 cost $19.75. 1971 value
$1,975

CPSIA information can be obtained
at www.ICGtesting.com
Printed in the USA
LVHW031143261121
704514LV00001B/1